Advance praise for

Zero Gravity

*Riding Venture Capital from High-Tech
Start-Up to Breakout IPO*

by Steve Harmon

"*Zero Gravity* offers an inside look on how garage geeks go to board-room barons."

JERRY YANG
Cofounder and Chief, Yahoo!, Yahoo, Inc.

"I wish this book had been around when I cofounded Netscape. Steve Harmon's book provides key insights on the new environment for creating businesses in the Internet era. A must-read for any entrepreneur looking at the Internet opportunity."

MARC ANDREESSEN
Cofounder, Netscape
Chief Technology Officer, America Online, Inc.

"Steve Harmon explains better than anyone the new metrics for success in the high velocity Internet economy."

ANN WINBLAD
General Partner, Hummer Winblad Venture Partners

"Finally—a handbook that sets us all straight on the flashpoint world of venture capital. There's no way to put a price tag on Harmon's *Zero Gravity*. To the right reader, it could be worth a cool billion. Maybe more."

THOM CALANDRA
Editor-in-Chief, CBS MarketWatch

"Steve has always been at the heart of the 'Net economy. With *Zero Gravity* he takes that experience and packages it into a "how-to guide" that no entrepreneur should be without."

BOB DAVIS
President & CEO, Lycos, Inc.

"A great read for any entrepreneur wanting to build a dominant, leading company. I wish all entrepreneurs would read this so they are ready for a great discussion with venture capitalists."

GEORGE ZACHARY
General Partner, Mohr Davidow Ventures

Zero Gravity

Also available from
BLOOMBERG PRESS

Smart Questions to Ask Your Financial Advisers
by Lynn Brenner

Clicking Through:
A Survival Guide for Bringing Your Company Online
by Jonathan Ezor

The Winning Portfolio:
Choosing Your 10 Best Mutual Funds
by Paul B. Farrell

Don't Die Broke:
How to Turn Your Retirement Savings into Lasting Income
by Margaret A. Malaspina

Investing in Latin America:
Best Stocks, Best Funds
by Michael Molinski

The Inheritor's Handbook:
A Definitive Guide for Beneficiaries
by Dan Rottenberg

A Commonsense Guide to Your 401(k)
by Mary Rowland

The New Commonsense Guide to Mutual Funds
by Mary Rowland

Zero Gravity

*Riding Venture Capital from
High-Tech Start-Up to Breakout IPO*

STEVE HARMON

Foreword by
JOHN DOERR

BLOOMBERG PRESS
PRINCETON

First edition published 1999
3 5 7 9 10 8 6 4 2

Harmon, Steve, 1964 -
Zero gravity: riding venture capital from high-tech start-up
to breakout IPO / Steve Harmon; foreword by John Doerr.
p. cm.
Includes index.
ISBN 1-57660-032-7
1. Venture capital. 2. Going public (Securities) 3. New business enterprises—Finance.
4. Internet industry—Finance. I. Title.
HG4751.H365   1999
658. 15'224—dc21   99-41689
                                                              CIP

Edited by MARIS WILLIAMS

Book Design by LAURIE LOHNE / DESIGN IT COMMUNICATIONS

Dedicated to my family

and the larger Internet family

that I am happy to be part of

Contents

Introduction

The Big Idea

The Firms

The Entrepreneurial Pitch

The People: Power Q & A with the Dealmakers

The Meeting

The Valuation

Zero Gravity: Definition by Example

Angels Among Us:
Alternatives to Venture Capital

Steve Harmon's Zero Gravity
Web Resource

Foreword
by
John Doerr

F o r e w o r d

IN 1994 WINDOWS 3.1 was established as the most important software product in the world. Nearly 50 million copies shipped every year, giving Microsoft a position of dominance few had the courage to challenge. At that time Windows didn't have a browser or even a TCP/IP protocol stack. That same year a twenty-three-year-old entrepreneur, Marc Andreessen, plopped down in the corner chair of my office. He confidently declared that his software (Mosaic, the first graphical browser for the World Wide Web) would change the world. Just five days later Marc Andreessen and Jim Clark presented their plan for Mosaic Communications to my partners at Kleiner Perkins Caufield & Byers. KPCB made our then-largest start-up investment—at the highest valuation we had ever paid. Over the next 120 days we scrambled to help Marc and Jim recruit five VPs and a CEO.

On August 5, 1995, the Netscape IPO rocked the world. As the first pure-play IPO, it ignited entrepreneurial energies and investor fever worldwide. Time had compressed. Less than twelve months had elapsed from Netscape's first product download to 40 million users and its Nasdaq listing. A new metric—Web time—was added to our vocabulary.

Fast forward to 1999: There are 500 million pages on the Web, with 1.5 million pages added each day. Seven new users are joining the 'Net every second. Netscape is acquired by America Online for $15 billion. Andreessen's software surely changed the world, transforming the pace and process of research, commerce, health care, news, entertainment, education, and politics. Steve Harmon's *Zero Gravity* features Andreessen's inside story on entrepreneurship in Web time.

Today more than one-third of the growth in America's GDP comes from technology. To reiterate a familiar maxim, "It's the New Economy, stupid." Strategy is easy. It's innovation, leadership, great teams, new business models, and execution that are key.

The Internet has been under-hyped. We're just at the beginning of a long boom, an unprecedented creation of powerful, personalized Web services and companies. New 'Net ventures have created more than $300 billion in value in the past three years.

Steve Harmon's book provides a clear snapshot of this growth from the entrepreneur's perspective. *Zero Gravity* takes you from idea to the start-up seeking venture capital to the IPO. It is the first book to really give entrepreneurs a glimpse into how venture capital works in Web time, offering practical advice on how to target VCs and how to get their attention.

There has never been a better time than now to start a new business or to transform an existing one. It's a zero gravity world of increasing returns and network effects. *Zero Gravity* helps you navigate where "information, entertainment, and communication all flow up, down, sideways, back and forth as easily in one direction as another."

JOHN DOERR, Partner
Kleiner Perkins Caufield & Byers
June 1999

Acknowledgments

I'D LIKE TO THANK all the wonderful friends in this book: John Doerr, Jerry Yang, Marc Andreessen, Ann Winblad, Neil Weintraut, Naveen Jain, Jerry Kaplan, George Zachary, Steve Jurvetson, Esther Dyson, Vinod Khosla, Mark Gorenberg, Bob Stavers, Susan Gore, Band of Angels, Venture One, and PricewaterhouseCoopers.

Some of the people behind the scenes who should be mentioned include Bloomberg Press's Jared Kieling, Maris Williams, Jacque Murphy, and the entire team there who edited my hypermind creation. Most of all I acknowledge the primordial entrepreneurial spirit in all of us that the Internet welcomes with open arms daily.

Zero Gravity

Get Big Fast, and Then Get Bigger

Introduction

THE WORLD NOW has a new clock, the Web. Think
Salvador Dali images merged with Stephen Hawking's
boundless universe, and that's the Webscape. With this
new surreal "timepace" come new opportunities to define time,
space, and the stars. The astronauts: venture capitalists.

The Internet enables great ideas to rapidly become great companies and to make the founders and original believers great wealth (at
least on paper). But getting from concept to capital daunts new
entrepreneurs in the Internet era where time is warped, black holes
are common, and turning hyper ideas into hyper businesses is a hair-
raising adventure.

The bumper sticker for the twenty-first century info-entrepreneur
is "GET BIG FAST, AND THEN GET BIGGER." To do just that,
more and more garage and grunge heroes turn to venture capital; it
can provide not only money, but also allies, partners, and a fast track
to initial public offering or sale to a larger company. The venture
capitalists (VCs in finance parlance) are the new power

brokers, banks, management providers, gurus, and mothers who hold the hands of the newbie idea-ites, taking them past the training wheels stage into rocket racers. It's smart money, the people and their capital. It has to be smart—there's no time to make the wrong moves in a world where every great idea has a half dozen imitators in sixty seconds.

To understand venture capital firms, it's important to take a look at the role of a VC today. Venture capital continually evolves as technology changes, new ideas seek capital, and capital seeks new ideas. Venture capital has made the funding process for Internet businesses happen faster than for any other single industry, and on scales unheard of in the predigital era. Similarly precedent-shattering is the size of the opportunities; entire industries being turned upside down by the Internet; the record volume of investments in private and public companies; and the hatching of new services, products, brands, ways of communications, buying, selling, and exchanging information. All these elements, the rattle and hum of the approaching twenty-first century, all of these and more, taken as a whole, define what I call *Zero Gravity*, the model for business in the new millennium.

The best venture capitalists understand the concept; they seed the ideas and make them grow into the "next big things." Getting to know the VC, therefore, is one of the basic steps of getting comfortable operating in this new environment.

If everything moves faster in the global computer network era, then a new term (and a new understanding to go along with it) is needed for raising money, plotting the future, or simply gaining an appreciation of the Internet's investment underpinnings. I call this "hyper-capital"—the combining of venture capitalists and Web entrepreneurs with connections of every kind to produce home-run investments and returns. It is a world as storied as Hollywood, as imposing as Manhattan, and as challenging sometimes as Mt. Everest.

In an era with information traveling as fast as light, the global computer network has become the place where gray matter (represented by your business notion) meets the sounding board of more than two dozen venture capital firms who've hung out a shingle saying, "Knock here." Sometimes your knock can be a simple e-mail with an executive summary, which can produce a phone call, a meeting (suit, tie, and all), and a check for real dollars to hire real people and take the next step. Other times it can bring a terse "Thanks, but no thanks." Firms that have had both replies have gone on to create multi-hundred-million-dollar valuation companies—with or without venture capital backing.

As if entrepreneurs didn't have enough to worry about by coming up with the great idea and tweaking a product or service, suddenly they also have to become experts at high finance in order to turn that idea into reality. Often, that's why the buck never starts for many great ideas—nobody knows where to start, whom to start with, what to say, how to combine the insanely great concept with the semi-sane capital it requires. That last part, the importance of capital, is the part nine out of ten entrepreneurs miss.

The capital pursuit begins to take shape as a business plan. (*Don't write it with the help of a business plan software program. Write it with real people, tailored to the plan at hand.*) The hopes and dreams encased in the biz plan get rushed via overnight express, e-mail, or pony and plopped on the desk of a venture capitalist with a hundred more just like it. This is the VC who's seen it all, heard it all, and has very little patience for how your idea is going to dethrone Microsoft or realign the planets. There may be a smile, but then the plan is filed—in File 13, that is. The reality is that more than half of all business plans sent to VCs get only a fifteen-minute scan (at best) and have between a 3 percent and 5 percent chance of making it past the cutting room floor to a funded deal. It's not rocket science to say that you must make sure you're prepared to go the distance, and to show them what you're made of. That requires passion.

Some examples of firms that have all gone through the gut-wrenching swirl of getting venture capital: AOL, Netscape, Amazon.com, Yahoo!, and GeoCities. All had venture capital behind them and more than that—the people behind the venture capital. It's not the idea per se that makes success; it's who gets behind the idea and how the idea is made flesh.

The Internet, more than any other medium in the past 100 years, turns dust into life. There's clutter with the old way of doing things and efficiency in the new way. Books. Who do you think of? Amazon! Pick an industry: communication, entertainment, retail, manufacturing, services. Each has been affected by the introduction of the Internet into the picture. Try going to the movies today and not seeing a Web site reference for upcoming movies at the bottom of the screen. Exchange a business card with someone in the Fortune 500 (5,000!) and chances are there's an e-mail address and/or Web site. Peek behind the scenes at staid manufacturing plants and see if the Internet is being used to link buyers, sellers, suppliers in real-time inventory systems—if not today, they will be sooner than you think. Maybe you'll be the provider of that service in some new way.

As the world turns the first pages of the twenty-first century, the Internet is the launch pad into the future. New millennium, new rules. As Internet pioneer Vint Cerf told me, "IP on everything!" referring to "Internet Protocol" that allows the global computer network to find and keep track of Web sites, e-mail, and data. The future is as wide open as the Internet. An idea can be worth a billion dollars.

Some already have been. Let's prove it.

PricewaterhouseCoopers surveys venture capitalists quarterly and gets the latest greatest stats on how much they're investing, what they're betting on, so on and so forth. Its latest pulse check shows more than $1.8 billion invested annually by VCs in Internet start-ups of various flavors. From 1995 to 1997 this inflow exceeded 1,300 percent in growth. The first quarter of 1998 saw $459 million, and 1998 moving into the first quarter through Fall of 1999 exceeded all of that as dollars increased.

Let's take a look at the capital journey from the early days of 1995 with some stats, courtesy of VentureOne:

Amount Raised in 1995 (*$ in millions*)

INTERNET SECTOR	1	2	3	4
Business Services	$7.23	$20.68	$46.53	$79.44
Content	$0.80	$21.50	$11.40	$14.76
Electronic Commerce	$8.27			$6.95
Infrastructure	$11.10	$28.30	$44.60	$54.44
ISPs	$64.50	$32.24	$16.30	$6.30
Software	$45.80	$58.36	$53.20	$141.44
Total	$137.70	$161.07	$172.03	$303.33

Number of Deals in 1995

INTERNET SECTOR	1	2	3	4
Business Services	3	10	13	17
Content	1	6	5	8
Electronic Commerce	3			4
Infrastructure	5	7	9	7
ISPs	4	2	3	1
Software	16	25	18	34
Total	32	50	48	71

Now, fast-forward to 1998 and see how the landscape shifted:

Amount Raised in 1998 ($ in millions)

INTERNET SECTOR	1	2	3	4
Business Services	$316.89	$360.78	$470.42	$507.79
Content	$30.10	$46.50	$80.35	$114.50
Electronic Commerce	$50.35	$132.77	$62.17	$147.50
Infrastructure	$240.30	$160.97	$131.25	$240.00
ISPs	$68.00	$38.60	$44.30	$146.00
Software	$213.20	$465.10	$458.26	$371.69
Total	$918.84	$1,204.72	$1,246.75	$1,527.48

On another front, Big Six accounting firm Pricewaterhouse-Coopers does the auditing for a majority of Internet firms and does a quarterly survey of venture capital in the Internet space.

Let's check with Bob Stavers, a PricewaterhouseCooper's partner who follows the pulse of venture capital in the Internet sector, and get some insights on the trends he sees emerging from the stats:

 **What's the biggest trend you've identified with regard to the Internet in the PricewaterhouseCoopers' quarterly venture capital surveys of the past few years?**

Stavers: We have a number of trends, but probably one of the most significant trends is the increase in average deal size. As I indicated, last quarter two years ago you had maybe one deal that received over $10 million in a single round, and within the last six months we have seen the average deal size increase significantly to the point that last quarter there were several companies that received in excess of $30 million in single rounds of financing. Some of the increase is the result of Internet start-ups becoming more mature, with these large rounds being the second or third rounds, which are typically used for sales and marketing launches versus the earlier rounds being used for product development. Secondly, there is a mad rush right now in the e-commerce space as there is the belief now that e-commerce is real, and accordingly, companies are having to move very quickly to get out into the marketplace to establish market positioning. Also, I would say that we have seen a trend of Internet start-ups positioning for a merger or acquisition much earlier in their life cycle and that the IPO (initial public offering) is not necessarily considered to be the ultimate [measure of] success as it was several years back.

Based on our survey results through June 30, 1998, Internet companies continue to garner a larger share of VC deals. They received 21 percent (24 percent of dollars) in Q2 compared to 15 percent (15 percent of dollars) in Q1 in 1998. The size of the deals continues to be large with all top ten deals getting over $15 million, compared to only five of the top ten getting as much in Q1 1998. As you know, the Internet IPO market is still alive with eBay's successful IPO. However, more Internet companies are likely to look at mergers rather than IPOs as the more likely exit strategy.

How many firms do you survey, and are they representative of the venture industry?
Stavers: We have over 600 VCs that respond to the survey on a quarterly basis.

Is the Internet the biggest venture capital investment area today out of all venture investments?
Stavers: This is a hard question in that the Internet really crosses all segments of business. It is clearly the fastest-growing area of investment. However, the survey results, I believe, would show that technology companies, of which Internet companies are a part, probably continue to lead in the dollars of venture capital investment.

Do you think the scale and growth of investment in the Internet will continue at this rapid pace?

Stavers: I would say that venture capital investments in Internet and related companies will continue to grow. The results of the study for Q2 1998 still have software- and information-related investments in the first place by a wide margin. These categories received just over a billion dollars, or about 30 percent of the investments in that period.

Which areas of the Internet attract the venture capitalist's eye today percentage wise and dollar wise? What's the breakdown of where the capital goes?
Stavers: Clearly the e-commerce/service area is the fastest-growing area. In Q2 1998, service received 37 percent of the Internet investments followed by software at 32 percent and access at 26 percent. Content is the least favorite of VCs; for a while it received only 5 percent. VCs continue to be concerned about the viability of content company business models. Their principal concern is that these companies rarely have the potential for really large-scale growth.

What stages attract the most venture capital, and what size rounds are being done at each stage?
Stavers: There are no clear trends here, although we continue to think that later stages are receiving more as VCs get reluctant to invest in start-ups, many of which they view as "me too" companies. In Q2, "expansion" money represented 36 percent of total investments. Initial and seed rounds received only 4 percent and second rounds, 36 percent. A year ago (Q2 1997) these amounts were 3 percent and 32 percent.

California dominates the funding parade. Do you see that continuing? Why or why not?
Stavers: California and Massachusetts continue to be the two primary areas where Internet companies are located; however, as our survey results indicates, it is not a requirement to be located in those states. We would expect California and Massachusetts to continue to lead from a location standpoint, just due to the significant talent and experience of engineers/entrepreneurship in those parts of the country. In addition, both states have unbelievable infrastructures (support organizations) in place to support start-up companies.

Internationally?
Stavers: We don't see that much activity in the Internet outside of the U.S. There are some notable exceptions, particularly with e-mail and access (Telcos).

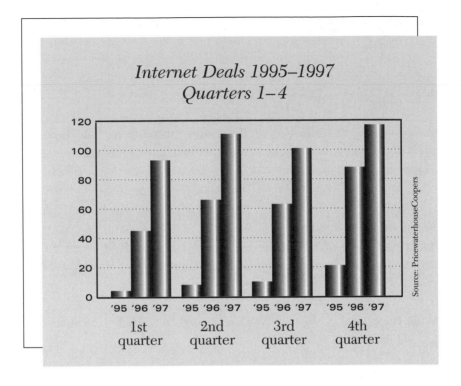

Internet Deals 1995–1997
Quarters 1–4

Source: PricewaterhouseCoopers

FAR FROM BEING a one-hit wonder or a biotech fad, the Internet reflects the diversity and dynamism of the people who experiment with selling its services or products. PricewaterhouseCoopers data echo the sheer raw growth of ideas getting funded. In 1995, as the commercial phase began bubbling out of college dorms, a total of forty-three deals were done. In what seems like decades later (in Internet time)—by 1997—ten times as many deals were funded, about 100 per quarter.

In fact, by first quarter 1998 and onwards more than 100 deals per quarter was quite common and holding. We're also seeing the dollar value per deal go up. Consider that Latin American Web portal Starmedia raised more than $100 million in private money on its way to the public markets. That makes it the leader in capital raised for any Internet company ever. Another start-up firm in the broadcast-Internet space was given $100 million by CMGI to get off the ground. The chart on the following page from PricewaterhouseCoopers recaps some early pops in size of the deals, the amount being funded.

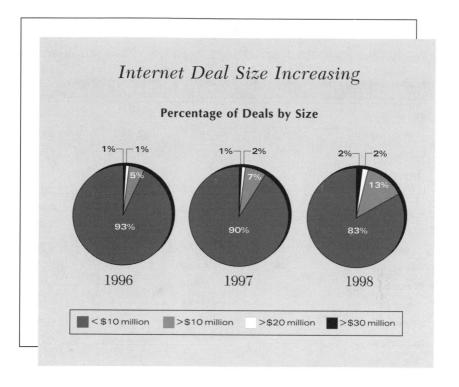

Following the money trail shows how widespread and fundamental—tectonic in California terms—the Internet's embracing new ideas. Notably, the percentage of capital invested in each sector remained consistent for 1996, 1997, and 1998. Translation: there's still a lot of software, access and infrastructure, services, and content to be invested in next year.

Notably, Internet percentages of all deals rocketed 66 percent in 1998 to $3.5 billion. That's 25 percent of all venture capital invested going to the Internet sector, which cuts across all industry groups. Why?

Venture capitalists are addicted to a good return. A 2x payback or return on investment is a bad day. 100x is a bases-loaded home run and 500x gets the partner's name on the firm's official letterhead. It's not surprising then that a majority of the investments go to companies of seed, start-up, or early stage. Don't be confused by the terms. Seed means getting the VC interested enough to develop the product or service and find the key management to do so. Start-up stage follows when you're ready to sell a product or service. And first, second, and

Venture Capital 1995–1998
from PricewaterhouseCoopers ($ in millions)

INDUSTRY	1995	1996	1997	1998
Software and Information	$1,191.8	$2,268.4	$2,887.7	$4,548.3
Communications	1,402.2	1,707.1	2,991.6	3,954.4
Healthcare Services	735.7	775.0	1,033.0	1,100.9
Business Services	316.4	443.0	462.6	636.7
Medical Devices/ Instruments	159.3	337.1	615.6	686.6
Consumer	584.1	419.5	448.1	586.3
Biotechnology	486.7	619.9	647.0	638.5
Computers and Peripherals	279.9	249.3	520.6	436.6
Industrial	201.6	232.1	440.6	424.9
Distribution/ Retailing	352.4	440.1	557.2	372.5
Electronics and Instrumentation	214.9	208.7	382.9	306.2
Pharmaceuticals	129.4	79.5	225.6	324.7
Semiconductors/ Equipment	67.7	99.2	175.7	226.9
Environmental	46.7	43.2	60.8	13.2
Other	47.5	96.2	33.1	9.4
Total	$6,216.3	$8,018.3	$11,482.1	$14,266.1

Source: PricewaterhouseCoopers

third stages (and more perhaps) progress as your firm starts to sell products or services and grows like crazy to reach the goal of every VC: a public offering of stock. The IPO is Wall Street's homage to successful ideas.

You need not worry that VCs may make the seed round and then abandon you if the firm is on track. They will help you in as many ways as possible to get more funding from themselves and others. Remember, smart money walks with you, sprints with you, and helps

Average Deal Size by Industry During 1995–1998 *($ in millions)*

INDUSTRY	1995	1996	1997	1998
Software and Information	$3.00	$3.52	$3.45	$4.78
Communications	6.84	5.16	6.37	6.74
Healthcare Services	4.13	4.19	4.34	4.30
Business Services	4.39	5.83	3.76	4.65
Medical Devices/ Instruments	3.01	2.70	3.62	3.97
Consumer	5.04	3.92	3.80	4.93
Biotechnology	3.96	4.66	4.83	4.56
Computers and Peripherals	3.33	4.79	5.78	5.08
Industrial	2.22	2.87	3.39	3.57
Distribution/ Retailing	4.00	4.00	4.72	4.49
Electronics and Instrumentation	2.39	2.46	2.74	3.19
Pharmaceuticals	3.16	2.34	5.25	6.37
Semiconductors/ Equipment	6.77	6.20	7.03	5.67
Environmental	1.73	2.70	2.43	0.94
Other	2.38	3.70	4.73	2.35
Total	$3.90	$3.97	$4.30	$5.00

Source: PricewaterhouseCoopers

hold up the tape in that last lap before IPO. To illustrate the point see the table on the following page for a breakout of what stages receive the most funding.

The table represents more than $1 billion per annum flowing into the ideaspace. Big dollars make big deals. The fact that over four-fifths of those dollars went to early/start-up/seed/expansion helps you understand that the folks getting funded started somewhere, somehow.

Getting to the VC often proves impossible. It may seem easier to get tickets on the space shuttle. How does one approach possible

Which Stage Gets Most Dollars?

STAGE	Q1 1998	Q1 1997
Early/startup/seed	48%	48%
Expansion	33%	42%
Late stage	9%	8%
Not categorized/other	10%	9%

Source: PricewaterhouseCoopers

investors? Who are "they" anyway? What's my idea worth? Do I really have the right stuff, whatever it is, to build a billion dollar or multi-million dollar valuation firm? Dozens of questions arise about company valuation: How much capital is required? What percentage do the founders own? Who invests in these ideas? Where does one turn for practical advice? But before you get to these questions, where do you begin?

In a word—here!

Zero Gravity

ZERO GRAVITY IS the little black power-book of movers and shakers. It's almost a necessity to know someone in the business when you're shopping around for venture capital. But, if you don't have an uncle in the VC community, this book will provide the proper (and necessary) introductions. It's also an insider's primer for what to say, how to say it, and how to mean it to find the capital to get the dream through the uncharted ether ahead.

This Introduction contains a clear snapshot of today's venture capital industry, clearly focused on the Internet.

Zero Gravity is sprinkled with real-world advice and insights from those who have started some of the biggest success stories of the new era: Jerry Yang, cofounder of Yahoo!; John Doerr, venture capitalist behind Amazon.com and Netscape; Marc Andreessen, cofounder of Netscape; Ann Winblad, venture capitalist behind many Internet firms; technology guru Esther Dyson; and more.

It all starts with The Big Idea (Chapter 1), that neuron-firing moment that keeps you awake at night, makes your brow sweat with possibility, creates a nervous energy that cannot be spent on the most vigorous workouts at the gym. Every invention since the dawn of humanity was first an idea. Planes, trains and automobiles, PCs, TVs—name it, it was an idea. In Chapter 1 we'll evaluate your idea according to the VC checklist, weighing its overall merit against financial reasoning, the why-would-anyone-invest-in-this? test. In short, we'll show you how to throw it against the VC wall to see if it'll stick.

Knowing which wall to throw it against is what Chapter 2 is all about. This fly-on-the-wall chapter takes you inside the top firms doing deals and shows you what they look for. What causes them to pick one firm over another? Check the list of who's who, what they invest in, and why. Find out if your firm fits their bill and what they typically offer firms who knock on their door. Insider insights are presented through descriptions of and interviews with the world's most famous and respected venture capitalists, including the aforementioned John Doerr, partner at Kleiner Perkins Caufield & Byers, and a backer of Sun Microsystems, @Home, Amazon.com, Netscape, and more in its twenty-plus-year history.

Even with a great suit, haircut, power tie, and business plan, only a small percentage of entrepreneurs actually get face time with a venture capitalist. Chapter 3 outlines how to make the e-mail, phone call, letter, or airplane skywriting pitch grab the VC's attention. One of the best ways is a referral from someone in the finance world. That can be a friend of a friend whom the VC backed in the past, a CEO or VP they respect, a notable industry analyst or pundit, or a contact with an industry for your services or goods. Nothing gets a VC's attention faster than deal flow. They then look for two of the most important ingredients—management and a great business plan. In the dead letter file (or PC trash can) lie thousands of pitches that have one but not the other. Preparing that plan and assuring leadership become central to the value equation. In a perfect world every VC would read every plan cover to cover. Truth be known, you have thirty seconds to set their world on fire. That means an executive summary worthy of Shakespeare. VCs want no fluff, but eloquent conciseness: Here's the team and here's how we'll make money—tons of it!

Chapter 4 offers one-on-one advice and anecdotes from Ann Winblad, who cofounded Hummer Winblad, and who is a good friend of Bill Gates; Neil Weintraut, who left a highly successful career as an investment banker to start his own venture firm; Bill Gross, Steven Spielberg's friend and colleague, who assists start-ups with his clout in networking people and businesses; and Esther Dyson, the philosopher-poet of venture capital, who sees the future better than most. These gurus of gurus set down the common denominator of what works and what doesn't for anyone seeking capital.

If you actually get to the meeting, how do you prepare? Chapter 5 talks about "face time." Knowing what to say and how to say it will be the difference between a "hi" or "goodbye." If you can't explain to one or two people at a VC firm in the quietude of Sand Hill Road, Boston, Austin, Tel Aviv, or London how your idea makes money in short order, how do you explain it to any possible buyer of your service or product? This is all about company growth, that very real exercise that goes beyond napkin scribblings and talks about the five- to ten-year growth window, how the firm will achieve success, what the milestones are, who the rivals and threats will be, where the road turns, and if yours is the road less or more traveled. The meeting is also about the VC selling you on them. Why should you take their money and for what? What's their track record, how is their money smarter than the VC's down the block? What allies, partners and deals can they plug your firm into right away? This is the "I'll show you mine if you show me yours" hour.

Lucky entrepreneurs who survive the first meeting may receive a call for a series of meetings that discusses valuations and how much the firm is worth (which is actually the sign that they're really interested) and how much you'll sell them for what. Chapter 6 revolves around the part they don't teach anyone in "B" school, but it's the part your grandchildren will remember if you sell the store and have nothing left to pass on. Basically it's how to find resources to value your business as practically and painlessly as possible. How much equity should a founder hold onto or a hired VP receive? What kind of valuation can a new firm expect in its first, second, or third round of financing?

Some of the world's best-known examples of Internet success share their stories in Chapter 7 and explain which firms they now find themselves investing in. Listen to the founders of Yahoo!, Netscape, Amazon.com, ONSALE, GeoCities, Earthlink Network, and more explain how they went through the financing process, what they learned, and how they structured their deals. This is the fireside chat that may make you think twice about how to achieve the seemingly impossible dream.

Traditional venture capital isn't for everyone, and there are other ways and means to find capital. For example, in Silicon Valley the most revered group is known as The Band of Angels™. Some of them ride motorcycles, but the band they're part of is an investment club made up of just about half of the who's who of high-tech. The angels pump smallish amounts of capital into seed and start-up firms, betting they'll hit it big with an IPO or sale to a larger firm. Similarly, corporate investors pull out the checkbooks in record number to fund start-ups that complement their own corporate goals. Intel, for example, has made hundreds of investments in Internet and other specialized firms that expand the need for high-speed chips and other products that it sells—seeding the fields, so to speak.

Chapter 8 expands on the growing role of nontraditional venture money, where to get it, and how to approach the corporate or angel investor. If traditional venture capital is knocking on heaven's door, as Dylan may have put it, this is rapping on heaven's gate.

What would a book about Internet venture capital be without a handy Web site reference for all the links and goodies you can explore to your modem's desire? In the closing pages we offer a power Rolodex of who's who and what's what—the firms, figureheads, and an overview of their Web sites and where to find them.

The Big Idea

Chapter One

YES, AT TIMES that concept scribbled on a napkin while under the influence of caffeine and a hot fudge sundae at your local all-night diner with the agreeing nod from your friend may appear as the greatest thing the world has ever seen. It may be. But once the caffeine wears off and the ice cream dish sits empty, the realization hits that molding the idea into a real business is a major task. So the next minute you may think you're going completely insane—maybe the idea lacks merit, making it a success seems overwhelming, or just knowing where to begin becomes too great an obstacle. Self-doubt creeps in. Your mind tells you that you're not an entrepreneur, your idea isn't that revolutionary, a gazillion other people have probably already started doing something similar, you're already behind, you've got a real job (and real bills). Childhood memories of success and failure return. You recall moments of glory, but mostly the agony of defeat on the school ground, sports ground, romance ground.

How can you make sense of your options?

Any journalist hunts for information with the five Ws and H: Why, who, what, when, where, and how? An entrepreneur with an Internet business idea must start in the same place and answer those same questions.

➤ Why would it be a viable business? (Why bother? What makes it a market opportunity?)
➤ Who will make it a business? (Who will make up the management team?)
➤ What are the key markets (global, regional, local)?
➤ When is the best opportunity for the business (profitability time-line)?
➤ Where will the headquarters and primary market be located?
➤ How will all of this be brought together? (Are you the glue that can make it happen? Do you want to be the glue?)

Why?

THE FIVE WS AND H are really the heart of your business plan. The first thing you should do is to determine the merit of your idea and whether it can be made into a business. If you strip away all of the clutter, just ask yourself: Does this idea address or solve a real need for businesses or consumers? Is this idea a business? Some ideas aren't. If it's a business, then you need to start thinking about how big the potential market is for your goods or service. In the red-hot Internet start-up space, today's venture capitalists look for the $500 million to $1 billion company valuation as a line of first reckoning for their payback. Can your idea be made into a $1 billion company trading on Wall Street? If not, think bigger!

See Through the Eyes of Your Customer
THINK LIKE A CUSTOMER or user of your Internet service or product. Sure, the general idea may be fantastic, but can it be "monetized"? Can it become a business that will attract real customers, users, clients, and hence, more investors—both privately and eventually through an initial public offering (IPO) of common stock? Your company's valuation, based on its potential sales/earnings, alliances, and market niche, will determine whether or not venture capitalists think they can expect a good return on their investment. Getting that valu-

Idea Checklist:
Moving from Idea to a Possible Business

✓ Is there a demand for this service, product, system, idea?

✓ How big is that demand likely to be?

✓ What's the potential size in number of people/customers/clients and, more importantly, what's the potential revenue for your business?

✓ Is there any way to protect the intellectual capital of your idea from copying or imitators?

✓ Is it a business that can grow rapidly? How large can it grow?

✓ What are the revenue sources?

✓ Would people pay for this service, product, system?

✓ What are they buying now?

✓ Who will pay, the end user or those who want to reach the end user through this channel?

✓ How much would they realistically pay?

✓ Is it a service for businesses or consumers or both? If both, will the offering differ? If so, how?

✓ Are there any firms providing this product or service now? What do they charge, or how do they generate revenue?

✓ Does your way of doing it offer a superior ability to generate net income or rapid growth?

✓ Who are the competitors today and who may they be tomorrow?

✓ How have successful Internet firms attained their success? How much do they spend on marketing, sales, promotion, salaries—in short, for growth?

✓ What sorts of business models exist in the Internet industry and which best suits your idea? Or is there a new model you thought of that benefits your firm and investors more than existing business models?

ation off on the right foot means moving the idea past the idea stage and into the business stage. Answering the checklist questions will help bring out the business from the "idea."

Not all great ideas are businesses. Venture capitalists invest in businesses, not hobbies or notions, unless those hobbies or notions are really businesses in disguise. Venture capitalists are accountable to the folks who have placed their hard-earned capital with them and expect them to increase it, not squander it. The venture capitalists who have the most hits attract more of other people's money. Good money follows good, not bad money.

First Come, First Served

A CONCOMITANT OF the accelerated time in Internet space is the fact that many great ideas began small. Sometimes things on the Internet grow by themselves of their own accord. We call it "viral marketing," and it's how all the big brands on the Internet became the big brands. Viral marketing relies on the power of your idea-turned-business to provide real value to users or customers—values they will tell their grandma and friends about. Often that means being first or one of the first to provide a new service or product. People tend to flock to those who are first in anything whether it's the Superbowl winner or the first man to set foot on the moon. Nobody cares about numbers 2 through 10. Being first provides an extreme advantage.

Yahoo! cofounders Jerry Yang and David Filo worked on the "Jerry Yang and David Filo Web Guide" in their dorm room at Stanford while they applied for regular engineering jobs around Silicon Valley. After initial reaction was favorable, they began to see their Web site as a business and not a hobby. So did Sequoia Capital, which invested in the two students to help the redubbed "Yahoo!" business get started.

CNET founder Halsey Minor worked as an executive headhunter before delving full-time into the hybrid cable-Internet media firm centered on technology news he now commands. Amazon.com founder Jeff Bezos worked on Wall Street before compiling a list of twenty-five possible business opportunities in the then virgin Internet commerce arena, settling on creating a Web-based book retailer. Netscape cofounder Marc Andreessen (who led the University of

Illinois–Champaign team that invented the Web browser Mosaic) was Silicon Valley bound, hunting for work, when he was tapped by Silicon Graphics founder Jim Clark and premier venture capital firm Kleiner Perkins to be part of Mosaic Communications, which soon became Netscape. Netscape went on to become one of the best Internet IPOs ever, beginning an era in Internet capitalism in which start-ups grow in flea years and go public with barely a scratch of revenue and less-than-zero earnings.

All of the stocks mentioned above have shown strong performance, had decent IPOs, and, here's the important part—provided liquidity for the venture capitalists who helped nurture them to that point. Being a business means being sellable as an investment. Being first means commanding more attention from users and investors and attracting more buyers and sellers to your firm once it's a stock. Being first also translates into a higher valuation, if you can stay first. Compare the stock values of category leader Yahoo! versus Excite or Lycos, and leading Internet book e-tailer Amazon.com with gravity-bound Barnes & Noble.

Remember: Venture capitalists require a liquidity event of some sort from their investments. You see your idea as a "business" and the venture capitalists see it as an "investment"—two sides of the same coin. Otherwise, without an IPO or sale of your business, you and the investors are simply playing valuation games without a real gauge, a real market, to confirm the belief. Going public or selling to another firm gives the venture capitalists payback for their investment. That's the number one goal for all of them. Payback. ROI.

If you make it past the "is my idea a viable business?" then the real work begins.

Who?

ONCE THE VENTURE CAPITALISTS agree that you've come up with a way to create a billion-dollar valuation company, they want to know who you are and who your team is. Can you and they get the job done? We popped in to the world's premier venture capital firm for a first-hand observation. In his office, a stone's throw from Stanford University, the world's most notable venture capitalist, John Doerr, partner at Kleiner Perkins Caufield & Byers, scribbled a three-part

SPOTLIGHT WE CAUGHT UP with George Zachary,
partner at Mohr Davidow Ventures (see
the Resources section at the back of this
book for a Web address) to get his take
on what he looks for in an opportunity—what criteria he uses
to evaluate the hundreds of proposals he sees.

What's your criteria for determining whether or not to invest in an Internet start-up?
Zachary: Can this be a category leader? Is it in a great category (not just an interesting or a good category)? Can this category support a $500M–$1B company? Are these the guys or gals to pull it off? What is the proof that they can or are pulling it off?

How does venture capital work, and what can an entrepreneur expect?
Zachary: Great early stage venture capitalists help build the company by investing money AND TIME. The time comes in the form of recruiting a management team, building partnerships, securing customers, brainstorming strategy.... A great entrepreneur should expect great assistance. VCs expect a chance for 10×+ return.

What's the ultimate risk/reward ratio for a venture capitalist?
Zachary: Again 10×–20× return based on area of speculative market.

Based on the thousands of business plans that fly across your desk annually, what are the best ways for anyone sending you one to position the idea and themselves as a candidate for venture capital funding?

Zachary: An exciting, accurate, and complete thirty-second description of why this company should exist and win.

Where is best the place to start after knowing the idea is a real opportunity?

Zachary: Think about architecting the business. Think about what is necessary for winning, not just revenues or product development, but also market domination.

process on a whiteboard like some mad scientist revealing the formula for world domination (which is actually not far from the truth, considering the $1 billion Kleiner Perkins manages). "All great Internet companies are built on three elements," Doerr said, "people, technology, and capital."

If Silicon Valley were Hollywood, Doerr would be the Duke (as in John Wayne). In dealmaking and turning out winners, Doerr is the fastest gun in the Web. The notches on his gun include Netscape, @Home, and Amazon.com. To hear Doerr tell it, contrary to what most entrepreneurs believe, capital is not the most valuable part of the equation. In fact, there's more capital than places to invest it. Capital is easy. By far the scarcest resource, Doerr explains, is the people—talented people. Great teams make great companies. Capital always seeks great people. So in many ways it's not you seeking capital, it's capital seeking you—if your idea is the golden goose. It's even better if you are the goose that's laid a few golden eggs and can brag about it.

Which brings us to you, the Who in the five Ws and H equation.

Are you the person to get the job done as founder/CEO/whatever of this new idea-turned-business opportunity? If you have the right stuff, are you asking for too much or asking too late in your capital cycle? Most venture capitalists spell out which stage of investment they prefer to invest in. They usually prefer start-up since that gives them the most control for the least amount of capital—and they can help steer your company, they hope, into better waters faster.

The right stuff comes in many packages, commonly past success, proven ability in some form, and an idea that's so huge (the $500 million to $1 billion valuation company) that even if you blow it it's still a home run. How extensive is your experience in the field you're proposing to enter as an entrepreneur? The venture capitalist wants to know who else in addition to you may have joined your effort. No one person builds a company.

The original team at Marimba, a Java software firm, created an "instant company." Many of the Java development team at Sun Microsystems followed Marimba founder Kim Polese over to the new effort. Venture capitalists lined up to fund it. It was a plug and play company. Never mind that before it really got its feet wet the market it thought it was in changed, and suddenly "push" (delivering Internet applications to end users rather than users retrieving them) was dead—or at least misunderstood. In that rough spell Marimba readjusted, refined its role in the big picture, and settled on its strength. Its flagship product became Castanet, Internet software that passes along other software through World Wide Web browsers. At Marimba's April 30, 1999, IPO, 6.1 million shares changed hands. The company closed trading that day with a market value of $1.38 billion and a share price of 60¾.

Marimba rival BackWeb had a very different scenario. It was begun by a former Israeli commando/software guru whose plan was to sell its knowledge management distribution system to some leading corporations. More than 250 corporations, including Compaq Computer Corp. and Cisco Systems Inc., deployed BackWeb applications, and BackWeb Infocenter 4.0 had won industry awards for excellence. A May 1999 IPO offered 15.7 percent of BackWeb's stock at $8 to $10 a share, with shares climbing past $200.

So the "Who" with these companies was three-fold: who the talented leaders really were as people, what the media thought they were doing, and, more than anything, how the market actually defined who and what they were. Marimba, with its visible SunMicrosystems team, generated confidence and high expectations from the media and from noted venture capitalists.

What?

THERE ARE TALES of venture capitalists who have taken raw sugar and made it into a viable concern despite the original founder's idea. If you don't understand how your business will make money, it's possible that someone else will. PointCast began life as PED (named after the pedestrian crossing the founder saw while trying to dream up a company name). Its original goal was to provide CompuServe members with custom news delivery. The venture team at Mohr Davidow played a role in renaming PED as PointCast and thinking of a wider audience than just CompuServe's members, which sounded stupid at the time (1994) since everyone knew CompuServe was the king of online services.

The founders of HotMail, the Web's free e-mail service, originally had plans for an altogether different enterprise. Free Web-based e-mail was an afterthought. But once it was part of the mix, HotMail and its backers saw free Web-based e-mail as the cash cow. Microsoft acquired HotMail for $425 million—many, many times what venture firm Draper Fisher Jurvetson invested.

So your concept may intrigue venture capitalists, but they will also play a role in developing it to its potential. On the Web no business plan is written in stone, and companies must change rapidly to embrace the opportunity or die. That said, however, venture capitalists want to see nuggets of greatness in your idea, polished jewels in you and your team. Knowing your service or product better than anyone else relies on your knowing the overall potential market for it and how you can get to the prize: market dominance.

Being first helps, as we mentioned, but being smarter helps more. If you walk into a venture capital interview and they know more about your idea for Web widgets than you, then it's obvious you're not ready. Remember, too, that they receive thousands of business pitches each year and may very well have seen a plan similar to yours. So they may know more about it. You have to be able to sell the venture capitalists on your idea, you, your team, your ability, your timing, your experience, and your personality. They are the easy sell since they want to invest in ideas—that's the business they're in. Think of the marketplace itself: consumers, businesses, the world at large, and the hecklers on Wall Street. All of them will be a tougher sell than the venture capitalists, because it's a constant sell once your firm goes public, and every quarter you have to report sales earnings. When nobody's keeping score but you, it's simple. When thousands of investors track your every profit and loss move, thousands more debate your company on the Internet stock message boards, and hundreds of customers call up and ask if your service can be adapted to their needs, the selling gets deeper and more complex on every level. So if you can't convince the venture capitalist why he or she should invest in your business in a fifteen-minute meeting, how can you convince the world?

When?

IN 1969 WHEN the precursor to today's Internet groped its way out of the primordial stew of the U.S. military's computer network, an effort to build a network that could link researchers at various scientific research labs, the original gurus couldn't have capitalized on the development. In other words, if Vint Cerf, credited by many as a founding father of the Internet, tried to get venture backing to create a computer network, he would never have received a reply. In 1969 not only was venture capital much less developed than it is today, but also the notion of the Internet was like Buck Rogers— science fiction.

Wall Street certainly had no clue, nor time for it either. And yet today more than $500 billion or more in market capitalization has been created by Internet firms going public or PC firms becoming Internet firms due to convergence of computers with networks. That value emerged from companies being formed at the right time in the cycle of things—PCs becoming household appliances, information proliferating at rapid pace, the network itself becoming global, software being created that made a PC or TV able to log onto the network, services and products being built on that, and so on. Think of how the ancient Greeks simply built new cities on top of the old. Eighth-century B.C. Greeks didn't build today's Athens, but they enabled it to be built.

Your product or service must hit in the right timeline for it to be successful. Timing gets extremely difficult to guess. Your business plan is basically a hypothesis in time—that at a certain time your enterprise will be viable, profitable, expandable. If they invest, the venture capitalists agree with your notion of timing, that you've found a window to go through to create a product or service to fulfill a need at this time and in the future. Virtually no Web browser software developers get funded today. Why? That window was 1993–1994. If you knock on doors in Silicon Valley or Boston or Austin for venture backing for your search engine firm that looks very much like the handful of firms long since public, you can forget it unless you have a new and better way. As you gaze into the "what ifs" and "might bes" of your business plan, knowing when the window opens for your service or product, that is, your business, is at the center of why you should receive funding today.

Where?

NOT ALL VENTURE CAPITALISTS invest globally. In fact, most invest in their neck of the woods. VCs want to be involved in the growth of your firm. They cannot do that very easily halfway around the planet. Often, when they invest they also get a board seat. So when your board meets they're there. Or if you need to hire a new "VP of just-fix-the-problem" the VC wants to be able to help fill the slot, to bring in the talent, and to keep the investment protected. Look for VCs in your area first, ones interested in your sector. Check the Web sites of several to see what their existing investment portfolios look like and if they've already done similar investments. If so, maybe they won't invest in yours. Yet they may invest if your firm complements one investment they've already made. You'll never know until you make the pitch to them.

The other "Where" is Where will you be selling your service or goods—globally, locally, or both? The Internet is a global medium, after all. Anyone with a connection can tap your Web site and see what you're selling.

English makes up about 80 percent of all Web sites today, and most users speak English, although more and more readers of Japanese, French, Spanish, Chinese, German, Swedish, and other languages log on to the Web. In a space that's delimited not by geography but by language, culture, and imagination, where is your business located, and where are its customers or users?

How?

START WITH KNOWING your strengths and weaknesses. Becoming an entrepreneur (which may be more of letting the entrepreneur you are come out) may be the first time in your life that you look in the mirror and really get to know who you are. We go from parents to corporations or organizations where others make the rules, dictate the path, determine the deadlines, create the criteria, and evaluate the results. Those decisions and choices are important, but you're only one part of someone else's vision—their business, their unit. You've been a cog in the wheel of someone else's vehicle—an important cog, but a cog by any other name is still a cog. Being a founder of a new business means you're now the wheelmaster. Are you sure you want to be the wheelmaster?

The first step is *not* to think like a wannabe-CEO, already planning which cherry desk you want, which leather chair, which window view in what office park, which yacht club you'll join, how much debt you can pay off if this thing flies. Being an Internet entrepreneur is like getting teeth pulled while skydiving—it commands more than all of your attention, creates supreme discomfort, and provides a heckuva ride. The Internet is 24/7 (open all the time), and if you want to hit the big leagues it will take you working at it day and night to do so. There are no 9-to-5ers in the start-up world of the Internet. No time for karaoke in the fast-paced, ruthless world of building a twenty-first century enterprise. Seven days a week your mind will churn the business, the people, the capital, the pitfalls, the rivals, the allies, the moves, the news. Holidays become distractions from pursuing the dream. TV bores, movies no longer provide the escape they once did. For better or worse, being an Internet mogul means sweat for equity. Real sweat. You will become a student of how to build a company while you're actually building a company. You and the company will become one and you will no longer be able to separate yourself from this new "body" of capital, people, and ideas that you have brought together under a corporate banner. Once you realize it's not instant success and instant retirement, you will learn to think about your idea not in the abstract, but as an entity producing cash flow.

Decide if you yourself with existing resources are able to pursue the opportunity of your business through personal bank accounts, friends, family, coworkers, or your present company. If you want to provide turnkey Web services to the Fortune 500, however, it's unlikely that your bootstrap effort can get the job done. Big ideas are like big gorillas—they consume huge amounts. If the idea is bigger than your own bank account, then start laying out just how big the opportunity really is and how much capital it requires.

Before you look for capital, take some time to prepare:

➤ Evaluate your managerial skills and interest in heading a company.
➤ Determine management "holes" and how they can best be filled. (Remember the VCs may prefer to help you locate talented team members.)
➤ Develop a detailed business plan.
➤ Double-check the latest developments and news related to your product.
➤ Contact people in the industry to find out which venture capital firms are good candidates for you to approach.

Various chapters in this book will provide you with more details on each of these points.

All entrepreneurs should be aware that the sooner venture capitalists get involved in their business the more ownership the venture capitalists will have in that enterprise. It's simple math. Venture capital works this way: you sell a piece of your company (equity) at an agreed upon valuation, and the investors own that percentage of your effort. If you sell them a piece when your company is what you and they agree is worth, let's say $5 million, for $1 million then they own 20 percent. If you sell them a piece when your firm is valued at $10 million for that same $1 million, they own 10 percent. Knowing when to sell a piece forms the foundation for your capital structure; it also determines how much you will end up owning in the long run, and if your grandchildren will praise your savvy or deride your selling out too cheaply and too soon.

"Other people's money" (OPM) from venture capitalists or other investors is not a magical mixture that you can spend from without accountability or consequences. Being an entrepreneur means having the vision, energy, time, commitment, honesty, faith, trustworthiness, desire, ability, resources, ingenuity, adaptability, and humility to develop an idea into a living, breathing business. Building a business means knowing how to bring people together to share a common vision.

Rounding off the big-idea-turned-big-business opportunity, the "How" is the dynamic element that sets in motion the Why, Who, What, When, and Where. It's capital meeting creativity; the people, talent, place, and timing, all moving in concert; your business plan moving out of the dream realm into the here and now. With much hard work and a bit of luck, it may become an Internet superstar.

The Firms

Chapter 2 *Two*

IT MAY SOUND OBVIOUS, but the golden rule of venture capitalists is to make money on investments. They manage other people's money, from large institutions to high-net-worth individuals. Being professional money managers first and foremost, their job requires that they make this money grow. If your idea or start-up can help them do that, then you have a chance of getting funded. Understand this rule, because as simple as it is, it is the powerful concept behind what VCs do. Their professional investment is the basis of their other functions, all of which are designed to protect their investment in you.

The VC will assist you in some or all of the following activities (and more): raising capital, finding the right management, structuring the company, designing strategy, making alliances, and networking. Many of the top VC firms prefer to create a *keiretsu* (a Japanese term for synergy and working together) among their investments so that the portfolio of start-ups add value to each other through technology sharing, complementary services, and more. That's not always possible, however, if two of its investments compete in some ways. Then a "Chinese wall" must be built between them. Once a VC funds an enterprise, it may also invest more and may help attract other investors. This isn't humanitarian—it helps protect the investment. A firm with a $50 million fund investing $2 million per start-up over a two- or three-year period is limited to twenty-five investments (of about 3,000 considered) with that fund. It cannot afford to lose money on these chosen few.

VC firms keep score with valuation of the firm. The goal (as we've seen in previous chapters) is at least a 10× return as soon as possible (no more than ten years, but two or three years is more likely in Internet space). If your idea cannot produce that kind of return on invested capital, they don't want to talk to you. It's not personal; it's just that they are focused on making money grow. Opportunity costs. Never forget that a venture capitalist wants to make all investments successful. If they are not successful, the firm won't be able to raise more funds with which to continue as professional venture investments.

It follows then that knowing something about the firms is a good place to start your education:

➢ What type of start-ups do they invest in?

➢ What do they want to invest in?

➢ Which companies have they already invested in?

➢ How are the investments structured?

Despite the catch-all phrase "venture capital," all VCs are not the same. That means research on your part is paramount to find the firm best suited for you.

Listen to this story about successful Web site auction firm ONSALE.com cofounder and CEO, Jerry Kaplan. Kaplan's prior firm created the first pen-based computing product in the 1980s, long before the success of 3COM's Palm Pilot. Unfortunately, the product burned its way through $100 million (a lot of it venture capital money) in a tale of techno-terror dealings with IBM, Microsoft, Lotus, and others before crashing and burning. Kaplan jumped out of the smoking capsule and onto the emerging Web. He began pioneering Web auctions that allow people using the Internet to bid and sell items, often at substantial savings over retail or discount clubs.

Kaplan was undeterred after the pen-computing debacle and built ONSALE.com from scratch. At first he had some difficulty getting VCs interested. So he plodded ahead without them, building a prototype

ONSALE.com auction site on a bootstrap budget. Within minutes of the auction site going live in 1996 he had bidders and knew it would go like gangbusters. Kleiner Perkins, easily the world's most renowned Venture capital firm, thanks to its cadre of talented partners, invested in ONSALE.com and helped steer it through the capital and strategic waters.

Here's a play-by-play of ONSALE.com's IPO moment: ONSALE.com had planned to sell 2.9 million shares to the public at $9 per share in early 1997. But as the Internet stock market weakened, it ended up selling 2.5 million shares in a soft market at $6 per share. Failure? Hardly. By October 1997 Internet stocks were hot and interest in ONSALE.com grew, generating a secondary offering of 2.3 million shares at a much higher price per share: $28.25. Of the shares offered, 1.7 million came from ONSALE, meaning it raised $48 million with this secondary. The original IPO of 2.9 million at $9 per share would have raised $26 million and probably not paved the way for a secondary. The actual IPO $15 million gross proceeds (2.5 million shares at $6—a lot for a start-up trying to keep the lights on), added to the secondary's $48 million, suddenly made ONSALE.com one of the better cashed-up Internet firms. It now had more than $60 million, or 2× more than its original IPO hopes. A short six-month timespan turned gloom into zoom and in summer 1999 they announced a merger with Egghead.com.

Our conclusion: In a nutshell Kaplan spells out the necessary core ingredients to being successful in the capital and business market, that is, have the right VC. There is no doubt that Kleiner Perkins (whom we profile in this chapter) had a few good tips about financing ONSALE.com, even after the stock went public below its desirable range. In the venture capital world Kleiner Perkins represents the top, the elite, the proven firm that has had so many successes that it's the legendary leader in VC. Every venture capitalist aspires to be like Kleiner Perkins. But that doesn't mean that every entrepreneur is a match for Kleiner Perkins or vice versa.

How do you find the right VC? Check with the library, talk to business associates, and plan your journey for venture capital with care. Examine the Web sites we mention here and others (see our handy Web guide, steve-harmon.com), attend Internet conferences, especially those with venture capital as a conference topic. Read industry

SPOTLIGHT

Q&A

With Internet Auction Pioneer Jerry Kaplan, cofounder and CEO of ONSALE.com

WE ASKED KAPLAN to provide a few sound bytes about the early days of funding.

How close was ONSALE to not getting funded by venture capitalists?
Kaplan: We weren't—at least initially. We launched in May '95 self-funded. The first and only private investment was September '96, long after we were profitable.

What was the key factor in getting funded?
Kaplan: The company was clearly leading in its field and profitable.

How important was the choice of venture capitalist?
Kaplan: Very important. We went with Kleiner Perkins, an excellent firm.

trade magazines and Web publications. Gather business cards from VCs; give them yours. Ask them if it's OK to e-mail them and what they want in that e-mail.

A wonderful set of data provided by San Francisco-based venture capital industry tracker VentureOne shows more than 500 investments by venture capitalists from 1995 through 1999. Any one of these VCs on any given day may be the best one for a start-up to approach.

Softbank has been extremely active, making some powerful bets on a slew of Internet companies in early 1996 in an "if it moves, invest in it" approach. That strategy has paid off. Softbank's few hundred million dollar investment in Yahoo! before and at IPO turned into billions in just three years! That one win cancels any other unprofitable Softbank bets made during the past decade.

CMGI (NASDAQ:CMGI) was an early believer in Lycos and GeoCities. As the original investor in Lycos, for example, it turned a few million into a few billion. CMGI got its start, in fact, in 1994 by selling Booklink to AOL for stock, which CMGI later sold at a handsome profit to launch what would become its phenomenally successful @Ventures unit. @Ventures' success has been led by Lycos and GeoCities among the bigger brands emerging from its stable.

You may be surprised to find Intel (not a VC in the traditional sense) among the top supporters of new companies. It usually invests in later stage firms that complement—guess ?— anything that helps sell more of its chips. Intel invested more than $300 million in the Internet start-up space in 1998. But Intel is not a venture investor per se, so don't bombard them with business plans. Look to the venture firms who do investing for a living. And just because a firm is near the bottom of this list doesn't mean you should factor them out. Maybe they're hungry for a particular good investment whereas the top ones listed may be overwhelmed by alternatives. At the smaller firms you'll get heard without shouting. Check the number of deals in the following table.

I don't profile every firm listed there but mention only a few in this chapter. By all means use this as a snapshot, but not as an exhaustive list (that's why I have a Web site with the links to more than 100 venture firms globally at steve-harmon.com).

Don't think just because you have an e-mail or mailing address and a partner's name that you're ready to contact a venture capitalist. You must know more about the VC firm and your start-up's potential fit with it than they do. Go about it as a zealot, but a zealot with a thinking cap and road map. Learning the goal and investing philosophy of venture capitalists by taking a peek at some of their portfolios is required due diligence on your part before you begin actually contacting them.

You wouldn't call a pizza deliverer and ask for a bucket of chicken wings or walk into a sports clothing store looking for a double breasted wool business suit, or try to sell cars at a comic book convention. But as ludicrous as it sounds, many times when entrepreneurs try to raise capital they go about it in a similar haphazard way that will cost them time, waste effort, and create endless frustration. Unfortunately, that's

Venture Capital Investments Since 1995

VENTURE CAPITAL FIRM	NUMBER OF COMPANIES INVESTED IN
Softbank Technology Ventures	29
Intel Corporation	21
Draper Fisher Jurvetson	18
CMGI @Ventures	16
Kleiner Perkins Caufield & Byers	16
Hambrecht & Quist Venture Partners	13
Sequoia Capital	13
Benchmark Capital	11
Accel Partners	10
Bayview Fund c/o Robertson Stephens	9
Comdisco Ventures	9
Draper Richards	9
Trident Capital	9
Bessemer Venture Partners	8
Chase Capital Partners	8
GE Capital Equity Capital Group	8
Geocapital Partners, L.L.C.	8
Highland Capital Partners	8
Internet Capital Group	8
Mohr Davidow Ventures	8
New Enterprise Associates	8
St. Paul Venture Capital	8
Technology Crossover Ventures	8
Venrock Associates	8
Altos Ventures	7
AT&T Ventures	7
Flatiron Partners	7
Greylock Management	7
Hummer Winblad Venture Partners	7
Labrador Ventures	7
Menlo Ventures	7
Patricof & Co. Ventures, Inc.	7
Scripps Ventures	7

VENTURE CAPITAL FIRM	NUMBER OF COMPANIES INVESTED IN
Trinity Ventures	7
TTC Ventures	7
Austin Ventures	6
Bay Partners	6
CE Unterberg Towbin Capital Partners	6
Charles River Ventures	6
Crosspoint Venture Partners	6
First Analysis Corporation	6
J.H. Whitney & Co.	6
Massey Burch Capital Corp.	6
Mayfield Fund	6
Media Technology Ventures	6
Microsoft	6
Sprout Group	6
Vulcan Ventures	6
Walden Group of Venture Funds	6
21st Century Internet Venture Partners	5
ABS Ventures	5
America Online	5
Attractor Investment Management	5
Battery Ventures	5
Boston Capital Ventures	5
Brentwood Venture Capital	5
Broderbund Software	5
Canaan Partners	5
Oak Investment Partners	5
Polaris Venture Partners	5
Sequel Venture Partners	5
Yahoo	5
Zero Stage Capital	5
TOTAL DEALS	**502**

Source: VentureOne

what many start-ups do—get so enamored with the quest for capital, usually for far more money than they've ever dealt with, that they toss bait to any and all venture sources to see if one will bite. Getting a bite becomes the goal rather than selecting a partner for a long and demanding journey. Funding is not the final goal but the starting point. Never forget that. Remember that you are joining forces with a partner who will become a vital part of your corporate life.

Part of planning also involves separating your business from your personal life. In your personal life, $5 million may be "big money." The same amount in your Internet start-up's life means about twelve to eighteen months of keeping the lights on—if you're lucky. Microsoft spends hundreds of millions of dollars simply marketing just one of its products. Proctor and Gamble blows more money changing the font color on packaging one of its products than your start-up would consume in three years. The world is a big place, and capital flow runs in the trillions. Take a business approach to capital, not a personal approach.

Know your venture capital firm better than they do: What is it invested in? Which companies are similar to yours, which are not? How many partners does the firm have? Which specialize in your area? and on and on. Never forget the golden rule, though. Venture capitalists are professional investors. Everything they do is aimed at increasing and protecting their investments.

How do you go about your VC homework?

VC Web sites will usually (or should always, by my reckoning) say which business areas they invest in, how much they usually invest, which stages (start-up, first, second, third) they invest in, which regions of the world they focus on, or a combination of all these factors. See our Web guide chapter at the end of this book for a list of sites. They are also easy to click to from steve-harmon.com.

VC firms invest according to a variety of criteria. Sometimes it's based on geography; others mix location and type of Internet sector or product; still others look for category killers, regardless of geography. All of them want to invest in Internet companies that can grow fast and attract higher valuations along the way.

Obviously, you don't cold call a VC or send unsolicited e-mail with a 100-page business plan attached. So what do you do? Attend investment conferences, ask your colleagues and contacts if they know any venture capitalists or top executives who may be willing to hear your pitch. In short, don't shoot yourself in the foot with lack of preparation. Leads can come from those top executives or from attending a VC conference and actually getting some face time with a potential venture capital investor who gives you a business card.

Try to find a referral. VCs appreciate it, and it validates your idea. Just don't go looking for a referral from someone who doesn't really believe in your idea. Find one who does or someone you can convince. If nobody does, then maybe you need to re-evaluate or refine your idea. Or ask yourself if you are the person to convert this idea into the successful business that you may envision. Visionaries and dreamers are not the same thing. Know your strengths and weaknesses. Quarterbacks would never say that they play wide receiver or can slam dunk a basketball. Put the skills and lack thereof right there on the table before yourself, before you talk to anyone else about them. Be brutally honest. The VCs will be brutally honest with you.

The best way to get heard above the noise is to get a referral from a notable person involved in an Internet business. I have had several people contact me for this purpose and am sometimes pleasantly surprised at the potential of their innovation. I actually do, on occasion, refer the better ideas to VC friends of mine (see our entrepreneurs' hotlist on steve-harmon.com).

Never "spam" the more than 500 venture firms begging for money or claiming that your business plan can create the monster to eat Tokyo or Microsoft. Do some mental preparation. **In your favor, however, know that without entrepreneurs there isn't a venture capital industry, PERIOD. They need you as much as you need them.** Evaluate the venture capital firms to find one that fits your idea and one that you can live with for the next several years.

Having VC involvement saves time, but it is also a trying experience. Keep your eyes wide open during this process as you and they discover each other's personalities and expectations. They want to make sure all the legal documents to protect their investment line up: tax structures, legal incorporation, accounting systems, employee benefits programs, stock option pools, preferred versus common share rights, and tons of other legal stuff. The good part is that VCs have done this before and know the process for setting up businesses legally. The bad news is that you may not know the first thing about

Things to Look for in a VC (your start-up partners):

Capital: How much do they invest, and what are some recent examples?

Connections: What influence do they have in the Internet and finance industries?

Commitment: How much time do they have to focus on you?

Portfolio: Where have they been and why?

Experience: Do they have proven success developing companies?

Enterprise: Are they innovative thinkers able to help you strategically and technologically—but humbly?

the legal mumbo jumbo. Have a credible venture lawyer represent you during this process (we delve into this in Chapter 6, where we discuss valuation).

The VC will also help you attract management if it's needed—for example, if a VP of business development or sales is required right away. Hardly any start-ups begin with an entire executive management team in place. The VC has contacts and can make things happen here when perhaps you cannot.

No one VC holds a monopoly on increasing value. Here's another now-classic case of venture capital and entrepreneurs working together to make a company take off, illustrating clearly why it's important to find the right venture capital firm:

In September 1993, UUNET did its first round of financing at a $6 million valuation. Venture firm Accel Partners invested $1.7 million in October 1993. By June 1994, UUNET had a $20 million valuation.

UUNET value was $48 million in October 1994. In January 1995 Microsoft agreed to use UUNET as the backbone for its soon-to-launch MSN online service. That watershed event propelled UUNET to a $400 million IPO in May 1995 (I recall analyzing this as a financial analyst when Internet stocks didn't yet exist, at least by name!).

By October 1995, UUNET had a $2 billion valuation. That dropped, however, in January 1996 as predictions of the "death of the Internet" from overuse came from industry luminary-turned-(false) prophet of doom Bob Metcalfe. The Internet didn't die (Metcalfe literally ate his words on stage about this), and by April 1996 MFS agreed to acquire UUNET for $2 billion.

In August 1996 UUNET was valued at $3.3 billion when Worldcom came calling and acquired MFS (with UUNET in tow). So you can see how the right idea and right capital propelled UUNET from $6 million valuation in 1993 to $3.3 billion in 1996. Some appreciation! You see why venture capitalists want "big ideas."

The key for UUNET? John Sidgemore told an Internet World trade show crowd in a keynote: The company was built with the mindset of a Silicon Valley start-up rather than that of a telecom company. Important insight into your approach—think like an Internet start-up. Throw away the assumptions of the heavy-gravity industries you may be re-inventing. Accel played a key role in helping UUNET grow to meet the demand—demand which you can see was incredible. With the demand, value grew. The venture capitalists were happy, UUNET was happy. That's the model for how it works.

Accel's focus as an ISP/telecom venture capitalist likely saved UUNET years by preventing mistakes that could have cost it time, market share, revenue/earnings, growth, and ultimately a sale to now one of the world's largest full-service telecom companies, Worldcom, where Sidgmore now serves as vice chairman and COO. Although surely Sidgmore and the top execs had more to do with this result than any other factor, having a VC who understood where they were coming from and where they were going was extremely valuable.

Landing the wrong venture capital firm can mean the difference between succeeding and failing. Ask the entrepreneurs at any of the dozen nonpublic Internet Web directories or other pioneers (or the VCs that may have backed them) why they didn't go public and you'll usually hear a horror story about an entrepreneur who missed the boat or a VC firm that should have seen the boat leaving. Don't be left dockside when the "big moment" (IPO or sale) comes or if the market for the company's product or services shifts. Sometimes a bad partner can tie the firm to an old model when a new one emerges, as was the case when scores of companies eagerly signed deals with proprietary online services like Apple's defunct e-world when the Web provided superior distribution.

We've covered the basic background about what a VC firm does and doesn't do. We know that the goal is to grow valuations, protect investments, and steer entrepreneurs clear of unnecessary mistakes that can blow the entire start-up out of the running. Now let's take a look at some of the higher-profile venture firms, see what they're about, and peek at a few portfolios.

Accel Partners (www.accel.com)

INVESTMENT FOCUS

Internet, networking, multimedia, wireless

PREFERRED STAGE(S)

Start-up, early

NOTABLE NOTES

Accel likes to invest in start-ups with technology that helps make the Internet faster, bigger, better

PORTFOLIO PEEK

- Avici Systems, products for next-generation networking
- Broadband Technologies, fiber to the home
- Biztravel.com, corporate travel services via Web
- Axent, Web security software
- RealNetworks, video-audio software pioneer
- CyberMeals, Web-based food order and delivery services

Although some VC firms are anonymous partners concentrating on sectors, others are personality driven due to the high-profile nature or the sensibility of the partner or founder. In the mid-1970s software guru Ann Winblad was programming in the mainframe days of computing (and pioneering personal computing with her friend Bill Gates). She sold her own software company for $15 million in the early 1980s, did some consulting, and then made the plunge into the venture capital arena. She teamed up with ex-NBA Seattle Supersonic standout John Hummer and sought slam dunks in the venture capital realm. Hummer Winblad, which sounds today like an all-terrain vehicle, actually prefers to tread in its selected landscape, software, because of Ann's background and expertise.

John added his know-how, degree from Princeton, and an MBA from Stanford, and the two set about investing. In the early 1990s the term *software* came to include the new-fangled Internet in more and more ways. By the end of the decade virtually all PC software had Internet functionality of one kind or another. Another trend: functions like e-mail, storage, and file management, which formerly resided in applications on the PC itself, began migrating more and more to the Web as the Web itself became the world's own PC of sorts, each computer being part of an organic whole. In step with the software shifts, Hummer Winblad is regarded as one of the elite venture firms using expertise in this area. In recent years it has added partners Mark Gorenberg and Bill Gurley to its lineup, rounding out a very strong team. Ann provides depth in software and has earned genuine visionary status in the technology field. Ann is one of my favorite VCs and business friends because of her human approach and thorough knowledge. Let's take a look at Hummer Winblad.

Hummer Winblad Venture Partners (www.humwin.com)

INVESTMENT FOCUS

Internet, enterprise, and desktop software in these areas—Internet, enterprise computing, networking, communications, engineering and scientific, graphics, education, and entertainment

PREFERRED STAGE(S)

Start-up, early stage

NOTABLE NOTES

Ann has been named one of the top movers and shakers of Silicon Valley/Bay Area by many publications, including *Upside's* "Digital Elite 100" for the past three years. Hummer Winblad looks for a number of criteria, including a huge market opportunity, how well the product or service meets a specific need, and whether the management can make it successful. It is a very thorough firm and works well with those who commit to it.

PORTFOLIO PEEK

- Adforce, an online ad management service for online publishers and advertisers
- BigBook, a business Web site of building and directory services
- BizTravel
- Liquid Audio, a maker of software to provide music over the Internet
- WindRiver Systems, embedded systems software (including Web devices)

If you've ever heard of or used HotMail, the free Web-based e-mail, then you can thank Draper Fisher Jurvetson, another of my picks for top leading-edge VCs in the Internet space. This firm moves boldly into the Internet, with a focus on early investment, which means they take more risks than other VCs, but it also gets them into the hot stuff sooner in some cases. HotMail began as an entirely different firm, a database product pitched by its founders Sabeer Bhatia and Jack Smith to DFJ in 1996. DFJ latched onto the free e-mail idea the two technologists mentioned, pumped in $300,000, and HotMail was born.

DFJ infused $4 million more as HotMail quickly defined the free Web mail space and attracted tire kickers, those seeking to acquire it. Fueling this explosion was "viral marketing" (users market the service by recommending it to others). Growth went from zero users to more than 12 million subscribers by the time Sabeer met with me at Spring Internet World in Los Angeles in March 1997 where he was talking to eager conference attendees about HotMail. Shortly after, HotMail was sold to Microsoft. Soon after that, venture capitalist Steve Jurvetson, a partner at what was then Draper Fisher and the lead guy on HotMail, was added to the venture firm's masthead and Draper Fisher *Jurvetson* emerged as the new name. DFJ bet boldly and won big.

I asked Steve about his approach on HotMail—how the first investment came about. This example clearly shows how the VC pulled the most valuable aspect out of the entrepreneurs' pitch and made that a resounding success.

Jurvetson recalls the tale: "They (Sabeer and Smith) had been turned down by twenty-one VCs. The twenty-first referred them to us. They came to us as JavaSoft, Inc., with a plan to sell Java database tools. Upon sharing our concerns about the challenge of rising above the noise of a thousand vendors on the Web, they shared their marketing gimmick of free Web-based e-mail as a way to raise awareness for their tools. We told them we'd fund the marketing gimmick if they would put the tools business aside. We were their only investors in the first, second, and fifth rounds. We also participated significantly in the third and fourth rounds."

By the time Microsoft acquired HotMail, its value was north of $400 million by my estimate. That would translate into a 300× return on investment, or 30,000 percent, for DFJ within two years of the first $300,000 seed investment by DFJ. Let's take a look at what else DFJ has done and is doing now.

Draper Fisher Jurvetson (www.drapervc.com)

INVESTMENT FOCUS

Internet applications, and services leaning towards those that users market; intranet applications (front office and back office automation); e-commerce (business to business and business to consumer); bandwidth improvement software and hardware

PREFERRED STAGE(S)

Early stage, seed stage, pushing the envelope, bright idea stage

NOTABLE NOTES

From DFJ itself: "We believe the Internet is a major technology dislocation which creates unfair competitive advantages for the nimble start-up. New distribution channels tend to favor the new entrants who lack the legacy of channel conflict. The Internet is a wonderful substrate where a good idea can spread like wildfire, untethered by the physical domain restraints of manufacturing ramps and physical distribution. We find that the rate-limiting factor for many Internet businesses is the availability of good people as a company grows. We also find that Internet businesses tend to thrive on partnerships. When a business model maps well to the medium, we tend to find that a 'Net business extensively exploits a network of partnerships. To that end, we have found enormous synergy within our Internet portfolio and within the broader network of companies with which they have partnered. We have now invested in over forty Internet companies, *more than any other venture capital firm.*"

PORTFOLIO PEEK

- Centraal, XML-based real name Internet addressing system
- Cybermedia, online PC repair and recovery
- Direct Hit, technology that improves search results
- Four11, Internet White Pages directory
- Globalsight, multilingual Web solutions

- GoTo, market-based directory services
- Homestead, private Internet communities and families
- HotMail, the world's largest e-mail provider
- C2B Technologies, complete Internet shopping platform
- Digital Impact, Java-based product catalogs
- Direct Stock Market, Internet public offerings
- FastParts, Internet-based semiconductor trading exchange
- Index Stock Photography, automated stock photo agency
- Internet Shopping Network, one of the Web's first shopping sites

One of the best investment bankers on Wall Street, Neil
Weintraut, was one of the bankers who took Netscape public in 1995
to much fanfare and became an instant global sensation in the capital marketplace. Weintraut, who parked his hat at Hambrecht &
Quist in San Francisco before crossing the chasm to become a venture capitalist in 1996, is one of the brightest VCs I know. Neil has a
tendency to think in bullet points and is fond of alliterative concepts.
Neil's acronym power tip for success is Timing, Innovation, Passion,
and Smarts (TIPS)." What does the twenty-first century look like?
Here's a snapshot:

21st Century Internet Venture Partners (www.21vc.com)

INVESTMENT FOCUS

As its name aptly implies, the Internet. Specifically, e-commerce and enterprise

PREFERRED STAGE(S)

Early stage, seed stage

NOTABLE NOTES

21st Century is a venture firm seeding and nurturing new-economy opportunities.
Spawned by Hummer Winblad Venture Partners, the venture firm that garnered
significant success by focusing on the emerging software industry, 21st Century
was founded by the head of Hambrecht & Quist's Internet group, J. Neil
Weintraut, in October 1996. 21st Century professionals include Peter Ziebelman,
previously of Thomson Ventures, and Rob Reid, author of *Architects of the Web*.
21st Century is capitalized at $55 million and to date has seeded eight new-econ-
omy companies.

PORTFOLIO PEEK

- AdForce, an ad management service for online publishers and advertisers
- AvantGo, an enabler of enterprise applications for the mobile Web
- CareerBuilder, a creator of an Internet/intranet recruiting system
- Employease, a provider of Internet-based human resource and employee benefits administration services
- GreenTree, an online nutrition store and information megasite
- Vicinity, a geo-enabler of Web sites
- When.com, an Internet calendar and event service
- BigWords, textbook sales via Web

We've already mentioned the elite of elites, the firm that tends to get more attention than any other VC firm on the planet (rightfully so, and one certainly operating in zero G). That firm, Kleiner Perkins Caufield & Byers, earned its reputation thanks to its roster of home runs in the technology arena and length of time in the game. One of the first VCs, KPCB was founded in 1972, when AM radio ruled the airwaves, bellbottoms were cool, and personal calculators weighed 5 pounds and cost $300. Its mantra was technology investing when technology was boring and IBM mainframes with punch cards qualified as "state of the art" computing.

The founding partners themselves are legends in the "Valley" (as Silicon Valley is known). The Internet team they assembled is unsurpassed by any other firm and it includes John Doerr, Will Hearst (of Hearst dynasty fame), Vinod Khosla (who cofounded Sun Microsystems), and Russ Siegelmann (original VP of Microsoft's first foray into the online world, MSN).

But the numbers tell the real story: KPCB has raised over $1.2 billion in capital and has invested in companies whose total market value exceeds $80 billion. Almost single-handedly KPCB has defined what venture capital and technology can do together and has helped spawn some of the best-known corporations in the world: AOL, Ascend, Compaq, and Intuit.

Nothing has captured the hearts and minds of Wall Street like Netscape, which KPCB rocket launched to one of the most memorable and best-performing IPOs ever in the Internet space. KPCB played a key role in the formation of Netscape when Silicon Graphics founder Jim Clark went in search of the "next big thing" and found wunderkind software guru Marc Andreessen and the few thousand lines of software code called Mosaic (the first Web browser). Andreessen and some pals put Mosaic together over pizza and soda at the University of Illinois–Champaign as a way to put a "face" on the text-driven Internet, to make it easy to use. Millions of people using the Internet downloaded Mosaic and made it an instant success. Clark, with Andreessen and many of the original software programmers, turned this early etching into Mosaic Communications and recast it as Netscape soon after in 1994. Netscape's phenomenal rise from an obscure college-born set of HTML code to the world's fastest-selling software company propelled at light speed KPCB and its Netscape's champion, John Doerr, into the new economy. By the time it went public just a year later, Netscape was one of the hottest IPOs ever, oversubscribed many times over by investors wanting in on this instant megastar company that many saw as the next Microsoft. I recall several times during this period that Clark would say, "Microsoft missed this one." It almost did. Netscape's explosion on the scene was probably the single biggest event in the history of Microsoft, turning the PC software giant's focus away from its primary interest at that time, interactive TV, to the Internet. Had Microsoft truly missed this one, Netscape may very well have been the Microsoft of the next era. If only.

KPCB also invested in start-up Amazon.com when its founder from Wall Street, Jeff Bezos, showed up with a crazy notion to sell books via the Web. Bezos spoke at one of my investment conferences and said he had listed twenty-one potential Web business opportunities before deciding on books. Doerr (who sits on Amazon's board now) described the key to KPCB's decision to invest in the idea was that Bezos, the Wall Street analyst-turned-Web business visionary, had top technical gurus creating what promised to be one of the Web's first commercial successes. In 1994, at a time when nobody was selling anything on the Internet and, indeed, the Internet was seen as a nerd's world entirely, Amazon created almost single-handedly what "e-tail" (electronic retailing) would become: large selection, discount pricing, and overnight shipping. It seems natural now, but at that time the Internet was still seen as a "publishing"-only medium, and a dubious one at that. Credit cards, security, billing systems, consumer trust—none of these were in place, so Amazon created its own. Now, of course, new browsers have security built in; credit cards and Web payment systems are commonplace. In 1994, only Amazon and maybe a few others were even thinking about this. As such, they established the beachhead while nobody was on the beach yet.

Key point: Although not a prerequisite, a start-up with business and technical know-how has a better chance of getting funded. And being first matters in the Internet. Dozens of booksellers emerged, but Amazon quickly dominated.

KCPB has more success stories. Six Stanford grads came to its offices with a notion about archiving the Internet; they called it *Architext*. KPCB's partner Vinod Khosla (who was founding CEO of Sun Microsystems, which KPCB invested in back in the early 1980s, by the way) was the point man on the project. KCPB put in some seed money to keep the grads going and worked with them and another VC, IVP, in figuring out a business plan for the bunch. They did, and the boring name *Architext* redubbed itself *Excite* with an advertising model, and voila! You know the rest.

KPCB's profile shows the depth of the partners and gives a nice roundup of their approach and portfolio. Let's take a look.

Kleiner Perkins Caufield & Byers (www.kpcb.com)

INVESTMENT FOCUS

Many VCs use the term *Internet*; KPCB prefers *"information sciences,"* which include the following: The 'Net, enterprise software, consumer media, communications. KPCB also invests in "life sciences": medical devices and diagnostics, drug discovery and therapeutics, health care services and Informatics.

You can see how the Internet could be part of any one of these, and KPCB's roster reflects that.

PREFERRED STAGE(S)

Seed, start-up, first stage

NOTABLE NOTES

KPCB was the first VC to blend the Japanese way of synergy, keiretsu. The term *keiretsu* describes modern Japanese networks of companies linked by mutual obligation. The companies in the KPCB keiretsu consistently share experiences, insights, knowledge, and information. This networking resource, comprised of more than 175 companies and thousands of executives, has proven to be an invaluable tool to entrepreneurs in both emerging and developing companies.

In some cases the VC and entrepreneur connect quickly and a start-up can find itself moving extremely fast in the finance cycle to an IPO, followed by more growth, more growth, and still more growth. That brings to mind another longtimer in the venture capital business, Sequoia Capital, founded in 1972. Sequoia earned its stripes investing in the start-up or early stage of a host of firms that became technology powerhouses, such as networking king 3COM, Apple Computers, Atari (remember them, the video game maker?), Internet router/traffic king Cisco, and database king Oracle. The overall value creation evident here exceeds hundreds of billions of dollars in market capitalization for these now public firms. Time for a portfolio peek:

Sequoia Capital (www.sequoia.com)

INVESTMENT FOCUS
Information technology and health care (again a wide swath that has "Internet" written all over it today)

PREFERRED STAGE(S)
Seed, start-up, very early stages

NOTABLE NOTES
Prefers companies in the electronic and health care segments of the economy. Rapidly growing firms are a key attraction.

PORTFOLIO PEEK
3COM; Cisco; Apple; E-loan, Web-based loan services; eToys, Web-based toy retailer; LinkExchange, Internet ad services; Oracle; Quote.com, Web-based financial info; Security Dynamics, Internet security software maker; Yahoo!, Web guide and content.

Bolstered by Cisco, 3COM, Oracle, Apple, and more, Sequoia clearly has made its mark on the networking and PC industries, and then some. But the one firm it invested in the Internet space that put it on the map was Yet Another Hierarchical Officious Oracle, the longhand name for what anyone using the Internet today knows as Yahoo!.

Yahoo! began in a dorm room at Stanford with Jerry Yang and David Filo, who created it as an afterschool hobby. In 1994 Jerry Yang and David Filo's Web Guide, housed on Stanford servers, began to get more and more usage by people who wanted to find things on the unorganized and cluttered Internet. Web users would follow Jerry and David's links and submit some suggestions for others. Usage continued to grow and the two figured this may be a business. It beat working for an old-fashioned (in Internet thinking) PC or database firm as many grads did at the time. Sequoia reportedly invested $1 million for a 25 percent stake in the two Stanford Web surfers who thereupon got paid to surf. Yahoo! was born as a business. Today, the now publicly traded Yahoo! is worth several billion dollars.

You're going to want to study any potential VC partner as closely as an engineering plan for your future, because that's exactly what VCs are—engineers of capital. If you go bungee jumping you want to make sure the cord is tied, by whom, and if they've done this before. Proper bungee jumping can be a thrilling, successful ride. Improper bungee jumping (going into a VC realm unprepared) could be fatal. Determining if your company fits the criteria of a venture capitalist requires looking at the VC firm's focus, philosophy, history, and whether or not it's currently investing. Some funds are and some are not. Typically a VC raises a fund and then invests that fund. It then raises another fund.

Sustenance for a start-up requires constant capital infusion. Landing your first round in venture capital is indeed cause for celebration, as it validates your vision—for one day. It equates with the newborn infant taking the first swallows of milk. The newborn is happy for a minute and then gets hungry again, and again, and again—all the time. So will your start-up need capital. Newborn is newborn—in Silicon Valley or the nursery.

With Internet Guide–Directory
Pioneer Jerry Yang, Cofounder,
Q&A *Yahoo!*

When did you first realize that venture capital was the way to go with your idea? How did that realization come about?

Yang: David and I were considering a number of options at the time, including bootstrapping the company by ourselves. We considered the venture idea very seriously around February '95 when we wanted to remain independent (neutral) and wanted to grow the opportunity fast. When we talked to a number of VC folks, we really felt that in order to take advantage of the market window, we needed an injection of capital as well as some expertise in helping us to grow the company in such a dynamic environment.

Did you know anything about venture capital before you began the process? What was your first step towards taking venture capital investment? What mistakes did you make or what right things did you do, if any, along the way?

Yang: Both David and I were familiar with the VC process since we've both had exposure through classes and friends at Stanford. We looked at a number of VCs, some via introduction by friends, others, just by name. It turned out we were introduced to Sequoia through a common friend, and we talked to three or four others. We really focused on bringing in a partner rather than just raising money, and focusing on partnering with someone who could help our business overall was the key.

How did you determine the value of something as new (then) as Yahoo!, without any revenue or earnings to speak of? What was Yahoo!'s seed round valuation and how did that valuation get determined? How many rounds before going public?

Yang: Our first round in April '95, we took $1 million for a $4 million post money (the valuation after the investment has been made. If a firm is valued at $X with $Y representing the investment, then it is valued at $XY after the investment). We then raised two more rounds before going public: the second round was November '95 at $45 million post money, and the third round was March '96 (right before going public) at $300 million post money. The first valuation was, of course, very fuzzy. We decided on it because it was the best deal we got and it was with a VC partner we wanted to work with.

Who were the venture capitalists behind Yahoo!, and what was their input on how Yahoo! ran things?
Yang: Sequoia was the first and only VC we've ever had. Mike Moritz (Sequoia partner) was very open to how the company should be run, but we all agreed on hiring a seasoned management team as quickly as possible. We set out to recruit a CEO, and brought on Tim Koogle three months later.

What was the biggest benefit of having venture capital behind Yahoo?
Yang: A couple of things: One, they have a network and relationships that got us off the ground quickly—things like legal expertise, space, PR, etc. Two, and more importantly, we were able to take advantage of having someone who'd seen other companies grow and to apply their experience in very hands-on fashion to grow our business. It's no accident that in addition to Yahoo! Sequoia has been involved with others, like Cisco and Apple.

What's the key for a founder to be able to hold onto as much equity as possible, so that if a company goes public they realize their sweat equity?

(continued on following page)

(continued from page 57)

Yang: The key for founders is to make the company as successful as possible. Those founders who try to hold on to too much equity may end up not growing the business as big as they want. Of course, we were judicious about dilution and making sure that each round we took we were adding real value and growing our business.

What advice do you have for any would-be Internet entrepreneur considering venture capital?
Yang: Picking a VC is like picking another founding partner. You have to make sure they can add the value to help your company grow. And, most importantly, you have to be able to get along with the VC.

What's the funniest moment Yahoo! had in trying to get funded in its early days or trying to make ends meet?
Yang: Our name was something that always took a little explaining. I remember talking to one vendor and for the whole conversation the vendor thought we were a chocolate drink. (Author's note: There is a chocolate milk drink called Yoohoo that's been on the market for decades.)

The
Entrepreneurial
Pitch

Chapter 3 Three

THE CHANCES OF a venture capitalist seeing and responding to your proposal depend on the time of year, the particular venture capital firm, the partners at that firm, and unpredictable things like how much caffeine or sleep they've had. Perhaps three of 1,000 proposals actually receive funding in any given year. At some firms as few as twenty-five of 1,000 submissions ever produce a face-to-face meeting, because the demands on the company's time are so limiting. There simply isn't enough time to invest in everything, to back all the things that should or could be backed, and "Internet time" moves at a 7-to-1 ratio compared to regular business ventures. Time determines the selection process for who will and won't get funded.

VCs want to invest in the billion-dollar bets, those firms that can achieve a billion-dollar valuation quickly via being sold or through an IPO. Time dictates a lot of that. Time to market. Time to raise capital. Time to hire employees. Time to deploy. Time to sell. Time to raise capital again. Time is the thread woven throughout any firm, but especially Internet firms. Windows of opportunity open and close in record time in this space, so something like Amazon.com became one of the world's most-recognized booksellers because of when it was founded and how quickly it grew. If Amazon were founded this year it wouldn't matter—its time would have passed. Speed. Efficiency. And more speed. Time, more than size, matters in the Internet. The right timing with hasty buildup will equal size in short order. Just look at AOL, Amazon.com, Netscape, eBay, Excite, and dozens more. Make time your friend here. Use it wisely.

How can you increase your odds for getting in synch with Internet time to reach a venture capitalist?

➤ Get a referral from someone the VC knows and trusts.

➤ Network your way to at least exchange business cards with a VC.

➤ Put together a business plan or executive summary that gives a glance at your story without creating a novel.

You've often heard "it's not what you know, it's who you know" that makes the difference in the business world. In the venture capital space you'll find that most VCs will look at a company idea or start-up pitch if someone in the VC industry refers it to them. This is the "who you know" part. So who's in the VC industry? Directly and indirectly, probably more people than you think: everyone from venture lawyers, accountants, other investors, industry leaders or notables, top executives the VC has backed before—all are good sources for a VC referral.

So, the first question you ask yourself must be, "Do I know any people well enough to have them refer me to a VC?" Think about all the positions you may have held at various firms, college friends that may be in the industry, family members who may be working in technology or Internet fields who may have some connections.

If you have none of these, then consider attending venture investment conferences, Internet industry conferences where VCs, execs, and others gather to share knowledge and exchange business cards. Once at the conference, highlight the sessions you think best match your concept or those with speakers you want to hear. And when it's time for questions and answers (if it's offered), ask a question about what one of the VCs said or what they may think generally about the area you're planning on building a business in. After the session is over walk up to the podium or try to get a few seconds of face time with a VC and exchange business cards. Ask them if they'd like to see an executive summary and find out the best way to send it to them.

Networking can save you endless anonymous e-mails, letters, or phone calls to VCs that fall into the ether. Once your idea has a face on it, you're already ahead of the other piles of paper and endless summaries with unknown names typed on them. The VC is interested primarily in people with great ideas—more so than great ideas without the right people.

Voila! You're on your way to getting your plan at least read by a VC. But the hard part is still to come. Beyond who you know, it's also what you know as well—and how smartly you to approach the next phase.

Once you get the referral (who you know) or have a VC business card from a conference, what do you do with it? How do you prepare? What are the things VCs want to know when you approach them? These are central to your next step: preparing a brief summary of the idea with these bullet points covered. You may hear a VC ask you to "send over an executive summary." This is not a 175-page business plan or *War and Peace in the Internet Era*. It's a quick summary of the opportunity, risks, talent, and time line involved in your venture. A VC should be able to read your executive summary in about ten minutes—or less! Leave them wanting more, not less. Consider the cookie dough analogy: how many people love cookie dough? Lots. But how many people want to consume an entire quart or roll of it at one sitting? None. Give the VCs a few spoonfuls, and if they like the taste of your idea, they will be in touch. Make sure, however, that you've mixed the ingredients well enough!

Your executive summary should explain your proposal in no more than three pages. That's three! Remember time is more valuable than capital to the VCs. Think about reading just one more page of an executive summary multiplied by the 1,000 a VC might receive— and you can see how this page is wasted time for you and them. Say it in three pages, two if you're able, or even one if it all fits and the VC can read it without looking through a microscope. In other words, keep it a readable font size.

The executive summary is the most important part of your entire package of information since it's the opportunity for the VC to decide if he or she likes the flavor of your idea. Executive summaries contain an overview; think of it as a *Reader's Digest* or *Cliff Notes* summary of

What to Ask a VC After a Referral

FIRST, CHECK THEIR Web site for information (see links from steve-harmon.com). Ask:

➤ Are you looking to invest in my area?
➤ Which rounds and size do you invest in?
➤ Are you actively investing now?
➤ Would you like to have more information from me?
➤ What is the best way to send you material: e-mail, fax, or overnight delivery?

your business plan. Dwell on the executive summary as the most important document between you and getting funded, because it may very well be.

Put simply, a disorganized and ill-prepared business plan or executive summary can cost you the chance of getting funded. Why? That summary may be the first and only thing a VC will see of your hopes and dreams. If the wording, forecasting, and vision aren't there, then the VC likely won't take the time to "fix" the plan. No time! Especially with dozens of other plans waiting to be seen. Don't be a time bandit and cost yourself a chance to be seen. When putting together your business summary, think efficiency and conciseness—no hype. VCs are experts at reading and knowing business plans, poring over them day and night all year. So keep it short and simple.

I recommend that a header or footer on every page of your summary have appropriate contact details: name, address, e-mail, Web site URL (if you have one), fax, phone, along with the name of your business or start-up proposal. That way if a page gets misplaced it can be replaced, a copy of one page will contain all relevant information, or a VC can contact you without having to search for the title page.

The complete business proposal should have a title page with the above contact info and title on it, followed by a table of contents pointing to what's what in your executive summary and business plan. The title page is essentially a "map" to your business plan. You may find books and software programs that assist in writing good business plans. Use whatever works best for you, but always keep your own imprint and ideas, ways of thinking and planning, evident in your plan. No VC wants to get a generic, software-generated document that looks like a template from "Business Plans 'R Us." Put your personality on it without losing sight of the necessary ingredients of the plan, in no particular order.

Essentials of the Internet Business Plan

➤ *What is your type of business?* Service, content, e-commerce, e-tail, software, hardware, or a hybrid? Oftentimes in the Internet your business may fit more than one description since content and e-commerce, for example, often mesh in many ways. One example of this: information about movies may lead to your site selling videos.

➤ *How big is the market for the type of business you want to create?* No VC is interested in funding a start-up with a goal of capturing 10 percent of a $10 million market. They want to see markets in the $10 billion or more range. Music is a $20 billion industry in the United States; Amazon.com first took aim at the book market, which is about $25 billion; AOL and Yahoo! are in a race for advertising, which comprises a market of about $200 billion across all mediums; the office supplies market amounts to about $140 billion, up for grabs. VCs want to tap a huge market potential—if your firm garners 2 percent of a $30 billion market, that's great. But 1 percent of $140 billion is fantastic. This may be difficult to achieve, but not impossible as the Internet opens up new opportunities to those who can see the path to market leadership in some area.

➤ *Who are you? Who makes up the team?* It's not always necessary to have a team in place, but the VCs will want to know the founder's degree of passion for achieving the goal. The VC wants to know your track record, what you've accomplished in past jobs or positions, and your technical or business accomplishments. Good technology is not enough unless you already have patents for an original, "hot" product. Beyond who you are, why are you bothering? How can you become a huge market leader quickly and cost-effectively, grow revenues and customers or users exponentially, and create barriers to competition by sheer momentum? 21st Century Internet Venture's Neil Weintraut calls this the "get big fast" method. I would add that VCs then expect to "keep getting even bigger, even faster."

➤ *How much of the market can you grab and how fast?* Given the background of you and the team you may have in place, can you scale an Internet company in Internet years, go from heavy gravity (in my parlance) to near zero G or even pure zero G and handle the pressure? Being at the helm of an Internet start-up is akin to captaining a ship through huge seas. Larger ships float on the horizon in the form of established market leaders that have yet to "Internetize" their operations. You must beat them with speed and agility. If Barnes & Noble bookstores had established Internet outlets in 1994 there might very well not be an Amazon.com today.

➤ *What kind of net income margins can this sort of operation generate?* Is this an attractive business after you've established a beachhead and strong revenues? Who are your competitors and can or will you ever work together with them in a co-opetition (a competitive but cooperative way)? Eventually Wall Street needs net income to support your valuation for the long haul. Early Internet IPOs such as Onsale, eBay, and CheckPoint Software posted positive earnings soon after going public or before. That has a big effect on the valuations of these firms. CheckPoint Software, maker of firewall software, had three big pluses when it went public: leading market share of more than 40 percent, positive earnings, and technological advantages. These are things that VCs drool over. The sooner you get any one of them, the better.

➤ *What are the necessary steps to get your start-up from garage to Wall Street?* Strategy? Marketing plan? How do they come together, with the help of the VC, to make it all happen? VCs talk about "risk points" and generally the first round or seed round of financing is all about overcoming one risk, say, creating a prototype of the Web site. Round two may be about overcoming another risk point, hiring experienced managers, for example. Later rounds will each have risks that you and the VC will target until you have a business with a clear or clearer path to predictable revenue and earnings. Step by step.

➤ *Board members, not bored members.* Many start-ups make the mistake of padding their boards with individuals who contribute nothing but a name that others recognize. These are bored members who may make first glancers notice, but who will, inevitably, just take up space on your board and offer no value to you, the employees, the shareholders, or the VCs. Go for board members who are interested in you and your start-up, who can help open doors to deals and offer insights into how industry works. The ideal is someone who is both known and has an interest in your firm. VCs will help you put together a strong board if you get funded and will probably want a board seat themselves in many cases.

➤ *The centerpiece for a business is capital inflow and outflow.* You must have some sense of at least three years' worth of financial plans: sales, expenses, income/loss, cash flow statements, and other standard balance sheet info. I say three years, because although many business forecasts go out five years—and you're welcome to do this also in yours—a lot can change in three years. Look at Netscape, which went from browser company to enterprise software maker to Web portal in thirty-six months. Projections are necessary, but flexibility and willingness to see the tidal changes in this industry are more important. Don't overestimate sales in the first twelve months. Aim low (not too low) and over-deliver. Kleiner Perkins targeted Netscape users at 10 million the first year. Netscape had 20 million. Once Netscape proved it could deliver, raising more capital was a breeze, with the company on its way to one of Wall Street's biggest debuts ever.

➤ *Be specific with what you plan to do with the capital.* Build Web site. Hire VP Marketing. Deploy Sales Force in Northwest. With each round of financing you will have to let the VCs and other investors know what you plan to do with the proceeds.

➤ *Consider how to spell out capitalization and return for investors.* Professional venture capitalists will work with you and your venture lawyer to do a "term sheet" that says how much of the company the VC is buying for how much and what type of security they're buying. I recommend that you find a good venture lawyer here and not try to do this yourself. Each area of the U.S. and some international cities have venture lawyers. Sometimes you can get referrals to one from a local university that may teach start-up financing as part of its business program. In Silicon Valley, Wilson & Sonsini is well known. Another is Venture Law Group. (See steve-harmon.com for more links.)

Here are some vital tips on your executive summary and business plan, which are really living, breathing documents, full of the hopes and dreams of you and perhaps of others who are reaching for the stars of the new Internet universe.

One of the major assumptions is that the VC knows all. Never assume that the VC knows everything. If you e-mail over a quick note that reads "We want to own the office supply market!" it may be quite clear to you that this represents something enormous and that the VC should fall at your feet from the magnanimity of the notion. Keep in mind the tons of business pitches VCs receive and that their minds may be focused on the current investments they're steering through the maze out there. A better approach would be to exclaim, "Our Web site makes ordering office supplies automatic and saves businesses an average of five hours a week they would've spent poring over office supply catalogs. It also saves $10,000 per year through our discounted and incentive buying program, something that we uniquely put together to reward customer loyalty. Studies by ABC research showed that the number one thing business managers wanted to make more efficient was ordering office supplies and saving time. We forecast that this approach may be able to take our firm to an x percent market share within twelve months of a $140 billion office supply market." That's an attention getter. It may not result in your getting funded, because the above factors all interrelate and bear on that decision, as does the VC's focus. But make it your own way of saying it, not a cookie-cutter pitch.

Another thing to remember is that you have to know the facts about your line of business up and down and twelve ways from sideways. If the VCs know something about the business area you're talking about, and they just might since they receive thousands of business plans, and ask, "What happens when your margin collapses because of XYZ?" and you look like a deer in the headlights, then you've blown credibility. If you come up with statements like "Nobody's ever thought of this before!" when two dozen business plans on the VC's desk have the same idea in them, then you're wasting your time and the VC's. Often ideas are a commodity, but the talent to execute them and make them a reality is rare. A billion people on the planet know what a slam-dunk is in basketball, but how many can defy gravity and dunk?

You have to know ten times more than the VCs about the start-up you hatched, because if you don't they won't fund you. There are simply too many great ideas ready to be funded with people who walk the walk and talk the talk—not with hype but real knowledge. Don't try to dazzle a VC with babble or gobbledygook about why 123 Protocol will revolutionize the planet. Talk about why customers or people will use this, how it fills an existing market need, improves by light years some process or service on BIG scales, how your chief technology officer was a leading force behind the creation and implementation of abc123 at a well-known firm. If it's a small firm and nobody knows about the accomplishment, it means zero and sounds like hype. Keep it REAL! Talk to the VC as if you're telling your mother or father, cousin or brother about the real potential of the enterprise. The VC will appreciate candor.

As I said, the good news is that VCs need you. The bad news is that they may not need you. It all begins with a solid business plan, a business plan with carefully thought-out financial projections in it. You cannot, however, predict such wild market antics as a rival giving away a similar product. You should, though, discuss the risks involved IF such a thing happened. Risk and reward always go hand in hand. Discuss both in your business plan with equal candor. Don't downplay risk as if it doesn't exist. Address risk by providing solutions for overcoming or lessening it.

Read sample copies of the forms produced by companies that have already gone public. They are called "S-1" in the SEC code. These effectively are business plans. In them you will see an example of elements your business plan should include: company overview, industry, risks, competition, alliances, partners, what the capital you raise will be used for, cash flows, profit and loss statement, and so on. If you've been in business and have actual data, that's good. If not, then be brutally conservative yet optimistic about the numbers—which sounds like an oxymoron. One way to make it work is to say if we get 1 percent marketshare it represents $x or if we get 5 percent it could generate $y. We're targeting 2 percent for this forecast but aim to beat it. Here's how...."

The industry section of your business plan lays out the obstacles and opportunities, risks and rivals you expect to encounter; government regulations, if any, or if any could be implemented which would hinder your business; and ownership structure. If you have existing investors (friends or family) or have doled out equity, then mention it. If you're a seed stage company, it's not a good idea to get into equity distribution before getting the VC involved. Ann Winblad of Hummer Winblad says this is a big mistake, especially if the cofounder who holds 25 percent equity just walked away with it while you have 75 percent of the company now to sell to investors and new employees. Your chances of getting funded went to just about nil if someone who helped you come up with that great idea wants part of your new company's equity without sweating to make it a reality. So don't get into equity distribution too soon. Let the VCs together with your venture-financing lawyer divide up the company appropriately (see Chapter 6 for more on this).

Future sales charts always look like a hockey stick, yet you must have the logic and reasoning behind the growth to make the chart believable. Explain why sales jump so fast, what drives growth, how you capture sales, what your marketing plans are to achieve this, who your allies are or will be to make the process go quicker, what your rivals may likely do to thwart your goals, which regions of the world you'll focus on first and last, and, with the Internet, which LANGUAGES AND CULTURES you'll be selling to and dealing with. For the Internet is global. Although English is the lingua franca of the Web, the opportunities to truly address a global audiences—in native tongues—are outstanding.

In a nutshell, the best way to approach a VC: get a referral from someone you and they both know or someone they've funded in the past who's seen your idea. Attend conferences and exchange business cards with a VC; put a face on your idea. Write your executive summary and business plan with passion and heavy doses of both the rewards and risks of your endeavor. It is a map to your Internet future. And remember, like the song says, "Time is on your side." The right VC, one that can move your business along with capital and connections, can help you tremendously to optimize that time.

The People
Power Q&A with
the Dealmakers

Chapter 4 *Four*

IME IN THE INTERNET space looks like Salvador Dali's melting clock. On any given day your friendly, neighborhood venture capitalists are out talking with prospects, making investments, attending board meetings, calling lawyers, scanning a gazillion new business plans, and putting out fires at portfolio firms. Virtually all of them experience what venture capitalist John Doerr calls a "time famine."

Therefore, getting past the letterhead and understanding important venture capitalists' key insights can save time for both you and them. In order to give you their own words, this chapter follows a question and answer format so you can get their unedited thoughts.

John Doerr—*Kleiner Perkins Caufield & Byers*

IF SILICON VALLEY were Hollywood, Kleiner Perkins's partner and the world's most notable venture capitalist John Doerr would be the Duke (as in John Wayne). In making deals and turning out winners, Doerr is the fastest sure-shooter in the Web. His gun includes notches for

Netscape, @Home, and Amazon.com. Doerr's being a partner is not the only reason his firm has been successful. Consider that about half of the top ten Internet and Web companies, measured in overall market capitalization, were backed by Kleiner Perkins Caufield & Byers. However, because of his success in recognizing winners early, especially the high-profile and pioneering role he played in landing Netscape and Amazon.com, Doerr has become the most visible partner in the Internet venture space.

As is the case with many VCs, Doerr comes from a high-tech background (surprise!), not finance. He holds Bachelor's and Master's degrees in Electrical Engineering from Rice University and an MBA from the Harvard Graduate School of Business Administration.

He was at Intel in the mid-1970s when the microchip kings-to-be debuted the first 8088 processor, a Magna Carta moment in the world of technology and the beginnings of what would become the personal computing industry. By the time Ronald Reagan ran for President in 1980, Doerr was taking office at KPCB with his focus on the emerging, yet still fuzzy, world of PCs. That was, after all, the era in which the Commodore Vic 20 was as good as it got in PCs and only the most die-hard Radio Shack customer gave a hoot about them.

Doerr rose to the top of Intel's systems sales force by recognizing the cutting edge of silicon. He could see that it would generate more and more uses. By watching the chips multiply, so to speak, he followed the silicon trail and began betting on a series of visionaries who were tired of the mainframe era. From his insights and instincts KPCB invested in firms that would later dominate PCs or PC computing in one way or another: Compaq, Lotus, Intuit, Symantec. And as newfangled things called *networking* and *multimedia* began to rumble in the early 1980s, Kleiner Perkins led the way with bets on Sun Microsystems and Macromedia.

It was no coincidence then that just as the PC world began to shift to an Internet world in 1994, Doerr once again saw the landscape changing long before most. KPCB, hence, bet on Amazon.com and Netscape, putting up $5 million for a 13 percent stake for the Web software pioneer in early 1994 when no other VCs would even touch the "absurd" valuation that Silicon Graphics founder Jim Clark wanted for his "next big thing." Recall, those were the days when Mosaic (the most popular browser in 1993–1994) ruled and Marc Andreessen was looking for a first job out of college. Netscape was born.

Shortly thereafter Doerr imagined a faster, better Internet access service sent via cable TV's bigger wires and recruited heavy hitter and world's leading cable firm TCI into the joint venture called @Home, which KPCB partner Will Hearst brought to fruition.

Let's let John explain his uncanny ability to see the big picture and also add the details, jumping right into a reply:

 *Doerr:* Steve, I was going to tell you the tale of Excite: seven Stanford students visited us with a superior search technology and the moniker Architext (remember that?). Our initial investment was $300,000. While the technology was superior, we knew it wouldn't carry the day, so forced ourselves over ninety days to develop three business alternatives.

Three years (and lots of deals later) the enterprise is highly regarded, well managed, aggressive, and worth $2 to $3 billion (I think, depending on the day). The Excite story is a story my partner, Vinod Khosla (the KPCB partner who oversaw the investment), could best tell.

I like the Excite story because it disproves the conventional wisdom that venture capitalists have become risk-averse money managers, that they have time to make only huge multimillion dollar investments, and that they will only do it when the team is pretty complete and sure about their plans. At KPCB, anyway, that generalization couldn't be more wrong. Year in, year out, with seven to ten active partners, we've helped entrepreneurs incubate, start up, and speed up new ventures, typically twenty projects a year. The founding of the ventures has created hundreds of thousands of jobs, billions in revenue, and billions of market capitalization. KPCB has made many of the leading investments in personal computing, networking, Internet software, e-commerce, and the life sciences (biopharmaceuticals, medical devices, and genomics).

Some of the fiascoes that failed (but provided lots of learning): pen computing, and of later vintage, MNI (MusicNet).

But, more recently I've been luckier:

➢ **Silicon Compilers** (the first company I incubated, and cofounded with Dr. Carver Mead)

➢ **Compaq**

➢ **Sun** (including Java, getting Java in the Netscape browser)

➢ **Intuit** (including trying to sell it to Microsoft, then abruptly shifting strategy to develop our own Web presence)

➢ **Netscape** (The first stab at a thorough accounting is in Michael Cusumano and David Yoffie's book, *Competing in Internet Time*, and the story's not over). Our main contribution was recruiting a first-rate team. Netscape made the Web accessible for everyone, which changed everything.

➢ **@Home** I was lucky to see an early cable modem, was blown away by the performance, and helped organize the cable industry to get them to consumers. I recruited technical founder/networking genius Milo Medin out of a GS-7 position at NASA and drafted my partner Will Hearst, who helped structure the business through launch. Then we recruited the president of Silicon Graphics, Tom Jermoluk, a phenomenal leader. I'm convinced @Home is an important, not-yet-understood, big part of the future of the Internet.

➢ **Excite** A great story, with terrific assistance provided the venture by Vinod Khosla.

➢ **Amazon.com** Not been written about yet. A "speed-up."

➢ **Healtheon** (A provider of Internet services to the medical and health care industries.) First rate time. A very important company in the important health care market. My first failed IPO. Bad time. They'll be back.

➢ Some recent projects, too early to brag about: **drugstore.com, realtor.com**, and **Handspring**, from the inventors of the Palm Pilot.

Counting AOL, which established momentum (but not profits) before the Web, KPCB has backed five of today's top ten largest market-cap Internet leaders: AOL, Amazon.com, @Home, Netscape, and Excite. The partnership (KPCB) has also helped other leaders/pioneers develop their net businesses, including personal finance **(Intuit)**, travel **(Preview Travel)**, sports **(Sportsline)**, parenting **(iVillage)**, health care **(Healtheon, drugstore.com)**, apartment renting/services **(allapartments.com)**, home buying **(realtor.com)**, home delivery of groceries **(homegrocer.com)**, and several business-to-business services, etc.

Kleiner Perkins was an original investor in Internet pioneer Netscape, which popularized the browser. What can you tell us about that?
Doerr: I had a series of meetings with Jim Clark and then a first vivid meeting with Marc Andreessen. Marc sat in that chair in the corner and told me that he had some software that would change the world. I knew of Mosaic (the first browser developed at the University of Illinois–Champaign by Marc and classmates); I had seen it in January 1994 and in May met with Marc. Marc is this hulking, wise, mature-beyond-his-years kid. He had this insight

that if you made this ubiquitous Web easy to access—one click, you get what you want—that everybody might use it. By the end of that year we had 20 million customers. The goal I had set was 10 million, but it had 20 million active users! So there's lots of stories to tell about Netscape. One meeting with my partners was all it took. We paid what we thought then was a very high price—$5 million investment on $20 million valuation. It was only Jim and Marc and five or six other engineers. We promised them that all the partners here (KPCB) would work as fast as possible to help the company recruit four to six world-class vice-presidents and a CEO. In 120 days we did that. The whole Kleiner team worked with management. I want to make it clear that Jim Clark and Marc Andreessen made the final decisions about these people, but we helped them recruit them.

So Netscape was a real turning point for you?
Doerr: Netscape was the real eye-opener for all of us, and led all of our partners to make Internet-related investments: the travel area with Preview Travel—Doug led that effort; the Excite story—these seven Stanford students that walked in our front door; Sportsline.

How did Sportsline come about?
Doerr: A Netscape rep met them on a sales call. They were looking for venture capital. The Netscape rep said, "Great. I'll introduce you to my friends at Kleiner Perkins." And we invested. Netscape set up a strategic deal with them around server software, and they charged forward. We thought it was key for Sportsline to have a large media partner, a broadcast partner, because of the role that television plays in major sports. Sportsline was originally targeted towards providing information, handicapping, and odds for office betting pools. But it's evolved into a full-fledged, head-on provider of sports information. Mike Levy, Sportsline CEO, and the team have done a great job. We got a guy by the name of Mickey Schulhof from CBS–Sony on the board and that helped us, I think, ultimately put together the important strategic relationship with CBS.

What are some of the latest e-commerce start-ups Kleiner's invested in?
Doerr: Lots and lots and lots of them. We've got this project, drugstore.com, which my partner Dave Wharton was instrumental in getting involved in. We're working on Chemdex, business-to-business lab technician online service; a bridal registry; lots of projects.

How big is the opportunity for the Internet? You've been quoted saying it's underhyped. What are your thoughts now?

Doerr: Fewer than 2 percent of the world's population is on the Internet right now. We've just scratched the surface of what's going to happen. This is only the fourth anniversary of the commercial Web browser—this has all happened within four years. And it's got very long legs, a long way to go, this phenomenon. It's not a fad. It's not a pen computer (an area that Kleiner invested in heavily in with a start-up called Go that ultimately failed to the tune of $100 million, but whose founder went on to start Onsale.com, which Kleiner backed). The Internet works. It matters. It's interesting to think about why the Internet is important. The PC was a big deal. That was the best investment area for venture capitalists in the 1980s. The PC was all about spreadsheets and word processing. When you punch through that and lower the cost of communicating, the Web is in a different place in the income statement. It's on the top line. It's something that educates, enter-tains, informs, sells, inspires, collaborates, governs, even makes meaning out of life and death. That's a much more powerful dynamic than lowering costs and it's why the Web-related companies are already worth $400 bil-lion. It took a decade—from 1980 to 1990—for the whole PC industry to be worth $100 billion. So here in half the time we've done four times that already. And we've just gotten started. Look at what's to come. This is a big deal.

The Internet is going global. Can enough capital be raised for a start-up to be truly global?

Doerr: Yes. Depends on the size of the market and competitors. Is Amazon.com a truly global Internet commerce company today? It is, yes. How much capital did it take to get Amazon to where it is? Well, about $50 million of equity and $300 million debt. The first venture capital investment was large. It was one of the largest investments we'd ever made; it was $8 million. Jeff (Amazon founder) used all that to go build brand at a time when it was cheap to build brand. But look at Excite. How much capital did Excite require? Our first investment there was $300,000. I think they may have consumed all of $5 to $7 million before they went public. So it all depends on what competitors are like and the point in time.

Not a lot has been written or told about Kleiner's investment in @Home, the cable Internet service that has agreements with most of the U.S. cable

operators to provide them high-speed programming. @Home seems to be a huge idea and very capital intensive.

Doerr: @Home itself has only cost maybe $100 million. They'd raised more than that. The truth is they're leveraging, working under contract, billions and billions of dollars of cable plant—getting the cable folks to make that a two-way infrastructure. So that's a real partnership. That's like an NBC-local affiliate model. @Home is to the cable operators what ESPN is to the cable operators, providing a programming service. People love it. We're up to a couple hundred thousand subscribers and I think could have a million in a year or two.

What's holding it back? @Home already passes 10 million homes, and entrepreneurs (many reading this book) would be able to offer a whole slew of new services over high-speed.

Doerr: Capital. All that's holding it back is capital. The cable companies have been short of capital. It'll cost about $36 billion total to upgrade the cable infrastructure to two-way communication. About $6 billion has already been invested, so that's $30 billion to go.

And there's DSL and other high-speed rivals coming from telco. So, who's going to win, cable or telco?

Doerr: That's a really great question. The experts disagree. Bill Gates has been on record as saying that in the long run he thinks DSL will win because you only have to invest for each line you upgrade, whereas the cable folks have got to upgrade a whole neighborhood. I think early on cable could have an advantage. But there'll be HDTV (high-definition TV) solutions; there are already satellite solutions. It's too early to tell who the broadband winners are.

What things do you look for in an entrepreneur or start-up?

Doerr: Let me tell you what it was like when I first visited Amazon.com. There may have been a total of twenty people in the whole operation. Jeff came bounding down from this loft with a big, genial grin on his face and said, "Hi, John. Let me show you the place." From that moment on I knew I liked this guy. We wandered into the technical area. Shel Kaphan, Amazon's CTO, was nursing along one *Alpha* server that was trying to keep everybody up and online. Jeff said the one thing that would limit their growth was the ability to hire software programmers, that this was a software company. We needed software talent to have this site scale with the demand. Jeff himself is a computer scientist from Princeton, so he showed me how he would run the command on the Unix-Oracle database to figure out how many book orders had happened that day. Jeff's wife, Mackenzie, was doing the finances at that time (she's not any more), and Jeff took me out to the warehouse where they were shipping all these books, and it was just buzzing. Growth was 6 percent per week, so you'd have to be dumber than a doorpost to not think this was an opportunity.

With something to show, it's far easier to get the venture capitalist's attention and also increases the competition among venture capitalists to fund the deal, right?
Doerr: Jeff made it plain to me that he had other very attractive offers from other venture capitalists. He had heard good things about Kleiner Perkins. So we had to compete to get the business.

What's the advice to entrepreneurs out of all this?
Doerr: I want them to think about these key success factors as well as some risks. I think entrepreneurs ought to work with or approach more than one venture capital firm.

View the signing of a venture capitalist like the signing of a vice president. Interview them and check out their references. They ought to ask them about their failures as much as successes. Most importantly, after their first and every meeting with a venture capitalist, make sure they ask them where this project stands. The worst thing to have is a slow maybe. And it's reasonable for investors to take several weeks to figure out if they're moving to a decision or not. So just ask: "Where does this project stand right now? Are you likely to invest or not?"

Some factors VCs look for:
➤ Attitude of excellence.
➤ Strategic focus.
➤ Outstanding management—usually experienced management, but not necessarily. One of the services we can provide a founding entrepreneur is a sober assessment on whether or not we think they're going to be able to grow the business or whether we should go right now to find a Barksdale (Netscape CEO) to run the business. If so, we'll help them do that.
➤ Reasonable financings. I've seen ventures raise too much money, squander it, get lost, and not have a cost-oriented culture in their company—

as well as ventures that have failed because they've raised too little money. Or they can't get any venture backing at all. Staging the financing is important, removing risks as you go.

Tell me about some of the lighter moments.

Doerr: I went to a cable trade show and saw these cable modems. I knew Mosaic (Netscape precursor) was going to be the Web. I said, "God, this would be great, if you could have high-speed access into all the homes." I asked a friend of mine at TCI, Bruce Raventhal, if we could start a business like that. It was more than five years ago. We met John Malone and a thirty-minute meeting turned into an hour-and-a-half and he gave us the green light. We promised John we'd hire a technical guru, a genius, to this venture because I knew you'd have to have one. All great technology companies have a technical genius: Apple had its Wozniak, Sun had Bill Joy and Andy Bechtolsheim (now with Cisco), and this needed a technical guru. So I asked everyone at Sun who would be an Internet guru and they all said Milo Medin, Milo Medin, Milo Medin. I said, "Who's Milo Medin," and they replied, "Well, he runs Mae West" (the Internet network hub for the Western United States).

And so, Milo is about a 31-year-old, conservative, God-fearing Christian, G-7 (government ranking) NASA employee, running probably the largest hub on the Internet. And I tried to call him to get him on the phone for over a month and I couldn't get through to this guy. One time I just got on the phone and I kept talking to people until they got me through. He was ignoring my phone calls. He thought I was some kind of lawyer. So I finally got him on the phone and said, "Milo, I've got to meet you. Everybody at Sun says I've got to meet you. Let's you, and I, and Kleiner partner Will Hearst meet as soon as we can." So on a Saturday morning we met at about 10 o'clock. Milo, who's a very blunt, outspoken, intellectually honest executive, met Will Hearst and me and I told him about this dream of @Home and how we're going to take all these cable modems and stitch them into the Internet, and it's going to be great. I couldn't tell him that we had the cable industry as partner—that was confidential. I did tell him we'd try to use cable modems.

Milo said, "Listen, John, there're at least three things wrong with your proposal. It's not going to work. If you take these cable modems and stitch them onto the Internet, it will melt it down. There may be a way we can solve that problem, but your idea is never going to work. Secondly, I don't believe that cable modems are ever going to work—not a chance. And third, these cable guys, they don't understand the Internet at all." And so, he basically said,

"Forget it." I said, "Milo, what if you were persuaded that cable modems, while they don't work now, could be made to work? And what if you invented an architecture, a broadband architecture that'd work to deliver streaming media to personal computers? Could you do it?"

So we turned the challenge back around on him. He pulled out a napkin and started sketching and said, "Well, yeah, if you and every headend (local cable plant) put a server and cached and replicated the content, and then you build an ATM cloud of high-speed backbone. It's a parallel Internet, but if you keep it open and had real good network management, it might even work." Those were his words. And so we challenged him to go meet with cable modem manufacturers, and meet folks in the cable industry and he gradually reinvented our idea in a way that is today @Home. He signed on with Will Hearst to be the first employee. The two of them started that business that today is worth several billion, building more consumer high-speed access than anyone else in the world.

Vinod Khosla—*Kleiner Perkins Caufield & Byers*

KPCB PARTNER Vinod Khosla is largely responsible for helping the Stanford grads who founded Excite create a business plan in the days when advertising on the Internet was unheard of and certainly not a business model. Vinod could imagine the future of a "now-what-do-we-do-with-this-new-fangled-thing-that-nobody-knows-what-to-do-with?" from his experience cofounding and writing the business plans for networking powerhouse Sun Microsystems and Daisy Systems. Vinod offers his view on what he looks for in an Internet start-up or idea.

Q&A **The Internet space moves very fast. How does a firm like KPCB adapt to this in its investment outlook?**
Khosla: We get educated by entrepreneurs every day! Our key strength is to be open to this education, to always seek out the best "teachers," that is, the thought leaders, and to be able to go on gut.
What remains the single biggest area of the Internet for growth?
Khosla: It is hard to come up with a single one but...

   (a) A complete overhaul of the worldwide communications infrastructure will happen. What is installed today for the $1 trillion ".com" market will become a fraction of the total infrastructure within five years.

(b) All commerce channels will be restructured with businesses contacting other businesses directly to buy, sell, and communicate via the Internet creating consumer markets with efficiency we have never seen before (I call it the ultimate visit of Adam Smith II). Present examples are auctions such as eBay and Priceline and low-cost channels like Cisco and Dell.

(c) Advertising will become accountable in the form of a new "merge" with the direct marketing business; consumers will want advertising, but what they want and when they want it.

What common element exists among firms such as Excite, Concentric, Juniper, QWEST, Netscape, Amazon, @Home?
Khosla: I am on the board of Excite, Concentric, Qwest, and Juniper. They all live or die by being able to adapt and to respond. Adaptability is more important than efficiency, low cost, systematic management, and many other traditional "success factors"; speed of response, the old "ready, fire, aim" is becoming increasingly important. Companies that try to build business plans and justification for new areas will perish at the expense of those with good gut, and a "judgment that there is a pony in here" and a fast "let's figure it out as we go along" attitude.

Having been founding CEO of Sun and cofounder of Daisy Systems, in other words, having been an entrepreneur yourself, what are the characteristics you look for first in an entrepreneur?
Khosla: The same factors as above. Add good people skills and good depth in intuitively understanding the markets, technologies, and a thoughtful but action-oriented approach.

Ann Winblad—*Hummer Winblad*

AT JUST OVER five-feet three, Ann Winblad, a former cheerleader, is more like a powerful quarterback of the venture capital and Internet arena. Besides being named one of the most influential people of the digital era by more magazines than we care to mention, Ann is at the same time one of the most personable of all the VCs—human in a business that moves at machine speed. Winblad knows the entrepreneurs' hopes, dreams, screams, frustrations, and successes more than most. In 1976 when Jimmy Carter was talking peanuts, Ann started her own business on $500 and the idea to produce accounting software. Her software outfit Open Systems was born. In 1983 Winblad sold it for more than $16 million. She shares valuable tips and traps.

Q&A

What are the biggest mistakes entrepreneurs make in pursuing venture capital?

Winblad: It appears entrepreneurs aren't making many mistakes, because everyone's getting funded! All the mistakes are getting hidden. There are a couple of classic ones. Mistake number one is that they assemble whole teams instantly, a "team in a box," thinking that they have to have a full team. Then we spend a lot of time figuring out which of the team is really the team and which has been "assembled" for the occasion. This leads to mistake number two, the initial capitalization of the company and the awarding of stock to doctors, dentists, angels, whatever, without thinking how to scale the capital structure for professional investors. An example: We had a company come in, it was a great little company, where they had effectively vested everyone's stock when they granted it and 25 percent of the stock was in the hands of the cofounder who had left the company fully vested. This means we're only dealing with 75 percent of the deck to start out with. So it does mean that if you're serious about pursuing professional capital in your company that you ought to learn how you should orchestrate the stock structuring of your company on day one, before you start giving it out, thinking it's just sort of à la carte currency.

It does happen more often than not that the capital structure is a train wreck that makes it uninvestable by venture capitalists without us having to go through a whole lot of negotiations with people no longer associated with the company or loosely associated with the company. We'd rather go with a deal that may be a little less good that we can get going immediately without arguing over capital structures with people who are no longer part of the company. We can't argue with any "founders for a day" over terms. We've got about $12 billion in uninvested venture capital in venture-capital-land. If we don't get the show on the road...time becomes our enemy, and any friction in getting the company off the ground is a competitive disadvantage. It means that there really is a shortage of resources. My buzzword is that you have to get in a position to firmly declare victory on day one. If day one gets delayed by months of capital structure negotiation, and not with people that are part of the company currently, don't go there. You will starve in the time famine.

Another common mistake is what I call the *direct mail approach* to venture capital. One of the silliest things is when I get e-mails saying, "I'm just getting ready to start this venture. I'd love to have you take a look at it. You're just the greatest venture capitalist." But they forgot that they had just blind CC:ed the entire listing of venture capitalists globally. First of all, that's not going to work. Take three or four venture capitalists to start out with, so you have the learning and pruning loop as well: who may or may not have a conflict here? Who's interested in this sector? Why or why not are they investable? There's a lot that an entrepreneur can learn making a quick loop to a small number of venture capitalists first.

What are some of the things someone looking to form a company should be thinking about?
Winblad: Most people talk about the role of just the venture capitalist, but it is a 360-surround-sound of quality strategy and competitive influences. A lawyer—the lawyer is almost a precursor to venture capital. And most cities in the United States have venture lawyers.

Is venture capital one of the best ways to fund an Internet start-up?
Winblad: In Internet time, capital-abundant time, most of the companies that are going public today are still primarily venture-funded. Why is that? All we do is company creation. Most Internet companies are taking more capital than less. That means that you've got to get someone on your team who's experienced in raising significant follow-on capital. Otherwise, you're doing this "find-it-somewhere thing" all alone. Sooner or later someone in the Internet space, if they're going to be a serious contender, has to find a venture partner.

How does a start-up determine what the initial company valuation is worth?
Winblad: Two things: (1) VentureOne is one firm that keeps track of valuations. (2) But, the real thing becomes how the pie is cut, not what the valuation is. Employee stock option pools are very important. From 1990, when we made our first investment, to 1999 the employee stock option pool has gone from 12 percent to about 20 percent. So it's 20 percent set aside that has to happen in a raw start-up. Then we decide how the rest of the pie is cut. Top tier venture companies cannot take just 10 percent of a seed-level company. As selective investors, we don't do that many deals, so we're looking for 20 percent or higher as well, independent of the amount of capital. It's possible that we can get the next round investor to invest at 10 percent, depending on

how well the company performs, how much that capital is needed, and who that partner is. It's the pie carving analysis: How many times will the pie be carved now and in the future? Entrepreneurs should consider that.

Do you recommend that a start-up hopeful talk with established Internet companies, ones that you or another VC has invested in, to see what the experience was like, to see if the arrangement was fair to them?
Winblad: The nice thing about the Internet is that someone can just send an e-mail to the CEO and say, "Hey, do you feel you got a fair valuation? I'm negotiating now. Do you want to give me any tips? Are these guys worth their salt?" As well as go to VentureOne. Overall, the first round valuations haven't changed much over the years, because we're all just carving the pie, and the valuations are small. The follow-on rounds have jumped up considerably. We're the ones who helped push those up.

The range seems to be about $3 million to $5 million seed valuation. Is it holding?
Winblad: That seems to be about the range, with some going as high as $6 million.

Mark Gorenberg—*Hummer Winblad*

A HOP, SKIP, AND MODEM from Ann is Hummer Winblad partner Mark Gorenberg. We wanted to highlight how within a firm the various partners add their own talents and skill sets to bear in the venture space. While the valuation ranges may be formulaic by nature, the VCs themselves are as individual as the business opportunity, applying their background and experience in bringing a start-up into being a full-fledged company. Mark provided us with this fantastic, itemized reply to help clarify thinking for any Internet powerhouse-in-the-making.

Q&A What should a start-up consider when beginning to raise capital?
Gorenberg: There are several issues that are important when selecting your investment partner. You should ask yourself a series of questions:
(1) Can the potential investor add more value than just money? There's lots of "green" capital out there, but there is still a shortage of "intellectual"

capital. Think about what value-add you need and ask for that first and the dollars second.

(2) Is the potential investor able to take a leadership role in this or subsequent financings? Ever hear, "I'd love to invest, but I'm not a lead"? You won't hear that from anyone on this panel.

(3) Is the potential investor willing to avoid conflict of interest situations?

(4) Does the investment preempt your company from customer opportunities?

(5) Has the potential investor demonstrated the ability not only to withstand, but also to assist in reversing downturns of a business?

(6) Is the potential investor willing to be a long-term holder of the investment, or can potential events force the investor to sell their interest?

(7) Can the investor be a proactive and useful sounding board?

(8) Do they really understand your business, and can they act like an extension of the management team, or will you spend most of your time educating your new investor? We are firm believers in focus—companies need to focus, and so should venture firms. Choose investors that you think you can learn from, not the other way around.

How does an entrepreneur do some "due diligence" on a venture firm?
Gorenberg:

➤ Look at our Web site—www.humwin.com. All top-tier venture firms now have Web sites.

➤ Determine their criteria.

➤ See what other investments they've made. Do they compete with you? Are they complementary, that is, would you benefit from others in their portfolio? Do they invest in your area?

➤ Check their success record. Do they have other winners? Will they need you to be successful in order to have a successful fund, or can they be more patient?

➤ At what stage do they invest? Is it the same stage that you're in?

➤ Ask people you trust—bankers, lawyers, accountants, etc.— if they would volunteer the firm on a short list. Would they recommend it?

➤ Talk with a CEO from their current set of investments.

How should you approach a venture firm? What is needed?
Gorenberg:

➤ Prepare an executive summary. Highlight the opportunity. Make it compelling.

➤ Interact early to get feedback. Use a digital introduction, that is, e-mail. It's easy to read, easy to return comments to. You receive once, read anywhere.

➤ "Leverage" your introduction with an influencer.

➤ Review the plan with your pre-funding team: lawyer, accountant, other sounding boards.

Prepare a fundraising presentation to control the flow of the first meeting:

➤ What is your mission?

➤ Who are you and why can you do it?

➤ What sets you apart from other companies?

➤ Who is your competition? Do your homework here and really understand your space.

➤ Build your plan from the bottom up (Revenue = Price × Quantity), not top down.

➤ Who is your customer? Ground your idea in market research by talking directly to the potential customers who would write the checks. Find the people who have the most pain.

➤ Positioning is critical. State it early and often. You will always be positioned. You either position yourself or your competitors position you for their benefit.

➤ What will drive your success? Leverage?

➤ How much money do you need to get to the next risk-reduction point?

How do venture firms determine valuation?
Gorenberg:

➤ Put the candidate on a curve against our other deals. Where does this fall with those deals—in line or out of line?

➤ Valuation is the wrong way to think about it. It's a trade of equity for dollars. Take fewer dollars to raise more later at a higher price from a new investor. It reduces the ownership given up. Get through the next risk-reduction point.

➤ What's the growth rate of company and industry? Value is very dependent on rate of growth, not revenues or profits. There are not patents if market is too small or unknown.

➤ Are there external risks that will make the deal higher risk? No deals are perfect. We love deals with internal risk, i.e., hire the team; don't like external risks; i.e., is there a market? Will this business model work?

➤ Staging was particularly important for Internet companies last year. There's huge differential between valuation of first and second venture capital rounds.

➤ Choose a first round investor who can help you clear the risk-reduction points that make you far more valuable in the second round.

How do you get the best valuation ?
Gorenberg:

➤ Don't have venture firms talk with each other until after a term sheet. It takes everyone in a firm to say yes, but only one person to say no to avoid a term sheet. Hearing negatives from another venture firm could tank the deal or lower the price. Don't tell us who you're working with. We don't want you to tell others you are talking with us.

➤ Stage funding, but don't take too little.

➤ Remember, highest valuation now is not necessarily the best valuation later. Concentrate on your ownership percentage, not valuation.

➤ The best venture firms are also more interested in ownership over valuation. Don't try to carve up a round to lots of different investors. Choose one key venture partner and make sure they have a good ownership position.

➤ Ownership is precious and dilutes over time. Be possessive from the beginning, that is, don't give out dribs and drabs to consultants, friends, and so on. In the end, you will give out about 20–30 percent to employees. The rest will be split between the founders and the investors.

J. Neil Weintraut—
21st Century Internet Venture Partners

21ST CENTURY IS A VENTURE firm seeding and nurturing new economy opportunities. Spawned by Hummer Winblad Venture Partners, a venture firm that garnered significant success by focusing on the emerging software industry, 21st Century was founded by the head of Hambrecht & Quist's Internet group, J. Neil Weintraut, in October 1996. 21st Century professionals include Peter Ziebelman, previously of Thomson Ventures, and Rob Reid, author of *Architects of the Web*. 21st Century is capitalized at $55 million and to date has seeded eight new economy companies, including When.com (sold to

AOL), AvantGo, CareerBuilder, Vicinity, AdForce, Employease, GreenTree Nutrition, and BigWords.

Q&A

What does 21VC look for in an Internet investment first and foremost?
Weintraut: Platform. Is the combination of opportunity, people, innovation, and capital structure a platform that will entice success-makers to the business? To be clear, success-makers aren't just top executives, but, rather, the top grade of talent in every position throughout the business. When you have a platform that attracts success, everything else falls into place.

What's the most practical advice you have for those seeking funding?
Weintraut: Listen. Entrepreneurs should view the interaction with venture capitalists as an opportunity to hone the edge-of-success of a business. Get backed. Bill Gates, Andrew Grove, and John Chambers are successful because they always listen—and then act on their best interpretation of what they heard. We, either the entrepreneur or the venture capitalist, can't know all the answers, and even if we did today, the market moves tomorrow. So listening is important for success at large, and tactically during the fund raising. Listening to the feedback from venture capitalists is key to honing a business—the offering, strategy, and organization—that is appealing for VCs to back.

How do entrepreneurs get funded? What's the first thing they should do after brainstorming that new idea?
Weintraut: Have the timing, innovation, passion, and smarts (we call this TIPS) for success. To make a point, the first question is in effect backwards. The question isn't how to get funded, but rather, what is a great business?; the funding will follow—in dump trucks.

After the initial brainstorming: Get a mentor. Ideally, the mentor is someone both knowledgeable and with contacts in the start-up arena. But whether or not a mentor brings these assets, a mentor is most important as a sounding board—a sounding board that will test your ideas and assumptions, help interpret the behavior of people, including VCs, through the process, and bring out both the passion and the essential elements of the business.

Is there a common denominator in the firms that you've funded?
Weintraut: Yes: TIPS. Timing, Innovation, Passion, and Smarts.

➤ Timing means hitting the market at the right time, rather than too early or too late. AvantGo, for example, hit the market with enterprise automation for Palm computers, just as the market had advanced from using Palm devices as personal information managers to field-service tools.

➤ Innovation is not just digitizing or better-automating a task, but rather by doing the task itself—such as the value proposition itself and business itself—with a change. BigWords doesn't just sell textbooks to college students at a discount; it enables students to do something they haven't been able to do before: rent books.

➤ Passion enables start-ups to do what existing or even new companies think is impossible. Landing the company-making first blue-chip customer, when everyone knows that blue-chip companies don't do businesses with two engineers in a garage. We bet on our vision, not passion, but we're betting that the vision is the correct one. And the passion to drive that vision must be there. AdForce won its first and company-making account, for better or worse, even before its technology was stable, based solely on the passionate charisma of the founder.

➤ Smarts both in key knowledge about either the domain (e.g., retailing) or function (e.g., marketing), and knowing what they don't know.

Is 21VC a "typical" VC? What makes your approach different?
Weintraut: Based on both my background and experience, I see professional VC firms differentiated into *two categories:* A-league and other. The A-league has a franchise that:
➤ "gets it"
➤ attracts talent and capital
➤ opens doors
➤ fuels rather than consumes energy
➤ has direct knowledge about the business models and nuances of new emerging opportunities

Differentiation beyond the categories is specific to both the company situation and the partner. I believe that there are thirty or so A-league firms; and as the new kid on the block, we are trying to prove ourselves A-league caliber. In this regard, we have found entrepreneurs particularly appreciative of our new economy wisdom and our active involvement not only to challenge the company to greater standards, but also to make things happen first-hand. Beyond the franchise, the differences are specific to both individual companies and partners.

Do you have geographic preference?
Weintraut: Silicon Valley.

What's the most humorous story of a company you've founded? Any napkin-scribbling business plans or meetings over coffee that produced a deal?
Weintraut: One incident happened on a New York City rooftop, with beer in hand, at a party hosted by a new-media publisher. We had previously declined having a first meeting with a company after reviewing the written business plan. Then we ran across these two charismatic and self-effacing "kids" at the party. That was it. At that party we saw success—both passion and smarts—in the entrepreneurs, and then we hacked through the business issues. Within ten intensive days, we floated a term sheet.

How big is the opportunity from the Internet from a venture capital perspective?
Weintraut: As I like to say, the Internet is bigger than itself. The Internet is actually two things—the entity and the phenomena. Internet, the entity, is the wires, routers, and software that shuffles bits around the world. It's big—perhaps a $100 billion industry by the turn of the century. But that's nothing compared to the phenomena catalyzed by the Internet. We are creating new commerce, culture, and communications applications as a result of the industry. For example, major established industries measured in tens or even hundreds of billions of dollars—be it diamonds, automobiles, entertainment, or securities—are up for wholesale and digital reincarnation. That's as big as it gets—trillions of dollars. That's what our fund is about: new economy ventures. If the Internet phenomena were any smaller, I'd be (only) overwhelmed.

What's the single-biggest area you invest in or are looking to invest in now?
Weintraut: We all but exclusively pursue with passion two arenas: E-commerce and Enterprise. Furthermore, it's not about investing, but nurturing—making success happen, rather than just investing in it after it occurs. Smarts and work, rather than money and reports.

Esther Dyson—*EDventure Holdings*

AS YOU'RE BEGINNING to discover with this book, venture capitalists are a diverse group. I wanted to include Esther Dyson, chairwoman of her own firm, EDventure Holdings, because Esther's angle is distinctive. In fact, she's not a "VC" per se, but invests using her considerable expertise and global knowledge. She's recognized as a technology industry guru, an author, and as someone active in conferences and organizations. In fact, she is the interim chairman of ICANN, the Internet Corporation of Assigned Names and Numbers; a member of the board of the Electronic Frontier Foundation and a member of the President's Export Council Subcommittee on Encryption. *Fortune* magazine recently named Dyson one of the fifty most powerful women in American business. I believe Esther's power comes from a fantastic mind, a mind not stuck on the traditional, as you're about to discover.

 **EDventure Holdings is different from traditional venture capital. You're not looking at things the same way as Silicon Valley or East Coast firms are doing. Tell me about your focus and approach. What do you look for first and foremost in an Internet investment?**

Dyson: What I look for in any investment: A good person in charge with some good ideas and the ability to change, because however good the idea, it probably won't last more than a year or two without needing some substantial revisit. So it's people.

What qualities are you looking for in people?
Dyson: Smart, passionate, intelligent—and everyone has their own definition of what that means. In essence, people that when something goes wrong, as it inevitably will, I'll be happy to be working with to help fix it rather than thinking, "This guy's a jerk, and I should have never given my money to him."

What are some of your Internet investment examples?
Dyson: One is a company called Orchestream, based in the U.K., which provides network administrative software with billing systems, management tools so a network administrator can assign priorities to network applications. So if the chairman comes on and wants to videoconference, the network admin can give him high priority. You can allocate bandwidth. And, if you're an ISP you can bill according to different levels of service.

What attracts you to invest in Europe?
Dyson: I'm not a rich venture capitalist. I'm just an individual, so one thing that attracts me is I can make more of a difference there than in the United States,

especially in Central and Eastern Europe. Since I speak Russian and have spent a lot of time knowing that market, I have a much better opportunity to find good companies than someone who doesn't have that experience.

E-pub is one of your investments. Tell me about that.
Dyson: Mike Simon. I really liked the guy; he had great ideas. To be honest, I wasn't that keen on what they did. I'm not a big fan of games. Believe it or not, I prefer accounting software. I thought that he would be successful and I liked him.

You are also an investor in some U.S. Internet start-ups, right?
Dyson: Yes, i-traffic here in New York. They manage a commercial presence on the Web. I'm on the board of Medscape also.

You seem to invest across boundaries more than others do. How do you discover investments?
Dyson: I tend to invest more in really neat people. I don't invest on the basis of a business plan; I invest on the basis of people. I've invested in about twenty firms so far. The best way to approach me is to have someone I trust call me and say, "Take a look at this." If somebody comes in over the transom, it's pretty hard. It's hard to tell, but if someone you know and trust refers someone, that means a lot. I had a meeting once with someone without a referral, and his business plan was good, but there was no passion. So I passed. Some people will say X told me to get in touch with you, and I don't even know who X is. Someone says, "I know Esther Dyson," and it turns out they heard of me in a magazine.

The role of the VC is part coach, part team player, part (to put a fancy name on one aspect of what a VC does) risk-reduction engineering—helping you avoid making mistakes. Now you've seen some of them close up. In the next chapter we'll take a look at how you prepare to present yourself to a venture capitalist—to propose a partnership based on much more than dollars.

The Meeting

Chapter 5 *Five*

WHEN THE TIME COMES for you to talk with venture capitalists, forget any notions you ever had about business meetings—they probably don't apply. There are no textbooks that spell out with real-life examples what to expect. But I will.

Passion wins. Be ready with passion twenty-four hours a day—not phony posturing, but real gut-wrenching, fly-to-the-moon, heart-moving confidence. Believe your idea matters, you matter, ideas are valuable, commitment counts, experience is key, you have the right stuff. Even then, that's just the underlying foundation to your future plans. But forget the ego. Simply get behind the idea, make the idea central, the opportunity central, not how great you may think you are. The idea and opportunity will speak volumes about you—more than anything you may say about yourself.

Also forget about odds and how many deals get funded versus the pitches a VC receives. Your chance with any VC is either 100 percent or 0 percent. They either invest or they don't. Which characteristics influence them to say yes?

Proper frame of mind for meetings is essential. Don't envision moguldom, wealth, cars, houses, boats, planes—all these are not the goal of a true Internet entrepreneur. True entrepreneurs focus on the business, because they believe in what they are doing and understand how it meets a real need in today's world, not some future science fiction era. They see a path to huge growth in every aspect of their enterprise and are passionate about it, carry it with charisma, and bring their heart into the enterprise. The world notices these types first and foremost. VCs do also.

So passion is rule number one for meeting anyone: investor, potential customers, allies, the press. Dozens of people probably have shared with the VC the exact same idea as yours—maybe better ones. So, passion is priceless; it's what can make the difference between a yes and no. Remember Esther Dyson's example of the entrepreneur who had a fantastic plan; everything looked great on paper. When she met the person he simply had no passion. No passion = no investment in many cases.

If you have more of it than the person before or after you does, your odds just went up tremendously. I'm going to dwell for a moment on this because I believe it is the single most important aspect of your idea and the most important aspect of any meetings you have from day one to day 10,000 in your enterprise. Be passionate. If you're not passionate about your idea, ask yourself why not? Focus more on it until you are passionate, or consider giving up being an entrepreneur. Why? Committing to a company is 24/7— every hour and every day. Internet leaders know no time zones, no days of the week. For myself, I'm always "on," that is, thinking about the Internet: opportunities, risks, rewards, deals, alliances, outlooks. It is not a choice but a real zeal for what I'm doing. I cannot turn that off and on with a timer. Passion keeps me going—the joy of doing what I do. Long before anyone recognizes you in the industry or anywhere else it will be your passion driving you forward. Passion is the fuel you go on when nobody believes in you. After they do, you find that passion is still what drives you. VCs are acknowledging your passion with an investment, a belief that your zeal will produce results.

So, if another VC or I call you, bump into you at the produce stand, or start hearing about you from industry publications or prominent industry folks, then express that passion. A venture capitalist or potential investor of any kind may meet you anytime, anywhere, often unscheduled, sometimes when you least expect it. In other words, you may not have time to put on your best suit, comb your hair, put the pizza down, and prepare your State of the Internet address. Why? VCs are on the prowl at trade shows, conferences, industry gatherings, and informal get-togethers. More often than you may think, the hungry venture capitalists are out scouring the dealscape, looking for hot young start-ups. John Doerr says that he oftentimes meets entrepreneurs at conferences or trade shows. That's not unusual; most VCs do that. But many entrepreneurs may not know that's where their first (and maybe only) meeting may take place.

In other words, all the e-mailing, overnight expressing, faxing, phoning, hounding in the world may not make up for that one moment when the VC stops by your booth at Internet World, drops in on your venture showcase or COMDEX and says, "Tell me about your company." And then it's up to you to make the passion and the business sense click.

To reiterate, I suggest you carry copies of your plan in an easy-to-read PowerPoint-type presentation. Also have a few floppies on hand with your executive summary, business plan, and biographical notes on yourself and all key people. Keep these in your briefcase, car, and home. A floppy is very easy to slip into your coat or shirt or purse. Label the disk with your name, e-mail address, phone number, date, Web site address, and title. Have these handy, especially when you're exhibiting or showing off your idea or company. Always. If your data is sensitive you could consider putting a password on the floppy—but this will also make it harder for the VC to open any files. Your disk might get tossed if it cannot be opened quickly.

Don't be on your toes only at formal industry functions. Your first meeting may in fact be when you bump into someone in the supermarket who overhears your Internet idea. Or your brother mentions that you're doing an "Internet thing" and his coworker knows someone who knows someone who suddenly calls you. That could lead to questions about what the idea is, and suddenly you're in a "meeting" with a potential investor. These possibilities require that you be 100

AS COMPANY FOUNDER or original idea person, you must be a walking, talking business plan, because the meeting can be any time. Here's the kind of setup I prepare that makes a spontaneous meeting out in public much more advantageous.

In a plastic, spiral-bound notebook—maybe twenty-five pages total—include:

➤ an easy-to-read executive summary and business plan in slide-show format printed on 8^1/$_2$" by 11" paper
➤ good charts, but not overdone
➤ bios of all key people
➤ company mission statement
➤ rewards and risks of the venture (Every enterprise or idea has both risk and reward, so don't try to gloss over risks as if they don't exist. Spell them out. VCs will assume you have a naïve approach to business if you don't know the risks of your endeavor.)

percent ready day and night to talk the talk and walk the walk. If not, then venture investors or others won't likely have the time to give you a second chance.

Consider that a coach overhears someone talking about the game of football in a local coffee shop and approaches that person and says, "Hey, I coach football. What position do you play?" Would you respond, "Well, I play running back" or "Let me check the rule book and see which position I could play"? You must tell the "coach" (the VC) what you're all about and your strengths, with plays and ideas for scoring. Then you have engaged in a meaningful "meeting." If that "meeting" (planned or not) goes awry then just getting back to that point can be difficult, at least with the same VC. If you stammer and don't think you performed well in this casual setting, learn from that experience. My advice is to be prepared for a successful impromptu meeting at any time.

How to Dress

➤ You can never go wrong by wearing a nice business suit (men or women), pressed and clean, white shirt, and tie. Don't go overboard with a pure wool or silk suit; keep it simple and not distracting. In Silicon Valley a casual look may work (long-sleeved shirt and khakis, tie optional), but wear a suit if it's expected for business in your area.

➤ At trade shows you may wear slacks and a pressed shirt.

➤ Don't get caught up in the clothing thing; VCs want to know how you think and what your goals are more than if you have the "right" wardrobe; it's not a fashion show, and the only time your clothes will be noticed is if they don't fit right. So dress as yourself within the basic business style of the area or region you're in. If a meeting comes up when you happen to be wearing a 1970s Hawaiian shirt and shorts with flip flops, don't worry! Focus on your business opportunity; you can always buy a suit later.

That was the unscheduled meeting. I mention it because it's quite common. If you get the scheduled meeting, that is, a call or e-mail from a VC who wants to meet you at the firm's offices, it's much the same as the unscheduled one, with more time to prepare. My point is that a meeting can be anytime, so plan on it happening anywhere. If you go to the VC's office, bring all of the slides and floppies we talked about before.

Passion is essential; but without substance it is misplaced and could lead to your sounding enthusiastic but green. The kind of passion I'm referring to is "confidence" and "belief" that your plan is going to happen with or without the investment from this particular venture capitalist. Your success cannot hinge on the investment from this VC. Your success depends on you. The VC only assists in parts of it. No one investment by anyone can "make" your company. You and the people around you who join the firm are the ones who will do that. Certain VCs are better at helping you succeed than others. But even the best VCs have backed $100 million flops. Sometimes the market is too early for the idea, the management lacks the right stuff, larger companies usurp market share and crush the start-up, and so on. Hundreds of things can divert success. Capital is not the only necessary ingredient.

In the first meeting in the offices with the VC you'll discuss broad concepts; it's really a getting-to-know-you meeting, and an opportunity for a demo of the product or service. Presumably by this time the VC has seen your executive summary and business plan, knows your strengths and weaknesses, and the opportunities and risks as you've outlined them.

The demo encapsulates everything your business plan says via a display. If you don't have a working prototype or example, use words to describe the process or idea: "paint" the picture of the market need your notion fills. A VC worth his salt will see the potential in your product or service fairly quickly if there's something to it. If that VC doesn't and you know the product is as good as you can make it, then try another VC. Not all VCs think the same, and not all of them are looking to make the same investments. Some may have made investments in products or services similar to the thing you're pitching. Don't waste your time with them; they've already bet on another horse. For example, we know VCs who have invested in various start-ups and later wished they had waited. When a better idea comes along, they may want desperately to invest in this new rival to the company they just invested in—but it's too late. Venture investors usually get behind one type of product or service and don't make similar investments that compete with that one. Why? Conflict of interests. So when they bet on you, they want to make sure you're the best in your category, that they won't regret it later.

Venture capitalists want you to be frank and open about the upside and downside of your Internet superstar company. They appreciate honesty, integrity, experience, and your ability to see the rewards and risks and to think like a leader. They will ask you about the marketplace, the need for your product or service, what problem it solves or addresses now and in the future, how protectable the idea is (patents or lead-in time to market), and why you and your team are able to pull it off better than the next guys. Keep the conversation moving in the right direction by knowing more about that aspect of the marketplace than the VC. If they're telling you what the outlook is, or if you stumble when they ask a basic question about something pertaining to your chosen market and you don't know the answer, the direction of the meeting can be short-circuited. Keep it on track by preparation and thorough knowledge of your endeavor in the big picture and in the little one.

Occasionally a VC may be excited about your plan and want to cut you a check right there. They may say, "Here's $x. Go and write a business plan (or improve this one)." Or "Develop this concept further and contact me again." Or "Call so-and-so and get their input here." Usually in the first meeting you won't negotiate any real valuation of your firm or idea. If they like the idea and believe you have the passion to pull it off, you'll have a few more meetings, each one getting more detailed and specific. Meetings past the first one may include other partners in the VC firm, some of them crunching numbers while you discuss the idea again. More in-depth questions may arise about your background; the VCs may ask for references, or make phone calls to industry people they know to see how your idea meshes with the marketplace, and so on.

A successful company will go through various stages of growth; a seed stage is very different from a viable stage. Venture capitalists view a raw start-up as risky; there are still many requirements: clear business strategy, prototype(s), marketing plan, rollout, and alliances. The VCs want to reach the point at which your business looks more predictable and provides a little more security than when all you had was scribbled notes on a napkin about how you're going to change the world.

At each stage new issues will dominate the company's actions and time. New personnel, from executive to staff, will be necessary to roll out a new business. This expansion will require more capital.

As growth creates a mature company, new management may step in to take it to the next level. Plenty of Internet founders have stepped aside and let professional managers run the companies once they reach a certain level. Yahoo! brought in Tim Koogle while Jerry Yang and David Filo focused on overall strategy and serving as company mascots; GeoCities founder David Bohnett brought in a media executive to run the show; EarthLink's Sky Dayton did the same.

These issues are important for you and your investors to consider, so that if your idea becomes huge, plans are in place to help keep it huge and yet stable. VCs and Wall Street want someone who can run a business with proven success at the helm. It's not always comfortable for founders to step aside, but the VCs and any of your investors want the best person for the job. If that's you from day one to day 10,000, that's great; if not, in the interest of growing value, forget your ego and take a strategy role instead of trying to manage a 1,000-person enterprise. Only you and your investors will know which you are. But be prepared to consider the company first and yourself second should the need arise. This means looking out for people you think could be valuable management team members, including someone who may take over your role. Think of value creation, not ego.

Jerry Yang and David Filo cofounded Yahoo! and have the titles "Chief Yahoos." Chairman and CEO is Tim Koogle, an experienced manager with proven skills for leading technology companies. President and COO Jeff Mallett is business centric. Jerry and David get to think about the future and ponder large issues for the firm; the management focuses on making money. Everybody wins. So be flexible in your thinking, or you may miss out on opportunity because your ego won't allow anyone to be called CEO other than you. It's better to be "Chief of .Com" or "Strategy Guru" of a billion dollar company than CEO or president of one that will never get to the big leagues. Think big. If you can take it there and your investors see it happening, then it may be you captaining the ship of your dreams. Keep an open mind, however, with the desire to grow the ship rather than your hat size.

So you must be ready in the meeting to discuss who's on board now or to suggest some suitable additions. A VC will also usually help draw in some talent to create value and establish the enterprise. It helps if you can lay out some candidates with their backgrounds and why you think they should be there. If you've already lined up some key people, then discuss how they help make things happen and why you selected them. Think about weak spots and how to fill holes in the firm. If you don't have anyone other than yourself and your cat, then say so. Don't try to "dress up" your business plan with names that you think may impress the VC. Just say "it's me and my cat" and the VC will kick in and try to work with you to find the right people (with you, not for you, since it's your company you're starting).

If those series of meetings go well then you may be presented with a term sheet. This document gives the VC's estimation of the value of the firm or idea, what they're willing to invest for what percent, the rights they have if they invest (board seats, preferences, bankruptcy claims, etc.). If you have arrived at the term sheet stage, consider hiring a venture capital lawyer or law firm to represent your interests and make sure the document terms agree with your expectations. Don't haggle valuation or terms without your venture lawyer—one you must trust. Discuss everything, making sure you understand all of the terms, and let the lawyer do the talking for you. But also keep in mind that at the pure seed stage your idea is probably worth about the same as most of the ideas that come through the VC's door—not much.

You and the VC may believe your chances of being big are fantastic, but it won't serve you or them to give you an initial high valuation. Why? (1) Until you prove your concept, it's just a concept. (2) Additional rounds of financing are easier if the seed round was reasonable, since the deal will be on more attractive terms for those second-round, third-round, and even IPO investors.

If you don't like the terms a VC offers, then maybe consider financing the company yourself with more lenient investors: those willing to invest less, control less, and maybe let you make more mistakes along the way (more on alternative financing in Chapter 8). "Angel" investors look for deals that some VCs won't do because of the small size of the investment and its subsequent opportunity. Angels, usually high-net-worth individuals with an interest in technology or the Internet, may offer you better terms that allow you to keep more of the company for yourself. True, you may have to ask for additional financing, but often the angels can seed the deal, and then when growth starts, the professional venture investor can step in. Sometimes you can do just fine without venture investment. The founders of Infospace (Nasdaq:INSP) and XOOM.COM (Nasdaq:XMCM), two of many examples, never took professional venture capital and financed their companies themselves with angels and friends who believed in their passion. Because, you see, passion is key, with or without the VC. You as founder are the fuel for the future. Passion is your mantra.

The Valuation

Chapter Six

JUST AS BEAUTY is in the eye of the beholder, so is value. Oftentimes in Zero Gravity ugly is as ugly does—and some pretty awkward, waddling ducklings have turned into high-flying, graceful swans. How crude were a few thousand lines of software code that Marc Andreessen and pals slapped together while cramming for final exams? Consider Jeff Bezos and family heading West in a beat-up Honda to start selling books on the Web or Jerry Yang and David Filo's rantings about links thrown together in 1993 while both were at Stanford. These efforts were not pretty by business standards, but each has become a billion-dollar beauty.

On the Internet value is subjective and often hidden in the most humble of efforts. That's a truism on the Web, where every truly great idea starts at the bottom and grows quickly in the churning nutrients of this living medium. Understanding what's behind valuation, therefore, is crucial to understanding what valuation should or shouldn't be.

The first thing that determines valuation is the enigmatic essence called potential: people potential, market potential, capital potential, technology potential, timing potential. On the reverse side of that is risk: market risk, capital risk, technology risk, timing risk.

Think about all the public companies, for example, and the very different prices per share and market capitalization each has. Many companies in the same line of business with similar revenue and earnings may be valued vastly differently on Wall Street. The same applies in that zygote state when your company is nothing more than a great idea scribbled on a breakfast house napkin with a splash of maple syrup on the corner. Why the difference in value? The interplay of people, market, capital, technology, and timing. I've covered these factors throughout the book in other ways so far but have not addressed them specifically. Indeed, you can almost value any business, Internet or not, on those five factors.

Management, market share, growth, leadership, innovation, leverage, cash, burn rate, total number of users, customers, and page views are the primary things that differentiate one Web company from another. However, when you're just starting up, the two things that matter most are the idea and what you can do with it. A football in the hands of Steve Young is a billion-dollar sport. A football in the hands of someone who can't throw a spiral is a piece of leather with laces. What talent does is draw other talent to itself, and suddenly you have a worthwhile team (note: *worth*; read: *valuable*. People are number one on the value equation. Who is on your side, and do they fit well together? Evaluate not only the people in the start-up but the people investing as well, because they are very much part of the total team effort. The last thing an exciting new idea needs is a needling investor—that's similar to an intrusive owner of a team.

But don't expect the venture capitalists to get this right every time—that is, seeing that the founders are the ones to make something happen. They often miss spotting potential during their speed-reading, abbreviated method of looking at and sizing up plans. Cisco, for example, had a terrible time getting any venture capital interest because a few VCs thought the people might not be the right ones for the job. More than $150 billion market value later who was right? The entrepreneurs who persevered despite the VCs. In other words, just because the value isn't obvious to the VC doesn't dismiss the potential if you know your stuff and can forge ahead. Value is always in flux also. So, if you're expecting clay tablets with unchanging rules, forget it. Any start-up can find various valuations depending on how many investors are interested. It's simple supply and demand. People are the magnet.

Market potential will be at the front of any discussion of valuation throughout the process. The market for polyester suits and disco balls is more limiting, for example, than the one for disco music. Selling an array of goods is obviously a bigger proposition than selling just one. Professional investors want to invest in potentially huge markets in which even if your firm doesn't win, losing looks pretty darn good. For example, if you garnered 1 percent of the entire apparel market with your Web company, you wouldn't beat Kmart in clothing sales, but investors wouldn't say the emperor has no clothes either. Books and music represent a $75 billion global opportunity, depending on what is included in those two categories. Boring office supplies is double that at about $150 billion in annual sales. Somebody's going to grab huge chunks of those kinds of markets—maybe existing "heavy gravity" firms like Office Depot, but maybe not.

Capital potential estimates the amount of cash you'll need to make your plan happen and the availability of that cash on terms favorable to you and the investors. Internet companies in 1993 and 1994 went public and routinely raised $25 million. Then that was considered "enough." By 1999 Internet firms with IPOs tried to raise from $60 million to $125 million, depending on how much Wall Street could swallow. That meant valuations had soared all along the chain from start-up to liquidity. But it also meant that more capital is now needed to compete in these billion-dollar market opportunities.

Getting to $100 million revenue in two or three years may take at least that much in invested capital. The turning point for profit relies on digital efficiencies of scale once a threshold has been reached. That's tricky. How big should an Internet company be? When does an Amazon.com or eBay stop growing? In Zero Gravity there are no walls, ceilings, or boundaries save cash on hand, deployed capital, and the talent to run unfettered. The heavy gravity world had boundaries: land, real estate prices, platforms that are incompatible. The Internet rides the global telecom infrastructure for almost nothing. Platforms talk to platforms, and you can e-mail a dozen friends to join you and chat or tell them to download a cool new software tool. They tell friends, who tell more friends, who tell more. In digital space time and distance are no more. Relativity is everything. Capital potential is very relative.

Which brings us right into the technology and the biological nature of how technology spreads on the Web. Freebie Web-based e-mail HotMail adds millions of users almost daily now. ICQ is its own nation of more than 30 million users. They tell each other about the technology, download it, and start talking, communicating. The potential of the Internet is unprecedented—an underlying global open platform for rollout of layers upon layers of value on top of itself. The ability of the technology is more limited by sociological and cultural mores than anything. Alexander Graham Bell didn't know what to do when he invented the phone. After talking to himself for a few minutes he concluded his invention was worthless. Thomas Edison questioned the value of electricity. When IBM forecast the need for a handful of mainframe computers, they didn't envision the PC. That's because the populations hadn't explored the technology potential. Even today's Internet hasn't been explored in terms of what it CAN do, not what it IS doing. Think about that for a second.

Timing potential. What if you're the only guy or gal driving your car to school every day, but it's the year 1840 and everyone else is walking or riding a horse? The drive will be dusty, bumpy, full of stares, and you'll have a heckuva time finding a gas station. You're timing would be off. Buck Rogers stories were all about going to the moon. Creators got there with a few scribbles in a comic book and their imagination. There was no space industry then, so what good would it have been to make rockets? Markets on the Internet open up and close all the time and sometimes the same markets re-open and get re-shuffled. Hitting it at the right time is best, but cannot always be timed.

The important thing to consider is that every corporation on the planet that wants to compete in the future will be Internet-based to some degree. In the wider view the timing then favors those venturing into this new realm as quickly as possible as smartly as possible.

The great thing about the Internet is that it levels the playing field, giving you and others the chance to throw the long bomb, or quickly learn how to. That's how people from all walks of life have become wealthy (at least with paper equity). The equity you have has everything to do with the equity you start out with, which has everything to do with your start-up valuation and how your company is legally structured. Sure, you don't want to be overly greedy with the percents and turn off investors entirely. But you also don't want to start handing out equity like candy on Halloween night. A look at market potential, therefore, gives you and the investors a sense of how big your firm can grow.

Usually VCs nowadays look to invest in companies that can produce a minimum of $100 million revenue in a few years (that's subject to change, but gives you a sense of today's valuations). Why $100 million sales? Because brand new ways of doing business are creating brand new markets. Big ones. It's think globally, act globally now. Think market potential. Investors want to put money on the number one firm in any space on the Web.

As you set forth with the people, market, technology, capital, and timing pieces juggling in your head, valuing your start-up is probably the most difficult thing you will do for several reasons:

➤ You've probably never valued an idea or business opportunity before, especially in the Internet where your idea could be brand new, so there's nothing to compare it to.

➤ It's sometimes hard for the entrepreneur to know where the start-up begins and he or she ends.

➤ You may think your idea is worth a billion dollars, but the venture capitalist may see a napkin scribble with some maple syrup on it.

In other words, determining what your start-up is worth is one of the most complex and novel experiences many entrepreneurs will ever go through. This process is one of highs and lows—highs when you get word from an investor that the investment is going through, and lows when you find out the terms involved or if the investor changes tune mid-song.

It may be a battle. Expect it. The start-up founders want to maintain as much control and get as high a value as possible, while the professional investors see that this is one of a dozen ideas they can invest in. If given a choice of two or more equally attractive investment opportunities it's safe to say the VCs will probably go with the one in which they get a bigger chunk for the same capital infusion. That's not to say the VCs will always do that. Kleiner Perkins invested in Netscape at a higher valuation than many other VCs would entertain. Why? It helped that the founders were Jim Clark and Marc Andreessen. Clark, for example, hailed from Silicon Graphics (which he had founded) and had a reputation of excellence. Andreessen, meanwhile, was the "Boy Wonder" who led the team that invented the browser (Mosaic), which had a few million users by the time this dynamic duo came calling on the VCs.

Superhero team. Valuation went up. Ironically, few VCs were willing to pay a premium for Clark and Andreessen. Not Kleiner.

In order to establish the "right" valuation it pays to know how the professional investor views things. First is the required rate of returns. I mentioned earlier that VCs often look for a 10× return. That's not always possible, depending on IPO market conditions or deal flow. A 10× return in three years means the required return is 115.4 percent. Even a 10× return in five years shows that the required rate of return is 58.5 percent. Generally speaking, venture capitalists investing in Internet start-ups or seed stage firms are on the hunt for required rate of returns north of 50 percent compounded annually. It's not a question of emotion; it's a question of the fund's viability and fiduciary responsibility to its investors, the limited partners who have handed their capital to the VC to make it grow. No grow? No go. So the VC is also on the line to perform, just as you and your business are.

The differences among rates of return have to do with the risks and rewards inherent in any investment. The first risk point is the market. Is there a real market for this? Will your product or service be a hit? Inventors of the pen computing industry in the 1980s, from start-ups to Apple Computer, discovered that nobody really wanted a pen computer. In those days nobody really wanted a PC with MS-DAH! Cryptic syntax. The market wasn't there.

Fast-forward: providers of an ad-based Internet service similarly discovered in 1995 that nobody was interested, no customers that is— the synch was out of synch. In both instances these efforts had bright, passionate people with high-profile venture backing. Kleiner Perkins sank millions in Go, the pen computing effort mentioned above. It did anything but go. Apple simply got too greedy and charged too much for its Newton handheld pen computer and it fizzled. The ad-supported Web firm funded by CMGI was ahead of its time. In the 1990s, however, US Robotics-3COM came out with an affordable handheld computer called Palm Pilot and it became a hit. The market was there and the price was right.

In another example, consumer online services have existed since 1969 in one form or another when CompuServe first turned on the juice. Prodigy and America Online arrived in the 1980s. All three had commendable subscriber bases in 1994 with well over 3 million between them. AT&T acquired Interchange about that time for $100 million.

News Corp acquired Delphi with a few hand gestures from Rupert Murdoch. And then the browser came along: the browser, a software application that allowed anyone with a PC and Internet connection to navigate an entire array of information across the globe on the World Wide Web. The browser was free and oftentimes so was information. Suddenly the online services looked stale and closed compared to this wide-open Internet. Before the online services knew it, by 1995 more than 10 million people had downloaded a browser and were using the World Wide Web, not their services. More people were using a browser than AOL, CompuServe, and Prodigy combined. Guess what happened to the value of AT&T's Interchange? Dropped to zero quickly. Prodigy was sold and so was CompuServe. AOL survived through brilliant marketing and maneuvering—and luck.

The market had shifted and so had values. Where had the value gone? To new firms born out of dorm rooms and zealots: Excite, CheckPoint Software, Infoseek, and dozens more. Prodigy was resurrected as an ISP and went public in 1999 with a valuation of more than $2 billion at one point. All of these are examples of how valuation, timing, and market presence come together or don't. To get the most valuation, be at the right inflection point at the right time.

On the other side of technology potential is technology risk. Technology was the basis for the switch from closed online services ("closed" in the sense that each required its own software to use the service). The browser, search engine, auction services, and more all rode a new technology whose time had come and a market that was growing, not ending. The new platform was based on HTTP or hypertext transfer protocol, the lingua franca of this newfangled thing called the World Wide Web. HTTP and the Web were wide open in that anyone could develop a Web site. Steve Kirsch, who founded Infoseek, didn't have to go to AT&T and ask them to license his product to put it on Interchange. He simply had to build a Web site with the search technology behind it all and he was in business as a global company from day one. The open platform spawns value creation.

The technology for providing news and information had switched into a new era, one that lies at the heart of the Internet today: every entrepreneur has the ability to leverage the entire global telecommunications' network for next to nothing. Every entrepreneur has the ability to leverage the standardized Web software out there because it speaks the same language as the other programs and services, the underlying TCP/IP, HTTP and Web protocols. Said another way, the technology risk shifted to a new underlying technology, but one that provided less for entrepreneurs in some ways. Although they needn't build an entire global telecom network to use it, there was also no need for a new spectrum of software that could be marketed. The collective open platform enabled the shift more from technology to ideas and services, to the people who could pull it off. The upside and downside of having a level playing field is that anyone can play.

Anyone can sell books on the Web. That meant Amazon had to be first and establish a lead in brand and sales. Its "technology" risk became "risk of execution." You wouldn't find any VC in 1995 investing in closed online services. You would find dozens, however, investing in companies trying to take advantage of the shift in technology to services and people. And in 1999 you wouldn't find many (if any) VCs investing in a company that wanted to make a better browser. The technology risk was too high for any new effort to surpass or catch the leaders Microsoft and Netscape. Amazon's pioneering affiliate program prevented rivals from getting as big as fast since it co-opted anyone who wanted to sell books into its own sales machine. Boom!

Let's think about the risks of flesh and bone. People manage the business; they make the decisions that affect revenue and profits. Management is a risk. Dozens of companies with great technology and great market opportunity fail because management loses sight of the market, technology, or its focus. Or it can get caught up in a political war inside the firm with other managers. Management in any Internet business must be flexible enough to shift to a better opportunity if the existing one closes up. Even old-fashioned retailers sometimes see that. Consider Egghead.com. It used to be just plain old Egghead, a chain of retail stores that sold software and hardware aimed at geeks. In 1998 the management saw the Internet taking over retail—especially the type of techno-centric retailing they were in—so Egghead took the bold and unprecedented step of closing its entire land-based franchise and going 100 percent as an Internet-based company, selling software and hardware over the Web. Egghead's stock went up, its value reflecting the new opportunity and market. But the management, led by George Orban, had to make that crucial and tough decision, to close a very popular chain of stores and go Web. People make the decisions;

management carries the risk and reward forward or back. Can you make the tough decisions that create value? Value is always in flux and the tendency investors want is for it to grow up, not down.

Therefore, in the digital space especially, valuation rests on bringing together the talent, technology, capital, and timing. Those are the starting points to value creation. Once a start-up is in place with a strong enough package of the above (even if it's not all of the above) the funding part might be really easy.

Let's talk valuation more specifically, translating the elements into capital. Not surprisingly, Internet valuations have gone up these past few years. In days long gone a start-up may find a $3 million valuation and sell 20 percent to 40 percent preferred equity. *Preferred* means preferential treatment for the VC's investment should the start-up shut down. They would get their investment back if it's there to get back. Yet as the public markets have bid up Internet valuations, it's pulled up the value of private firms. A gap still exists, but today you may see an Internet start-up at $5 million or more, depending on the combination of people, ideas, talent, and industry opportunity it addresses. Does that mean more equity for the founders to hold onto? Not if the capital investment by the VC is still about the same percent regardless of valuation—30 percent is 30 percent.

Let's say you're one founder/CEO in a garage bringing key people on board. How the equity is distributed could look something like this (this is not a one-size-fits-all template so please use it only for discussion and reference):

	COMMON STOCK	SHARES	PERCENT
MANAGEMENT	CEO	3,000,000	30%
	VP Operations	1,500,000	15%
	VP Marketing	1,500,000	15%
	Reserve for Stock Option Plan	2,000,000	20%
	TOTAL	8,000,000	80%
PREFERRED	Issued to the Investor at $.50 per share	2,000,000	20%
	TOTAL	10,000,000	100%

Source: Ann Winblad, Hummer Winblad Ventures

In the pre-Internet era Hummer Winblad's Ann Winblad explained that the stock pool for employees was much smaller, with 10 percent being a sizable amount. With the Internet driving incentives via stock options and the tremendous competition for talent in this space, the stock option pool for employees has gone up 10 percent to 20 percent, maybe 25 percent in some cases. The important thing is having enough to disburse in incentive stock options to new hires that will make the enterprise more valuable.

Keep in mind that every financing is unique, so trying to figure out how much the founder should own by the time the company goes public (if it makes it that far) has everything to do with how effectively capital has been deployed. The wiser you deploy, the more equity you hold. That doesn't mean to be a penny pincher if more capital is needed to scale and compete. But every time you raise more capital your equity percentage gets diluted. Every round the pie gets fatter and your slice gets thinner in relation to the expanding valuation. Many founders struggle with this. But 100 percent of nothing is nada, and 10 percent of Yahoo!, as cofounder Jerry Yang knows, is something. Dilute! Create value. Grow the valuation. Have a venture lawyer represent you every step of the way if you need to; you'll see how typical deals are done and where yours fits into the overall range.

VentureOne in San Francisco provided me with some fantastic profiles in dollar terms of dozens of Internet companies, some well known and others not so well known. By delving into these real-world examples we'll see how the value creation began and progressed, providing a valuable map to the valuation trail. The amount raised from the assorted Internet companies totaled more than $6.7 billion. They turned that into a $38.8 billion post money valuation as a group. That doesn't count the aftermarket, post-IPO runs.

Among the list, which I encourage you to pore over at will, find America Online. In the summer of 1986 AOL was a development-stage effort that raised $1.5 million. Note the "step ups" from there to $61.6 million in 1992. That makes AOL one of the first "Internet stocks" to go public, although in those days it was all closed, proprietary online services.

Amazon.com raised $8 million in June 1996 as it was already shipping books. Kleiner Perkins's John Doerr explained that he got on a plane to Seattle, visited this humming warehouse with books being shipped everywhere, and saw the potential in action. Amazon has proven to be one of Kleiner's best Internet investments to date with a market valued that has soared north of $20 billion.

In August 1995 Doerr was on the hunt again and dreamt up @Home, putting $10 million on the line to lure NASA's Milo Medin away from the government. Post money valuation got big fast at $156 million.

Look at CNET, only a computer cable channel with a Web site in 1993 when it raised $650,000. That will hardly keep the lights on at CNET these days.

Benchmark Capital bet on a guy who had created a Web site to allow his girlfriend to trade Pez candy containers. That humble effort grew to include more and more items people wanted to sell. In its first round in June 1997 that humble Pez-candy trader, eBay, took $3 million. We all know the story of its IPO and performance afterwards as this multi-billion-market cap firm trades in the big leagues now.

GeoCities in January 1996 was fresh off the heels of being a spiffy, cool part of a firm called Beverly Hills Software, a leading Microsoft developer-type of Web site. GeoCities served an odd function that allowed people to post Web pages—hardly a business. More than 3 years later Yahoo! agreed to acquire it for $3.6 billion. A little-known fact: GeoCities is the world's largest publisher of content if you count all the millions of pages its members have made and continue to make. Ponder that according to GeoCities, its members produce more than the New York Times Co., GANNETT, News Corp., and Times Mirror, all which produce volumes and volumes of content daily. If you can understand that phenomenon you better understand Zero Gravity.

Look at Jim Clark's second time at bat with an Internet start-up, Healtheon, and see the nearly 10× valuation increase from first launch to shipping. It also went on to IPO at a higher valuation.

The quintessential example? Yahoo! It's almost inconceivable that in April 1995 Yahoo! was a seed deal and raised $1 million from Sequoia Capital. Also unbelievable is the valuation supernova since then with this one. Browse the list, jot down notes. Have some fun here with this fantastic resource on the following page.

I've taken that same group of data and now show the jump over time from pre-IPO valuation and amount raised. Note how Netscape, the first truly "big" Internet offer, broke the mold with amount raised at more than $140 million, an unheard of figure on those nascent days

COMPANY NAME	INTERNET BUSINESS	FINANCE ROUND	CLOSE DATE
24/7 Media	services	Later	1/15/98
24/7 Media	services	IPO	8/14/98
Actuate Software	software	Seed	12/1/93
Actuate Software	software	1st	9/15/94
Actuate Software	software	2nd	1/23/96
Actuate Software	software	3rd	4/25/97
Actuate Software	software	IPO	7/17/98
Allaire	software	1st	6/1/96
Allaire	software	2nd	9/1/96
Allaire	software	3rd	5/1/97
Allaire	software	IPO	1/22/99
Allegiance Telecom	ISPs	1st	8/14/97
Allegiance Telecom	ISPs	2nd	10/15/97
Allegiance Telecom	ISPs	3rd	1/29/98
Allegiance Telecom	ISPs	IPO	7/1/98
Amazon.com	ecommerce	1st	6/1/96
Amazon.com	ecommerce	IPO	5/15/97
America Online	ISPs	1st	6/1/86
America Online	ISPs	2nd	2/1/87
America Online	ISPs	3rd	6/1/88
America Online	ISPs	Mezz	9/1/91
America Online	ISPs	IPO	3/19/92
Asymetrix	software	1st	10/1/96
Asymetrix	software	IPO	6/12/98
@Home	ISPs	1st	8/1/95
@Home	ISPs	2nd	5/1/96
@Home	ISPs	3rd	8/1/96
@Home	ISPs	IPO	7/11/97
Beyond.com	ecommerce	1st	1/15/95
Beyond.com	ecommerce	2nd	7/1/96
Beyond.com	ecommerce	3rd	12/1/97
Beyond.com	ecommerce	Mezz	3/15/98
Beyond.com	ecommerce	IPO	6/17/98
Broad Vision	software	1st	11/1/93
Broad Vision	software	2nd	4/1/94
Broad Vision	software	3rd	8/31/95

YEAR	STAGE	AMOUNT RAISED	POST VALUE
1998	Shipping	$10.00	$160.00
1998	Shipping	$45.50	$284.00
1993	Start-up	$1.00	$3.00
1994	Development	$3.50	$10.50
1996	Shipping	$4.00	$30.00
1997	Shipping	$5.90	$65.00
1998	Shipping	$33.00	$159.30
1996	Development	$2.32	$11.56
1996	Shipping	$1.00	$14.00
1997	Shipping	$9.35	$28.00
1999	Shipping	$50.00	$209.20
1997	Development	$5.00	$6.00
1997	Shipping	$25.00	$30.00
1998	Shipping	$20.00	$50.00
1998	Shipping	$150.00	$778.00
1996	Shipping	$8.00	
1997	Shipping	$54.00	$503.67
1986	Development	$1.50	
1987	Shipping	$0.80	$3.00
1988	Shipping	$5.00	$30.00
1991	Profitable	$5.00	
1992	Profitable	$23.00	$61.60
1996	Shipping	$5.00	$60.00
1998	Shipping	$33.00	$185.87
1995	Start-up	$10.00	$156.00
1996	Development	$10.00	$275.00
1996	Shipping	$24.73	$568.00
1997	Shipping	$94.50	$1,285.95
1995	Development	$1.00	$12.00
1996	Shipping	$5.14	$26.00
1997	Shipping	$6.00	$46.00
1998	Shipping	$3.00	$55.00
1998	Shipping	$45.00	$284.50
1993	Development	$2.60	$6.02
1994	Development	$1.60	$15.40
1995	Development	$6.60	$31.80

Source: VentureOne; values in millions

(continued)

COMPANY NAME	INTERNET BUSINESS	FINANCE ROUND	CLOSE DATE
Broad Vision	software	4th	4/12/96
Broad Vision	software	IPO	6/21/96
CDnow	ecommerce	1st	7/15/97
CDnow	ecommerce	2nd	8/14/97
CDnow	ecommerce	IPO	2/10/98
CheckPoint Software Technology	software	1st	11/29/95
CheckPoint Software Technology	software	IPO	6/27/96
CNET	content	Seed	8/1/93
CNET	content	1st	1/15/94
CNET	content	2nd	10/30/94
CNET	content	3rd	1/15/96
CNET	content	Mezz	4/26/96
CNET	content	IPO	7/1/96
Computer Literacy Bookshops Online	ecommerce	1st	9/20/96
Computer Literacy Bookshops Online	ecommerce	2nd	5/29/97
Computer Literacy Bookshops Online	ecommerce	3rd	1/15/98
Computer Literacy Bookshops Online	ecommerce	Later	5/21/98
Computer Literacy Bookshops Online	ecommerce	IPO	11/20/98
Connect	software	1st	4/1/89
Connect	software	Later	7/1/94
Connect	software	Later	12/20/95
Connect	software	IPO	8/14/96
Consilium	software	1st	8/1/83
Consilium	software	IPO	5/9/89
Covad Communication	ISPs	1st	6/1/97
Covad Communication	ISPs	2nd	7/16/97
Covad Communication	ISPs	IPO	1/22/99
Crosscomm	infrastructure	1st	7/12/91
Crosscomm	infrastructure	2nd	11/12/91

YEAR	STAGE	AMOUNT RAISED	POST VALUE
1996	Shipping	$5.10	$136.30
1996	Shipping	$21.00	$137.30
1997	Shipping	$1.25	$27.00
1997	Shipping	$8.74	$40.00
1998	Shipping	$65.60	$315.00
1995	Development	$10.10	
1996	Profitable	$58.80	$457.80
1993	Shipping	$0.65	$2.80
1994	Shipping	$1.00	$8.40
1994	Shipping	$5.00	$16.00
1996	Shipping	$7.60	$68.20
1996	Profitable	$8.40	$97.20
1996	Profitable	$32.00	$212.10
1996	Shipping	$4.09	$7.00
1997	Shipping	$2.50	$15.00
1998	Shipping	$7.25	$32.00
1998	Shipping	$5.52	$55.50
1998	Shipping	$30.00	$118.00
1989	Start-up	$4.80	
1994	Shipping	$2.20	
1995	Shipping	$29.30	$44.00
1996	Shipping	$14.40	$110.60
1983		$1.10	
1989	Profitable	$14.00	$54.00
1997	Shipping	$0.25	$5.00
1997	Shipping	$8.50	$16.96
1999	Shipping	$140.40	$810.84
1991	Development	$1.32	
1991	Development	$2.50	

Source: VentureOne; values in millions

(continued)

COMPANY NAME	INTERNET BUSINESS	FINANCE ROUND	CLOSE DATE
Crosscomm	infrastructure	IPO	6/18/92
Cyberian Outpost	ecommerce	1st	5/30/97
Cyberian Outpost	ecommerce	2nd	10/31/97
Cyberian Outpost	ecommerce	3rd	2/15/98
Cyberian Outpost	ecommerce	IPO	7/31/98
CyberMedia	software	1st	1/1/95
CyberMedia	software	2nd	9/29/95
CyberMedia	software	3rd	7/2/96
CyberMedia	software	IPO	10/23/96
Daou Systems	services	1st	10/19/95
Daou Systems	services	Mezz	11/1/96
Daou Systems	services	IPO	2/12/97
Digex	ISPs	1st	3/24/95
Digex	ISPs	2nd	5/31/96
Digex	ISPs	IPO	10/16/96
Digital Link	infrastructure	1st	11/1/87
Digital Link	infrastructure	IPO	1/31/94
Digital Transmission Systems	infrastructure	1st	12/27/91
Digital Transmission Systems	infrastructure	2nd	8/9/92
Digital Transmission Systems	infrastructure	IPO	3/4/96
DoubleClick	services	LBO	6/10/97
DoubleClick	services	IPO	2/20/98
Eagle River Interactive	services	1st	9/29/95
Eagle River Interactive	services	IPO	3/21/96
EarthLink Network	ISPs	1st	12/31/95
EarthLink Network	ISPs	2nd	5/10/96
EarthLink Network	ISPs	Mezz	9/30/96
EarthLink Network	ISPs	IPO	1/22/97
Earthweb	services	1st	10/25/96
Earthweb	services	2nd	6/1/97
Earthweb	services	IPO	11/11/98
eBay	services	1st	6/1/97
eBay	services	IPO	9/24/98

YEAR	STAGE	AMOUNT RAISED	POST VALUE
1992	Profitable	$29.26	$69.30
1997	Shipping	$2.30	$9.89
1997	Shipping	$1.50	$13.88
1998	Shipping	$22.00	$31.36
1998	Shipping	$72.00	$516.30
1995	Shipping	$1.10	$1.90
1995	Shipping	$4.50	$8.30
1996	Shipping	$5.10	$48.30
1996	Shipping	$40.00	$183.70
1995	Profitable	$11.50	$44.90
1996	Profitable	$2.20	
1997	Profitable	$18.00	$102.08
1995	Shipping	$4.00	$17.50
1996	Shipping	$8.00	$79.60
1996	Shipping	$45.56	$107.40
1987	Development	$1.00	$8.00
1994	Profitable	$35.70	$116.20
1991	Shipping	$1.75	$7.00
1992	Development	$0.85	$10.00
1996	Profitable	$8.00	$27.28
1997	Shipping	$40.00	
1998	Shipping	$59.50	$304.00
1995	Shipping	$6.00	$11.60
1996	Shipping	$52.00	$145.12
1995	Start-up	$6.30	$14.90
1996	Shipping	$8.70	$58.40
1996	Shipping	$15.00	$81.30
1997	Shipping	$26.00	$166.76
1996	Development	$6.70	$18.81
1997	Shipping	$10.00	$35.79
1998	Shipping	$29.40	$117.60
1997	Profitable	$3.00	$30.00
1998	Profitable	$63.00	$740.00

Source: VentureOne; values in millions

(continued)

COMPANY NAME	INTERNET BUSINESS	FINANCE ROUND	CLOSE DATE
Entrust Technologies	software	Later	1/15/97
Entrust Technologies	software	IPO	8/17/98
ETrade	services	1st	9/28/95
ETrade	services	2nd	4/10/96
ETrade	services	3rd	6/6/96
ETrade	services	IPO	8/16/96
Excite	software	1st	7/28/95
Excite	software	2nd	11/1/95
Excite	software	3rd	12/11/95
Excite	software	Mezz	3/8/96
Excite	software	IPO	4/3/96
Exodus Communications	services	1st	3/15/96
Exodus Communications	services	2nd	10/2/96
Exodus Communications	services	3rd	6/24/97
Exodus Communications	services	Later	12/12/97
Exodus Communications	services	IPO	3/18/98
Extended Systems	infrastructure	IPO	3/4/98
faxSAV	services	Seed	10/1/90
faxSAV	services	1st	4/8/91
faxSAV	services	2nd	10/1/91
faxSAV	services	3rd	6/1/92
faxSAV	services	Rest	11/1/94
faxSAV	services	Later	1/18/95
faxSAV	services	Later	3/5/96
faxSAV	services	IPO	10/11/96
FTP Software	software	Later	1/15/93
FTP Software	software	IPO	11/16/93
GeoCities	services	1st	1/15/96
GeoCities	services	2nd	1/13/97
GeoCities	services	3rd	10/15/97
GeoCities	services	Later	1/7/98
GeoCities	services	IPO	8/11/98
Giga Information Group	services	1st	7/1/95
Giga Information Group	services	2nd	11/13/95
Giga Information Group	services	3rd	5/1/97
Giga Information Group	services	Later	4/1/98

YEAR	STAGE	AMOUNT RAISED	POST VALUE
1997	Profitable	$25.75	$96.00
1998	Profitable	$124.27	$880.46
1995	Profitable	$12.30	$43.00
1996	Profitable	$2.85	$51.50
1996	Profitable	$9.00	$198.50
1996	Profitable	$59.50	$367.50
1995	Profitable	$1.50	$2.70
1995	Profitable	$1.50	$6.50
1995	Profitable	$0.90	$16.50
1996	Profitable	$12.30	$57.60
1996	Shipping	$34.00	$183.10
1996	Shipping	$3.22	$5.50
1996	Shipping	$6.50	$17.64
1997	Shipping	$21.50	$53.00
1997	Shipping	$7.50	$117.00
1998	Shipping	$67.50	$295.00
1998	Profitable	$12.40	$89.00
1990	Start-up	$0.75	
1991	Shipping	$1.50	$2.50
1991	Shipping	$2.00	$9.00
1992	Shipping	$5.00	$9.60
1994	REST	$1.20	$6.50
1995	Shipping	$4.20	$13.50
1996	Shipping	$8.00	$32.60
1996	Shipping	$12.00	$77.40
1993	Profitable	$1.10	$127.60
1993	Profitable	$95.00	$377.00
1996	Development	$2.50	
1997	Shipping	$9.00	$90.00
1997	Shipping	$11.00	$165.71
1998	Shipping	$18.95	$200.00
1998	Shipping	$80.75	$640.51
1995	Shipping	$2.85	$10.48
1995	Shipping	$25.74	$58.00
1997	Shipping	$10.73	$69.00
1998	Shipping	$2.00	$73.00

Source: VentureOne; values in millions

(continued)

COMPANY NAME	INTERNET BUSINESS	FINANCE ROUND	CLOSE DATE
Giga Information Group	services	IPO	7/30/98
Global Telesystems	ISPs	1st	1/1/94
Global Telesystems	ISPs	2nd	1/1/95
Global Telesystems	ISPs	3rd	11/15/96
Global Telesystems	ISPs	4th	9/10/97
Global Telesystems	ISPs	IPO	2/5/98
HealthDesk	services	Seed	8/31/95
HealthDesk	services	1st	12/31/95
HealthDesk	services	IPO	1/17/97
Healtheon	services	1st	1/26/96
Healtheon	services	2nd	10/2/96
Healtheon	services	3rd	7/1/97
Healtheon	services	4th	11/15/97
Healtheon	services	Mezz	11/6/98
Healtheon	services	IPO	2/10/99
Hybrid Networks	infrastructure	Seed	8/1/92
Hybrid Networks	infrastructure	1st	11/10/94
Hybrid Networks	infrastructure	3rd	5/31/95
Hybrid Networks	infrastructure	2nd	10/1/95
Hybrid Networks	infrastructure	4th	7/12/96
Hybrid Networks	infrastructure	IPO	11/12/97
Individual	content	Seed	11/1/89
Individual	content	1st	1/1/91
Individual	content	2nd	3/1/92
Individual	content	3rd	12/16/92
Individual	content	4th	9/13/93
Individual	content	IPO	3/15/96
Infonautics	services	1st	7/22/94
Infonautics	services	2nd	9/22/95
Infonautics	services	Mezz	2/9/96
Infonautics	services	IPO	4/29/96
Information America	services	2nd	1/1/87
Information America	services	IPO	11/21/91
Infoseek	software	1st	6/30/94
Infoseek	software	2nd	6/30/95
Infoseek	software	IPO	6/11/96

YEAR	STAGE	AMOUNT RAISED	POST VALUE
1998	Shipping	$37.50	$150.05
1994	Profitable	$65.00	
1995	Profitable	$46.00	
1996	Shipping	$110.00	$600.00
1997	Development	$39.00	$750.00
1998	Shipping	$222.00	$974.10
1995	Development	$1.20	$2.20
1995	Development	$2.20	$6.60
1997	Development	$8.50	$35.44
1996	Development	$5.14	
1996	Development	$6.00	$49.00
1997	Shipping	$6.00	$67.60
1997	Shipping	$25.00	$167.00
1998	Shipping	$46.00	$455.00
1999	Shipping	$40.00	$475.40
1992	Development	$0.60	
1994	Development	$0.94	$2.77
1995	Shipping	$5.55	$10.91
1995	Shipping	$1.24	$5.10
1996	Shipping	$12.53	$43.68
1997	Shipping	$37.80	$225.80
1989	Development	$1.00	$2.60
1991	Shipping	$2.60	$6.40
1992	Shipping	$0.50	$8.60
1992	Shipping	$3.80	$15.50
1993	Shipping	$3.00	$28.00
1996	Shipping	$35.00	$163.49
1994	Development	$2.40	$9.90
1995	Development	$6.70	$22.60
1996	Development	$13.70	$84.00
1996	Shipping	$31.50	$131.40
1987	Shipping	$4.40	
1991	Profitable	$14.50	$33.80
1994	Development	$1.20	$6.40
1995	Shipping	$4.50	$15.40
1996	Shipping	$41.45	$304.80

Source: VentureOne; values in millions

(*continued*)

COMPANY NAME	INTERNET BUSINESS	FINANCE ROUND	CLOSE DATE
Inktomi	software	1st	4/14/97
Inktomi	software	Mezz	3/4/98
Inktomi	software	IPO	6/10/98
Intraware	services	1st	6/1/97
Intraware	services	2nd	12/5/97
Intraware	services	Later	5/13/98
Intraware	services	IPO	2/26/99
ISS Group	software	1st	2/15/96
ISS Group	software	2nd	2/15/97
ISS Group	software	IPO	3/24/98
Lycos	software	Seed	6/6/95
Lycos	software	1st	10/1/95
Lycos	software	IPO	4/1/96
Masstor Systems	software	2nd	3/1/81
Masstor Systems	software	Mezz	2/1/82
Metatools	software	Seed	4/1/92
Metatools	software	1st	2/1/94
Metatools	software	Later	1/15/95
Metatools	software	IPO	12/12/95
Mobius Management Systems	software	1st	5/12/97
Mobius Management Systems	software	IPO	4/28/98
N2K	ecommerce	1st	8/15/94
N2K	ecommerce	2nd	2/13/96
N2K	ecommerce	4th	4/15/96
N2K	ecommerce	3rd	5/29/96
N2K	ecommerce	5th	4/1/97
N2K	ecommerce	IPO	10/17/97
Netcom On-line Comm.	ISPs	1st	12/29/93
Netcom On-line Comm.	ISPs	2nd	9/9/94
Netcom On-line Comm.	ISPs	IPO	12/15/94
NetGravity	software	Seed	9/1/95
NetGravity	software	1st	1/1/96
NetGravity	software	2nd	3/1/97
NetGravity	software	Later	11/1/97

YEAR	STAGE	AMOUNT RAISED	POST VALUE
1997	Shipping	$8.00	$58.70
1998	Shipping	$12.00	$104.00
1998	Shipping	$40.57	$405.00
1997	Shipping	$2.64	$11.00
1997	Shipping	$1.50	$21.49
1998	Shipping	$11.70	$58.50
1999	Shipping	$64.00	$376.50
1996	Shipping	$3.65	$12.50
1997	Shipping	$5.28	$40.00
1998	Shipping	$66.00	$360.00
1995	Start-up	$1.00	$2.50
1995	Shipping	$1.00	$5.30
1996	Shipping	$48.00	$218.50
1981		$0.65	
1982		$0.14	
1992	Start-up	$0.80	$3.20
1994	Shipping	$3.40	$19.00
1995	Shipping	$5.00	$27.00
1995	Profitable	$54.00	$201.97
1997	Profitable	$12.00	$44.00
1998	Profitable	$47.85	$291.00
1994	Shipping	$1.45	
1996	Profitable	$3.00	$12.32
1996	Shipping	$0.73	$13.05
1996	Shipping	$15.27	$21.64
1997	Shipping	$7.40	$24.18
1997	Shipping	$63.27	$310.38
1993	Shipping	$2.00	$8.10
1994	Shipping	$8.15	$37.10
1994	Profitable	$24.10	$85.70
1995	Shipping	$0.15	$0.26
1996	Shipping	$4.45	$4.80
1997	Shipping	$4.30	$12.80
1997	Shipping	$8.68	$34.00

Source: VentureOne; values in millions

(continued)

COMPANY NAME	INTERNET BUSINESS	FINANCE ROUND	CLOSE DATE
NetGravity	software	IPO	6/12/98
Netscape Comm.	software	1st	9/1/94
Netscape Comm.	software	IPO	8/8/95
New Era of Networks	software	Seed	5/1/95
New Era of Networks	software	1st	9/20/95
New Era of Networks	software	2nd	6/3/96
New Era of Networks	software	IPO	6/19/97
Object Design	software	1st	8/1/88
Object Design	software	2nd	6/29/90
Object Design	software	3rd	7/1/91
Object Design	software	4th	3/21/92
Object Design	software	5th	3/18/94
Object Design	software	Mezz	2/13/96
Object Design	software	IPO	7/23/96
Onewave	software	Seed	12/15/94
Onewave	software	1st	2/20/96
Onewave	software	Mezz	4/6/96
Onewave	software	IPO	7/2/96
OnSale	ecommerce	1st	9/1/96
OnSale	ecommerce	IPO	4/17/97
Open Market	software	1st	5/1/94
Open Market	software	2nd	4/1/95
Open Market	software	Mezz	1/15/96
Open Market	software	IPO	5/22/96
Peapod	ecommerce	Later	4/16/96
Peapod	ecommerce	IPO	6/11/97
Pegasus Systems	services	LBO	7/1/95
Pegasus Systems	services	1st	6/26/96
Pegasus Systems	services	IPO	8/7/97
Performance Systems Int.	ISPs	1st	3/11/93
Performance Systems Int.	ISPs	2nd	10/14/93
Performance Systems Int.	ISPs	3rd	5/31/94
Performance Systems Int.	ISPs	Mezz	1/15/95
Performance Systems Int.	ISPs	IPO	5/1/95
Pilot Network Services	ISPs	Seed	1/15/94
Pilot Network Services	ISPs	1st	3/13/95

YEAR	STAGE	AMOUNT RAISED	POST VALUE
1998	Shipping	$27.00	$156.60
1994	Shipping	$6.40	$20.80
1995	Shipping	$140.00	$1,068.52
1995	Development	$2.00	$4.18
1995	Development	$1.90	$6.50
1996	Shipping	$7.50	$42.30
1997	Shipping	$33.10	$134.55
1988	Development	$2.75	$5.25
1990	Profitable	$6.10	$14.70
1991	Shipping	$5.00	$23.00
1992	Shipping	$4.50	$35.80
1994	Profitable	$7.00	$150.00
1996	Profitable	$5.00	$87.90
1996	Profitable	$21.00	$184.00
1994	Shipping	$0.30	$1.73
1996	Shipping	$7.40	$97.10
1996	Profitable	$6.00	$93.50
1996	Profitable	$60.00	$236.12
1996	Profitable	$4.20	
1997	Profitable	$15.00	$120.71
1994	Development	$1.80	$5.00
1995	Development	$9.40	$36.30
1996	Shipping	$27.80	$229.40
1996	Shipping	$72.00	$484.90
1996	Shipping	$17.25	$60.00
1997	Shipping	$64.00	$336.58
1995	Shipping	$8.65	$52.10
1996	Shipping	$7.50	
1997	Shipping	$46.50	$146.58
1993	Shipping	$3.60	
1993	Shipping	$2.10	
1994	Shipping	$5.20	$70.00
1995	Shipping	$13.20	$120.00
1995	Profitable	$45.60	$361.50
1994	Development	$0.61	$2.00
1995	Shipping	$1.30	$5.60

Source: VentureOne; values in millions

(continued)

COMPANY NAME	INTERNET BUSINESS	FINANCE ROUND	CLOSE DATE
Pilot Network Services	ISPs	2nd	7/18/96
Pilot Network Services	ISPs	3rd	3/31/97
Pilot Network Services	ISPs	IPO	8/11/98
Preview Travel	ecommerce	1st	8/1/93
Preview Travel	ecommerce	2nd	1/31/95
Preview Travel	ecommerce	3rd	6/29/96
Preview Travel	ecommerce	IPO	11/20/97
Raptor Systems	software	1st	10/1/94
Raptor Systems	software	2nd	5/15/95
Raptor Systems	software	IPO	2/6/96
RealNetworks	software	1st	10/26/95
RealNetworks	software	2nd	11/27/96
RealNetworks	software	IPO	11/21/97
RoweCom	services	1st	4/1/97
RoweCom	services	2nd	5/4/98
RoweCom	services	3rd	12/11/98
RoweCom	services	IPO	3/9/99
Sportsline USA	content	1st	5/25/95
Sportsline USA	content	2nd	3/1/96
Sportsline USA	content	3rd	9/27/96
Sportsline USA	content	IPO	11/13/97
Spyglass	software	1st	11/1/90
Spyglass	software	2nd	10/1/91
Spyglass	software	IPO	6/26/95
Stratacom	infrastructure	1st	2/1/86
Stratacom	infrastructure	2nd	8/1/86
Stratacom	infrastructure	3rd	7/1/87
Stratacom	infrastructure	IPO	7/21/92
Sync Research	infrastructure	1st	6/10/91
Sync Research	infrastructure	2nd	2/26/93
Sync Research	infrastructure	IPO	11/9/95
TGV Software	software	Later	12/2/93
TGV Software	software	IPO	2/28/95
Ticketmaster Online-CitySearch	content	1st	10/31/95

YEAR	STAGE	AMOUNT RAISED	POST VALUE
1996	Shipping	$1.57	$18.00
1997	Shipping	$6.10	$49.05
1998	Shipping	$45.50	$237.20
1993	Shipping	$2.40	$14.00
1995	Shipping	$6.27	$30.10
1996	Shipping	$22.67	$75.00
1997	Shipping	$27.50	$154.20
1994	Development	$1.90	
1995	Development	$3.00	
1996	Shipping	$45.00	$178.30
1995	Development	$5.70	$39.19
1996	Shipping	$17.90	$177.60
1997	Shipping	$37.50	$537.50
1997	Development	$4.00	$15.00
1998	Shipping	$8.00	
1998	Shipping	$15.00	$68.80
1999	Shipping	$49.60	$154.00
1995	Profitable	$2.95	$9.15
1996	Shipping	$11.09	$30.56
1996	Shipping	$15.93	$66.50
1997	Shipping	$28.00	$163.70
1990	Development	$0.90	$2.00
1991	Shipping	$1.60	$6.05
1995	Profitable	$34.00	$85.06
1986	Start-up	$4.50	$5.00
1986	Profitable	$7.00	$26.00
1987	Shipping	$3.50	$30.00
1992	Profitable	$17.50	$103.00
1991	Shipping	$3.50	$5.60
1993	Shipping	$7.80	$23.00
1995	Shipping	$78.00	$261.50
1993	Profitable	$7.00	$27.70
1995	Profitable	$32.00	$85.20
1995	Shipping	$1.78	$10.00

Source: VentureOne; values in millions

(continued)

COMPANY NAME	INTERNET BUSINESS	FINANCE ROUND	CLOSE DATE
Ticketmaster Online-CitySearch	content	2nd	10/31/95
Ticketmaster Online-CitySearch	content	3rd	5/15/96
Ticketmaster Online-CitySearch	content	Later	12/13/96
Ticketmaster Online-CitySearch	content	Later	11/11/97
Ticketmaster Online-CitySearch	content	IPO	12/3/98
TSI International Software	software	IPO	7/2/97
Tut Systems	infrastructure	Seed	8/1/91
Tut Systems	infrastructure	1st	7/20/93
Tut Systems	infrastructure	2nd	5/1/94
Tut Systems	infrastructure	3rd	11/1/94
Tut Systems	infrastructure	4th	5/1/95
Tut Systems	infrastructure	5th	8/2/96
Tut Systems	infrastructure	Mezz	12/16/97
Tut Systems	infrastructure	IPO	1/28/99
UOL Publishing	content	1st	7/1/95
UOL Publishing	content	IPO	11/26/96
USN Communications	ISPs	1st	5/15/94
USN Communications	ISPs	2nd	6/23/95
USN Communications	ISPs	Later	9/30/96
USN Communications	ISPs	Later	9/30/97
USN Communications	ISPs	IPO	2/4/98
USWeb	services	Seed	12/1/95
USWeb	services	1st	2/21/96
USWeb	services	2nd	1/1/97
USWeb	services	3rd	7/1/97
USWeb	services	IPO	12/5/97
UUNET Technologies, Inc.	ISPs	1st	12/22/93
UUNET Technologies, Inc.	ISPs	2nd	6/10/94
UUNET Technologies, Inc.	ISPs	3rd	9/19/94
UUNET Technologies, Inc.	ISPs	IPO	5/25/95

YEAR	STAGE	AMOUNT RAISED	POST VALUE
1995	Shipping	$1.00	$46.20
1996	Shipping	$11.30	$57.50
1996	Shipping	$28.90	$134.50
1997	Shipping	$40.00	$192.00
1998	Shipping	$98.00	$333.00
1997	Profitable	$36.00	$120.00
1991	Start-up	$0.20	$1.60
1993	Shipping	$1.75	$7.40
1994	Shipping	$1.60	
1994	Shipping	$2.40	
1995	Shipping	$6.00	
1996	Shipping	$11.50	$34.20
1997	Shipping	$15.00	$109.00
1999	Shipping	$45.00	$197.40
1995	Shipping	$3.50	$10.00
1996	Shipping	$18.59	$41.40
1994	Shipping	$15.21	$30.96
1995	Shipping	$26.24	$60.00
1996	Shipping	$10.00	$69.00
1997	Shipping	$30.21	$99.50
1998	Profitable	$128.00	$496.00
1995	Shipping	$0.50	$5.56
1996	Shipping	$10.00	$21.30
1997	Shipping	$5.66	$34.10
1997	Shipping	$17.50	$159.80
1997	Shipping	$37.50	$473.40
1993	Shipping	$2.70	$9.40
1994	Shipping	$3.30	$15.80
1994	Shipping	$8.20	$48.70
1995	Profitable	$66.20	$386.30

Source: VentureOne; values in millions

(*continued*)

COMPANY NAME	INTERNET BUSINESS	FINANCE ROUND	CLOSE DATE
Verio	ISPs	Seed	3/15/96
Verio	ISPs	1st	7/1/96
Verio	ISPs	2nd	12/5/96
Verio	ISPs	3rd	5/20/97
Verio	ISPs	IPO	5/12/98
VeriSign	services	Seed	4/15/95
VeriSign	services	1st	4/20/95
VeriSign	services	2nd	2/15/96
VeriSign	services	3rd	12/5/96
VeriSign	services	IPO	1/30/98
Verity	software	1st	5/1/88
Verity	software	2nd	5/1/89
Verity	software	3rd	7/1/90
Verity	software	4th	9/30/94
Verity	software	Mezz	8/1/95
Verity	software	IPO	10/6/95
VerticalNet	services	1st	9/1/96
VerticalNet	services	2nd	7/1/97
VerticalNet	services	3rd	10/1/97
VerticalNet	services	Mezz	5/1/98
VerticalNet	services	IPO	2/10/99
ViaGrafix	services	IPO	3/4/98
Vignette	software	Seed	2/1/96
Vignette	software	1st	6/1/96
Vignette	software	2nd	7/28/97
Vignette	software	3rd	4/1/98
Vignette	software	Later	5/11/98
Vignette	software	Later	12/9/98
Visual Networks	infrastructure	Seed	12/15/94
Visual Networks	infrastructure	1st	12/30/94
Visual Networks	infrastructure	2nd	8/11/95
Visual Networks	infrastructure	3rd	1/15/96
Visual Networks	infrastructure	4th	9/19/96
Visual Networks	infrastructure	IPO	2/6/98
Voxware	software	2nd	3/5/96
Voxware	software	IPO	10/30/96

YEAR	STAGE	AMOUNT RAISED	POST VALUE
1996	Start-up	$1.00	$3.00
1996	Shipping	$18.02	$25.83
1996	Shipping	$60.00	$106.00
1997	Shipping	$20.00	$158.00
1998	Shipping	$126.50	$785.00
1995	Shipping	$0.56	$0.12
1995	Shipping	$5.17	$10.79
1996	Shipping	$5.10	$27.17
1996	Shipping	$29.00	$118.00
1998	Shipping	$42.00	$317.00
1988	Shipping	$3.00	$7.00
1989	Shipping	$6.00	$15.80
1990	Shipping	$3.50	$19.50
1994	Shipping	$4.50	$30.90
1995	Shipping	$3.30	$52.50
1995	Shipping	$40.00	$114.00
1996	Development	$1.00	$2.30
1997	Shipping	$2.00	$6.50
1997	Shipping	$0.20	$10.00
1998	Shipping	$16.00	$50.00
1999	Shipping	$56.00	$262.80
1998	Shipping	$28.60	$95.00
1996	Start-up	$0.40	$2.50
1996	Development	$3.05	$10.20
1997	Development	$3.72	$40.00
1998	Shipping	$1.75	$65.00
1998	Shipping	$14.30	$125.00
1998	Shipping	$8.50	
1994	Start-up	$0.12	
1994	Start-up	$1.20	$2.50
1995	Development	$2.00	$5.67
1996	Shipping	$4.00	$12.00
1996	Shipping	$5.02	$51.00
1998	Shipping	$43.75	$213.30
1996	Development	$6.00	$17.60
1996	Shipping	$20.25	$90.00

Source: VentureOne; values in millions

(continued)

COMPANY NAME	INTERNET BUSINESS	FINANCE ROUND	CLOSE DATE
White Pine Software	software	Later	2/16/95
White Pine Software	software	Mezz	3/19/96
White Pine Software	software	IPO	10/11/96
Whittman-Hart	services	Later	8/30/95
Whittman-Hart	services	IPO	5/1/96
Worldtalk Comm.	software	1st	3/31/93
Worldtalk Comm.	software	2nd	3/10/94
Worldtalk Comm.	software	3rd	3/3/95
Worldtalk Comm.	software	Mezz	12/1/95
Worldtalk Comm.	software	IPO	4/12/96
Xylan	infrastructure	Seed	7/9/93
Xylan	infrastructure	1st	2/4/94
Xylan	infrastructure	2nd	9/18/94
Xylan	infrastructure	Later	10/15/95
Xylan	infrastructure	Mezz	12/22/95
Xylan	infrastructure	IPO	3/11/96
Yahoo	software	Seed	4/7/95
Yahoo	software	IPO	4/12/96
TOTAL			

of 1995 when just finding your way onto the Internet took an engineering degree. The $100-million-plus-amount-raised club has been an exclusive set even since then. I expect that to change, and indeed it already has. Many Internet companies now routinely do an IPO and then a secondary offering a few months later as capital requirements have gone up to be competitive in a global marketplace. Check out the list *(on pages 140–142)*, sorted by year.

Interesting in the chart beginning on page 140 is the average pre-IPO valuation of about $240 million with $50 million raised. Those values will probably look small indeed as time goes on. Underlying what the chart shows, not evident in the numbers at first glance, is the difference in valuations. All Internet companies are not valued equally, are they? There is no template for valuation; it's always in flux. Each of the companies on pages 140–142 that took venture money

YEAR	STAGE	AMOUNT RAISED	POST VALUE
1995	Profitable	$0.70	
1996	Profitable	$2.00	$34.60
1996	Shipping	$27.00	$81.27
1995	Profitable	$5.50	$37.50
1996	Profitable	$43.20	$143.20
1993	Shipping	$4.20	$10.20
1994	Shipping	$3.30	
1995	Shipping	$3.75	$15.00
1995	Shipping	$2.00	$34.00
1996	Shipping	$16.80	$76.86
1993	Start-up	$0.25	
1994	Development	$2.00	$6.60
1994	Profitable	$6.20	$23.70
1995	Shipping	$5.00	$140.20
1995	Profitable	$5.00	$189.15
1996	Shipping	$109.20	$1,024.50
1995	Shipping	$1.00	$3.00
1996	Shipping	$33.80	$334.10
		$6,741.35	**$38,760.53**

Source: VentureOne; values in millions

had to go through the process you may be going through now.

All the discussions and debates on valuations, percentage, and amounts comes together in one document that's the most relevant to you and your future, the document that all of the above firms also signed, entered into, debated, argued over, and lost sleep over: the term sheet. It's simply that: terms. How much will they invest and for what percentage and what rights? Depending on the size of the venture firm and its risk tolerance, the term sheet may vary. Large firms routinely include these items in the preferred stock term sheet. The following bullet points are to give you a sense of the terms, but an actual term sheet would have much more legalese and other clauses. (Get a sample term sheet from a VC if you wish.) The list below will give a sense of what to expect the VC as preferred shareholder to receive; this is for informational purposes only, avoiding unnecessary legalese:

Pre-IPO Valuation
and Amount Raised

COMPANY	YEAR OF IPO	PRE-IPO VALUATION	AMOUNT RAISED
Allaire	1999	$159.20	$50.00
Covad Communications	1999	$670.44	$140.40
Healtheon	1999	$435.40	$40.00
Intraware	1999	$312.50	$64.00
RoweCom	1999	$104.40	$49.60
Tut Systems	1999	$152.40	$45.00
VerticalNet	1999	$206.80	$56.00
24/7 Media	1998	$238.50	$45.50
Actuate Software	1998	$126.30	$33.00
Allegiance Telecom	1998	$628.00	$150.00
Asymetrix	1998	$152.87	$33.00
Beyond.com	1998	$239.50	$45.00
CDnow	1998	$249.40	$65.60
Computer Literacy Bookshops Online	1998	$88.00	$30.00
Cyberian Outpost	1998	$444.30	$72.00
DoubleClick	1998	$244.50	$59.50
Earthweb	1998	$88.20	$29.40
eBay	1998	$677.00	$63.00
Entrust Technologies	1998	$756.20	$124.27
Exodus Communications	1998	$227.50	$67.50
Extended Systems	1998	$76.60	$12.40
GeoCities	1998	$559.76	$80.75
Giga Information Group	1998	$112.55	$37.50
Global Telesystems	1998	$752.10	$222.00
Inktomi	1998	$364.43	$40.57
ISS Group	1998	$294.00	$66.00
Mobius Management Systems	1998	$243.15	$47.85
NetGravity	1998	$129.60	$27.00
Pilot Network Services	1998	$191.70	$45.50
Ticketmaster Online-CitySearch	1998	$235.00	$98.00
USN Communications	1998	$368.00	$128.00

COMPANY	YEAR OF IPO	PRE-IPO VALUATION	AMOUNT RAISED
Verio	1998	$658.50	$126.50
VeriSign	1998	$275.00	$42.00
ViaGrafix	1998	$66.40	$28.60
Visual Networks	1998	$169.55	$43.75
Amazon.com	1997	$449.67	$54.00
@Home	1997	$1,191.45	$94.50
Daou Systems	1997	$84.08	$18.00
EarthLink Network	1997	$140.76	$26.00
HealthDesk	1997	$26.94	$8.50
Hybrid Networks	1997	$188.00	$37.80
N2K	1997	$247.11	$63.27
New Era of Networks	1997	$101.45	$33.10
OnSale	1997	$105.71	$15.00
Peapod	1997	$272.58	$64.00
Pegasus Systems	1997	$100.08	$46.50
Preview Travel	1997	$126.70	$27.50
RealNetworks	1997	$500.00	$37.50
Sportsline USA	1997	$135.70	$28.00
TSI International Software	1997	$84.00	$36.00
USWeb	1997	$435.90	$37.50
Broad Vision	1996	$116.30	$21.00
CheckPoint Software Technology	1996	$399.00	$58.80
Cnet	1996	$180.10	$32.00
Connect	1996	$96.20	$14.40
CyberMedia	1996	$143.70	$40.00
Digex	1996	$61.84	$45.56
Digital Transmission Systems	1996	$19.28	$8.00
Eagle River Interactive	1996	$93.12	$52.00
ETrade	1996	$308.00	$59.50
Excite	1996	$149.10	$34.00
faxSAV	1996	$65.40	$12.00

COMPANY	YEAR OF IPO	PRE-IPO VALUATION	AMOUNT RAISED
Individual	1996	$128.49	$35.00
Infonautics	1996	$99.90	$31.50
Infoseek	1996	$263.35	$41.45
Lycos	1996	$170.50	$48.00
Object Design	1996	$163.00	$21.00
Onewave	1996	$176.12	$60.00
Open Market	1996	$412.90	$72.00
Raptor Systems	1996	$133.30	$45.00
UOL Publishing	1996	$22.81	$18.59
Voxware	1996	$69.75	$20.25
White Pine Software	1996	$54.27	$27.00
Whittman-Hart	1996	$100.00	$43.20
Worldtalk Communications	1996	$60.06	$16.80
Xylan	1996	$915.30	$109.20
Yahoo	1996	$300.30	$33.80
Metatools	1995	$147.97	$54.00
Netscape Communications	1995	$928.52	$140.00
Performance Systems International	1995	$315.90	$45.60
Spyglass	1995	$51.06	$34.00
Sync Research	1995	$183.50	$78.00
TGV Software	1995	$53.20	$32.00
UUNET Technologies, Inc.	1995	$320.10	$66.20
Verity	1995	$74.00	$40.00
Digital Link	1994	$80.50	$35.70
Netcom On-line Communications	1994	$61.60	$24.10
FTP Software	1993	$282.00	$95.00
America Online	1992	$38.60	$23.00
Crosscomm	1992	$40.04	$29.26
Stratacom	1992	$85.50	$17.50
Information America	1991	$19.30	$14.50
Consilium	1989	$40.00	$14.00
TOTAL		$22,311.75	$4,679.27
AVERAGE		$239.91	$50.31
MEDIAN		$159.20	$41.45

Source: VentureOne; values in millions

➤ dividend provisions, if any
➤ liquidation preference—the VC as preferred shareholder has rights in the event of liquidation
➤ conversion rights—allow the preferred shareholder to convert preferred to common stock at a specified ratio
➤ auto conversion rights—preferred turns to common at IPO or if preferred and common holders approve
➤ voting—preferred shareholders' votes in relation to converted common shares held
➤ anti-dilution—stock splits, dividends, change of control via merger, and so on adjusts the number of shares to be received. Anti-dilution may include "ratchets," that is, provisions protecting the preferred holders if you have to do a "down round," or to try to raise capital at a lower valuation than during previous rounds.

There are several more clauses that appear on the term sheet. My purpose is not to try to present a legal template but to give you a sense of some of the items. It can be confusing to anyone the first time through. But each term sheet will have specifics relating to your agreement only. Get an example from your friendly neighborhood venture capitalist—or, if you're negotiating a term sheet, you should get very familiar with it through your venture lawyer. The important thing is that the VC is trying to maximize equity while minimizing risk, the same thing you're trying to do from the opposite side of the table. Use VentureOne as a resource, venture lawyers on your side, and talk with funded companies of the venture investors you're in discussions with about what their experience has been like. Valuation is in the eye of the beholder and always changing as the table above shows. More often than not, the ugly idea may be a hidden gem.

Zero Gravity

Definition by Example

Chapter Seven

" The best VCs can see ahead and are willing to think they can fix things, put the management team together, do all this stuff. Any huge success story like Netscape or Apple...[is] like a sausage factory. Everybody likes to eat sausage; no one likes to see how it gets made (laughs). These things are all sausage factories inside. "

—MARC ANDREESSEN, COFOUNDER OF NETSCAPE

A S WITH THE FIRST attempt to send humans into orbit, there must always be a first success, a trailblazer, to cut through the stratosphere and open up new possibilities. Netscape embodies Zero Gravity, a rocketship into the future. Someone, some elements had to come together at the right time, with the right thinking, right fuel, and right approach to lay down the foundation for launching Web firms into orbit.

In heavy gravity a platform for communication commerce includes buildings for writers and production processes, newsprint, trucks, news racks, ink, newspaper deliverers, and an entire system based on transporting paper with information on it. Ads, subscriptions, and marketing create a medium through which consumers and businesses connect. This model, which represents heavy gravity, moves paper around the planet, fells trees, makes pulp. You won't find many (if any) venture capitalists throwing money at newspaper start-ups. The opportunity for operating in heavy g prohibits the kind of return on investment they require to remain viable as money managers.

Broadcasting, on the other hand, works as electronic "e-media," and therefore is more in line with a mid-gravity commerce platform. It's not zero gravity because the information flow is more up to down, top to bottom, one-way. Your local news, for example, is aimed at the city or town in general but perhaps not at you specifically.

Zero gravity represents the ability to operate in a purely digital environment one-to-one, one-to-many, many-to-one (or even one-to-none!). Information, entertainment, communications all flow up, down, sideways, back and forth as easily in one direction as another, similar to the way in which an astronaut can move in all directions in a weightless environment. In that way the Web provides information humming along in a constant stream of (forgive me for sounding too ethereal) "consciousness" in which information is tailored to your interests, needs, locale, and tastes in a boundless package.

The evolution of information flow coincides with the development of technologies to make the flow efficient and relevant at the same time. Mass media and mass commerce meet the Web and allow customer media and custom commerce. One way of looking at this is to consider Amazon.com or CDNow. Each can sell a book or music title, thousands of them even, in a single hour or even minutes. Certainly an entire chain of bookstores or music shops can do that also, but how efficiently and at what cost? Obviously, they can't do it as easily, or as cheaply; nor as globally; not 24 hours a day, 7 days a week.

Operating in zero gravity is fundamentally a very different way of doing business. Zero gravity changes every business. Let's check out the table below that reads left to right. On the left are businesses or companies operating across the gravity spectrum, from heavy to zero. As they move more and more into being Web-based enterprises, they lose the tug of gravity and gain the benefits of the weightless environment. Follow the movement from left to right as industries and companies move into Zero Gravity.

As you can see, industries intersecting with the Web create a new purely digital way of doing business, without being encumbered by

	HEAVY GRAVITY	MID GRAVITY	ZERO GRAVITY
PLATFORMS	Newspapers Telegraph	Broadcasting Telephone	Web Web
BOOKS/MUSIC	Barnes & Noble	barnesandnoble.com	Amazon.com
MEDIA	Gannet Co.	USAToday.com	Yahoo!/Excite/ Lycos/Infoseek
ENTERTAINMENT	Disney	Disney.com	Go Network
TRADING	Charles Schwab	eSchwab	Etrade
AUCTIONS	Sotheby's	Onsale/Egghead.com	AOL
DISCOUNT	Costco Cendent	Netmarket	Surplusdirect.com Xoom.com
MUSIC/ RECORDING	Warner Records	MTV	CDNow MP3/RealNetworks
SPORTS	Sports Illustrated	Fox Sports ESPN cable network	Sportsline.com or ESPNSportszone.com
TRAVEL	Travel agents	travel clubs Expedia/ Preview Travel	Priceline.com
WEATHER		CNN/WeatherChannel	Accuweather
TRADE PUBLISHING	Ziff Davis/CMP	ZDNet/CMPNet	Internet.com/CNET

Source: Steve Harmon

moving real goods and services via land, sea, and air. Online personal auction service eBay, for example, never touches any merchandise, but sells more of it than some of the largest flea markets or antique shows in the world—and generates sizable revenue doing so. This is zero gravity.

Priceline.com allows consumers to name their own price on air travel and hotel rooms in a way that only a digital environment could allow. MP3 and other audio formats for Internet recording and distributing music don't require CDs, pressings, inserts, jewel box cases, trucking, shipping, boxing, racking, ringing up at a register, transporting home in a car, or inserting into a CD player. Just download and zap onto a flash memory card, and voila! The essence of what the listener wants is delivered without the baggage of the wrappings and trappings. This is zero gravity.

Consider Disney, the global media and entertainment conglomerate. Much of what it does lies in the heavy and middle gravity range: theme parks, books, videos, movies, and souvenir stores. It bought into Infoseek, a leading Web firm, to gain exposure into the tens of millions of users of the Internet. Getting that access didn't require building a shop or a new ride, publishing a new comic book, or creating a new animated film. It required paying $430 million for 43 percent of Infoseek.

Paying $430 million made a footprint in the digital realm. Not bad, considering that many studios now approach that cost to make a few movies. Until that buy-in Disney was being outrun by those firms gobbling up digital space like Yahoo! or Excite. In zero gravity Yahoo! expanded from two guys in a dorm at Stanford into a global media powerhouse in just three years. There are local news weeklies that may increase circulation by 10,000 in three years if they're lucky. Yahoo! went from a few thousand users to more than 30 million per month in short order and in more than a dozen languages.

Now, is zero gravity starting to make sense—how it fundamentally changes everything to do with communications, commerce, community, and context?

The downside of zero gravity is that it's brand new. Companies on and off the Web are learning its nuances, strengths, and weaknesses (can't smell perfume before you buy it in the Internet!). Also, when does a company stop adding products to its virtual shelves? Do you just sell pencils, or office supplies, or home and office supplies? In a digital environment a company can grow in any direction, but that can introduce lack of focus and wasted effort. You can shoot for the moon but end up on Mars.

As firms move and explore this newfound space, people often ask me, "How do you value an Internet company?" One way is to use Ben Graham's classic text of securities analysis, using standard price-to-earnings, book value per share, marketing and overhead costs. I complement Graham's and traditional Wall Street metrics with a set of analytics I invented over the past five years to help me and investors get a handle on Internet companies. I call these "digitalytics."™ Basically, these are a set of ratios that compare digital firms to digital firms but allow for them to be compared to land-based firms. Digitalytics all point to earnings and operating efficiencies, so they go hand-in-hand with price-to-revenue and price-to-earnings. Comparing AOL to

Viacom is like comparing apples to pears—they're similar, but very different. Comparing AOL to Yahoo!, however, is pear to pear. As "Internet" firms there are certain intrinsic natures about AOL and Yahoo! that don't apply to Viacom. One metric that's grown quite popular from my toolbox is called *value per user*. It's determined by taking the market value (public or private) and dividing it by the number of unique monthly users to yield a value. Here's a table showing the top Web sites and how each compares on this metric. The values are dated but the metric itself is what's important to focus on.

	MONTHLY USERS (MILLIONS)	6-10-99 MARKET CAPITALIZATION (MILLIONS)	6-10-99 VALUE PER MONTHLY USER
Yahoo	31.2	$29,583	$948
Lycos	28.9	$3,890	$135

Source: Steve Harmon valuation metric; monthly users from Media Metrix

Note that valuation gap between the two firms, both with similar levels of users at the time. Why the difference? Perceived value had something to do with it, a variable that will influence the valuation of your firm as an investment from day one to day 20,001 and beyond. Market ignorance is also a factor to contend with. Sometimes being first or being the pioneer leads to a premium in valuation. Just as the Apollo astronauts even today are held in high esteem (another word for "value") for being some of the first to defy terra firma, which firm in the Internet space deserves a similar status? Who took that one small mouse click, one giant leap for Webkind? Which firm can serve as an example of the many that were to follow? Netscape.

To be sure, there are dozens of success stories flowing out of the Internet space. One example is the guy who spent his evenings making a Web site that allowed his girlfriend to trade Pez candy containers. That effort turned into eBay. The two founders of HotMail pitched their Java tools to venture capitalists, along with 1,000 other brave souls making the rounds in Silicon Valley. They almost gave up before hitting on the one thing about their business plan that was new and truly unique at the time: Web-based free e-mail. They sold the firm to Microsoft for $425 million shortly after founding it. There are more equally fantastic examples of drive and spirit overcoming the odds for new Internet enterprises.

But the one story that defined the World Wide Web belongs to Netscape. In 1993 the company created the first Web browser with a few lines of code (Mosaic) slapped onto a chaotic electronic mess called the Internet. This was both the launch pad and launch vehicle for thousands of entrepreneurs who now had a medium for doing business in a digital environment.

Yes, other firms made browsers and still do, and Microsoft's browser is just as popular or more popular than Netscape's. That's now. But in 1993 and 1994 the groundwork required someone setting up basic standards for content flowing across the global computer network so that people could easily access it. Even Netscape built on previous layers on the Internet. But the phenomenon of the Internet really got its kick when Netscape built this new structure.

Netscape provides another key example of zero gravity success in the background of its mascot and cofounder Marc Andreessen, who I think could be dubbed *The Everyman Entrepreneur*. Why? Marc embodies someone with a non-techie or finance family background. His father sold tractors, and the closest venture capital firm to his hometown was perhaps 1,500 miles away.

I sat down with Marc for what turned out to be a walk down Internet memory lane for both of us, considering we've been in the industry since its beginning in 1994—what seems to be aeons ago in some ways, and like yesterday in others. The interview began at that defining moment August 9, 1995, when Netscape went public with a value of several billion the first day, a moment that set the tone for every Internet investment since then, and perhaps for all time. The following valuation table illustrates clearly how value creation in a zero gravity environ can be quick and huge.

How Digital Value Is Created: Netscape Valuation from Start to Merger with AOL

ROUND	DATE	POST VALUATION (MILLIONS)
First Round	9/1/94	$20.80
IPO	8/9/95	$1,068.52
Sale to AOL	3/17/99	$10,133.00

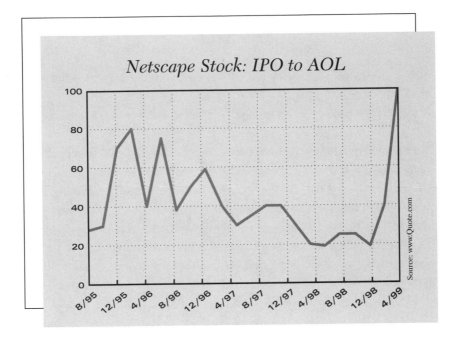

Netscape Stock: IPO to AOL

Source: www.Quote.com

What did you think when you saw the Netscape ticker symbol flash across NASDAQ that very first day, whereas only months prior you were smelling pig farms in Illinois?

Andreessen: To go out and pop the very first day and have a $3 billion or $4 billion market cap—it was "holy s——!" It happened so fast. It was amazingly fast, especially when you looked at the stock jump the first day. My first thought was that the investment banker screwed us (meaning Netscape could have priced higher, perhaps, and not left as much money on the table). It went at $28, double its original offering. Opened at $71 and closed at $58.

Did you get phone calls from other entrepreneurs after they saw the IPO?
Andreessen: No, they were too busy trying to get their own companies ready to go public!

In those days only a few people really saw the potential of the Internet. Who do you credit?
Andreessen: I'll tell you who really figured it out sooner than anyone: Jim Clark (Netscape cofounder) realized that this was going to happen early on, in 1995. At that time we were hunkering down to try and grow revenues and

be profitable. The wisdom at that point was that we were a software company. But Clark saw this would be different.

Netscape's focus was software. Did this cost you a chance at being more than that early on?
Andreessen: By mid-1996 we began charging for advertising on Netscape.com.

Yahoo!, Excite, Infoseek, and Lycos, in particular, built businesses on Netscape's Web site as a launching point—and look at what happened to their valuations. What did they pay to be on Netscape? Essentially, what turned them into huge firms overnight?
Andreessen: The initial deal was $5 million per year that each paid to be listed under Netscape search. At the time that was incredible, and nobody had ever done anything like that before. At that time the business model was the VCs behind those firms write the check and they turn the check over to us. There was a moment in time when that was a great business! (laughs)

Before they each became multi-billion competitors on Netscape's back...
Andreessen: On Netscape's back. This is a great example. The software industry's going to go through this big change as value is migrating further— has migrated further—the value chain has migrated away from software.

As in television, the value is in programming, not the box or technology per se.
Andreessen: Exactly. That only happens once you reach mass media status.

Netscape was the RCA of the Internet then. Somebody had to build the fundamental platform and that was Netscape.
Andreessen: So, yeah. Clark saw this. The conventional wisdom was to get four profitable quarters under your belt and then you can go public. The other thing then was that concept IPOs had a bad name because of General Magic and 3DO. 3DO was the pure concept IPO, let's go public without a product. And so going public without four profitable quarters under your belt felt like a concept IPO. But Clark was like "Gotta do it. Gotta do it."

What was the advantage of going public?
Andreessen: I bet there are multiple reasons, and I don't know all of them, but Clark thought it would be a fantastically successful IPO, the ultimate marketing event. He thought it would succeed beyond anybody's expecta-

tions, and he was absolutely right. No one else was willing to take the leap that he took, say that this event could be a big deal, and get that much attention. And it even made sense to do it purely as a marketing event. We literally didn't need the capital. I don't think we ever spent the capital from our series C financing because we were essentially cash flow positive since March 1995 and profitable the quarter we went public.

The Marc Andreessen sitting here today is finance savvy, but tell me about Marc circa 1995.
Andreessen: I was involved in the writing of the prospectus, the due diligence, and I did a little of the road show.

Doing a road show must have been an entirely new experience. You were fresh out of college.
Andreessen: So, I went to...what was it?...the Deutsche Bank or Morgan Stanley sales force, and on our way out, I didn't own a suit. So I was wearing a white shirt, tie, and khaki pants, and I remember Peter Curry (Netscape CFO) got this page and it read, "Doesn't Andreessen own a f——ing suit?" (laughs)

And your reply was, "I don't need to." (laughs)
Andreessen: Right! But I think by the time we did a secondary I owned a suit. It was just fascinating, the whole process.

There was a period when Netscape's stock languished, shortly after Bill Gates had a gathering in Redmond to announce Microsoft's Internet strategy, December 1995.
Andreessen: Then Netscape spiked up again, then back down. Then the stock was floating around. Then the AOL deal brought it to an all-time high. The broader AOL story is a fantastic story. Netscape plus AOL is a more powerful story than AOL alone. It's the story of the number one company in the Internet space.

Let us focus on entrepreneurs. You were once a college graduate looking at job offers, heading West to take a job or hang a shingle somewhere, make your fortune—and actually did so.
Andreessen: Clark was the key to the whole thing. He needed to exist for this to happen, because I didn't have any contacts or any knowledge of any of this stuff.

Had you heard of Kleiner Perkins before then? You wouldn't have known whether it was a dentist or law firm?

Andreessen: Would have assumed a law firm. (laughs) No, Clark was the guy who put it together. Fair to say he couldn't have done it without us. We all brought different things into it. What I'm not a good model for is an entrepreneur that has an idea but doesn't have a Jim Clark. Jim Clark was the guy who could go to the venture capitalists and say, "I'm going to do this; if you want to invest in it let me know and I may let you invest in it."

But if Marc Andreessen in those days had walked into Kleiner Perkins...

Andreessen: Now, Kleiner...and this is one of my theories: the dividing line between good VCs and bad VCs is the good ones would be willing to look at a Marc Andreessen off the street. A bad VC wouldn't. But even still it's a real challenge to get their attention. The Kleiners...you know, they don't have a 100 percent success rate. Kleiner only expects to see...what do they say? They only expect to see half the good deals on the West Coast. The good VCs recognize that the home runs tend to look nontraditional at first, which is why they end up being home runs—whether that's Steve Jobs at Apple or Pierre at eBay or Jerry and David (Yahoo!). The big home runs start out looking like oddballs because there are people doing things that to conventional wisdom makes no sense.

And that's when you get the opportunity to gain the leverage. You're not going to get a pre-built management team with suits and ties and years of experience with this radical new idea. So the best VCs...and if I had been able to figure out who they were, and if I had been able to figure out some way to get a meeting, I don't know what would have happened—but the odds would have been far, far, far less. It would have been a miracle to put Netscape together. The good VCs rely so much on the people they know to filter out the best deals. They don't have time to filter it out.

What is your advice, then, for entrepreneurs? What are the common elements you see for success?

Andreessen: There are a few different models: There's the fighter Jim Clark model. Maybe it's not Jim Clark, but find someone with a little money who has some experience and contacts. And there are actually quite a few more people around today then there were a few years ago. That's one way to do it.

Another way to do it: be in the right place at the right time, when the VCs are already out looking for what you're doing. That was part of the Yahoo! story. Michael Moritz at Sequoia started to figure out what was going on, and when he saw Yahoo! he was able to put two and two together in a way that others weren't.

Bootstrap is another way. Raise the money from angels, family, mortgage your house, and get it to the point where you have something to demonstrate, and get some decent managers on board.

Spinning it out of an existing company provides another example. And there are a few examples. CNET and Amazon were started by people coming out of financial or investment banker background or hedge fund management background. Amazon and CNET both exist because the founders knew how to work the financial back end already and had some credibility because of that.

By far, however, the best thing to do is have something succeeding, and they will seek you out. And you can identify them on the 'Net also.

Is it getting more expensive to start a firm on the Internet?
Andreessen: Not if you're doing something new. If you're doing something that's being done by others who have cash, then it is. But something radically new, then it's not. You can still do radically new things with very little money and just a couple of people in the garage. The challenge is coming up with the right radical new idea. Many of the logical categories are expensive. But there absolutely will be more radically new ideas, more Yahoos!.

You didn't come from a finance or technology venture capital background. You came from Illinois, which is not a place where venture capital is prominent. So when you were developing the browser, did you ever think, "This is a business!" or was it just sort of a cool thing?
Andreessen: Never as a business. And a big part of it is I had never heard of venture capital until I moved out here (Silicon Valley). Urbana-Champaign–Illinois is typical of a lot of college towns, especially at that time: major research university, lots of opportunities for commercialization. No venture capital. No success stories. My university had a complete lack of interest in having there be successful start-ups coming out of the research that was happening there. In fact they were hostile to that very idea. No concept that you could build a business out of this. None.

So you had no encouragement to make the browser a business? Did you say to yourself, "Let's make a company based on this browser," or you thought it was time to get a job after graduating?
Andreessen: More the latter. Mosaic had kind of taken off and had 1 or 2 million users at the end of 1993. Mosaic was originally paid for by National Science Foundation grants for super-computing research. The program I was in was to help scientists use super computers.

That was how this got started. It was completely within standard operating procedure to build software and put it on the 'Net for scientists to use. By December 1993 I was graduating, and it still hadn't really occurred to me. I thought once or twice maybe there would be a business here, because we were getting so much interest. Some companies were trying to license it from us.

But I never thought seriously about that. I had no clue. The idea you could actually do that was alien, foreign. Nobody had ever done that before in the Internet or the University of Illinois. There were a few start-ups around the university and they made it look so difficult as to make me not even want to try. I mean the local industry around Urbana-Champaign supports the college town, or it's pig farming, and that's it.

You don't need venture capital for pig farming.
Andreessen: You generally don't. (laughs)

What did your family do?
Andreessen: My dad was on the right side of the table, which is he worked for an agriculture products company selling to the farmers, both big farms and small farms. So for Internet and venture capital for me there were no books, no success models, and no knowledge. No classes at the university. There was no university involvement with start-ups.

In fact, when we ultimately started, it was Mosaic and then Netscape the company. The university was incredibly hostile to us and tried to kill it— which turned out to be a large, big, big, big, tens of hundreds of millions of dollars mistake. Ultimately, billions perhaps. We offered them stock that would have been worth hundreds of millions today.

But when I was just leaving the university, I left to go get a job. I had an offer from a small company called EIT. I did an intern stint at IBM, so could have gone there. Sun was sniffing around. I wanted to start at a smaller firm.

So the browser was kind of left behind?
Andreessen: It was still taking off with lots of users and starting to get some press attention. But if you picked up a newspaper every day, the big story then was that interactive TV was the wave of the future. The superhighway as brought to you by...

I believed in 1994 that the Internet would be bigger than interactive TV, that it was real...
Andreessen: You were one of the only ones who believed that. At the time I just thought it was strange reading about these interactive TV efforts companies defining the future, and I could never really find one or see it work. And so, it took me about two or three months with Clark to figure that out.

How did Clark find you?
Andreessen: He e-mailed me, and he said, "I hear you're in town and worked on Mosaic, and I want to start a software company with programmers who don't work for SGI" (Silicon Graphics, which Clark founded, because he didn't want to rip people out of SGI). So he said, "Let's talk," and I said, "Sure."

We got together and started talking and I was sort of available. Highly interested. We talked for a couple of months about what area: interactive TV, Nintendo 64, which he had also been working on. We looked at those two paths and concluded neither one would work as a start-up in the course of a year, year and a half.

Interactive TV wasn't going to get rolled out, and the Nintendo 64 wasn't going to ship in that timeframe. He wanted to do something as a software rather than hardware company—interactive/online/network something. By the end of March we decided that this Internet thing was probably going to be a really big deal after all, and you could build a really big business on it.

You were tracking Mosaic downloads still?
Andreessen: Yes, and it was still taking off. That was March 1994. I would just run into people on the street or at a party and they were talking about it. It was starting to dawn on me that this was going to be more of a mass-market product than people suspected at the time.

Once we locked onto that, we said let's recruit the team from the university, so we did. We incorporated April 1994 and hired all but one of the original Mosaic team and then started hiring more broadly. Jim did the first round, brought in Kleiner for the second round, brought in the corporate guys for the third round, and then went public.

Netscape going public defined what an Internet company financing is— how fast, how big.
Andreessen: At the time to be a software and move that fast was unheard of. We thought of ourselves as a software company. There weren't "Internet" companies. Yahoo! and eBay later defined more service-oriented ways that drew out the Internet. Netscape was a prototype Internet company, but not in the Yahoo! sense. But in those days Yahoo! was two guys in a trailer at Stanford. The convenient thing about starting as a software company was that it ramped very fast. It let us go public easily with the revenue we had. If we had adopted the services model...

You would have needed someone else to do the software layer.
Andreessen: Right. It would have been a much less attractive model at that time or near that valuation, because our financials wouldn't have been any-where close to where they were.

The software model was understood then as being the model. Somebody had to build the infrastructure. Navigator and the server software were part of the infrastructure. Other layers came on top of that.
Andreessen: The Internet is the world's first software-based medium. Everything is enabled and happens by software. If you want to start something like a Yahoo! or eBay, you can't because the software it takes to do it doesn't exist. And by the time you get to the size where there would be software that does it, the scaling issues are huge. And then there's the issue of differentiation.

It may be necessary that software, to run an online business and succeed, may always be largely custom. That may be different than any other medi-um we've ever seen—TV, radio, movies. It's never commoditized. Always updating. Not only that, the Internet is the carrier for its own changes. It's the world's first completely, instantly mutable medium.

(It's) all software-based and constantly changes. I've got a feeling that in five, ten, fifteen years e-commerce companies, whatever they're called then, will be employing very large numbers of programmers, and they'll be com-pletely pissed off about it, but they won't have any choice. It's a permanent addition to what you're going to need to succeed. The value of being Amazon the service is much greater than the value of being Amazon the software company that developed its software that allowed Amazon to succeed. Yet Amazon could not succeed without its software.

What software companies need to figure out is that being a software company and letting others get all the downstream value is a losing proposition. Instead, that's why every software company is going to end up being a Web services company. The successful companies will be the ones who employ the most programmers.

Best advice for entrepreneurs?
Andreessen: Do something new and have it start to be successful. It's wide open. The nuclear engineer in New Mexico doing Gnome on top of Linux. The sixteen-year-old girl in Ireland who now has the ten-times-faster e-mail encryption. It's by far the lowest barrier to entry. If you have the right idea, there can be a way to get it jump-started. The final thing is persistence. It takes persistence.

What if the venture capitalist says, "We really like this, but thank you anyway."
Andreessen: Try to find out why they don't back it, and then go fix those things. Or say, "Screw you," and come back in six months with a winner. The thing is, VCs get things wrong all the time—plenty of them pass on great ideas. The less-than-stellar VCs often come up with too many reasons why they shouldn't invest in something, whereas the good VCs are willing to completely disregard all the reasons they shouldn't invest in something. The best VCs can see ahead and are willing to think they can fix things, put the management team together, do all this stuff. Any huge success story like Netscape or Apple or any of these other things, there was always a lot...it was like a sausage factory.

Everybody likes to eat sausage; no one likes to see how it gets made. (laughs) These things are all sausage factories inside—things get screwed up inside. There are always things going wrong and eighteen different reasons why your firm is going to die an imminent death, and if it's the right idea at the right time and the market's growing, then all those things end up getting fixed when they need to get fixed.

And often it doesn't matter. This is again why the best VCs are the best. They don't have to fix it before they invest; they can do that afterwards. They know that, accept that, and that's fine. Part of their job is to help the entrepreneur. One piece of advice is to focus on the top VCs. If you can get in with one of them, your chances of succeeding go up dramatically. I would rather focus all my attention on one or two than four or five.

There's a ton of angel investing also. It's not always that useful if they don't have the time commitment, but it's something to start with.

And the sausage still tastes good?
Andreessen: And the sausage still tastes good!

And so you're probably asking yourself if you're going to be in this Internet sausage business, what flavor will you make, what types are being linked today with venture capital? What are the ideas now? VentureOne provided me with a list of some of the start-up companies and the business opportunities they're addressing. Not surprisingly, even as you read this, some of these have since gone public or been acquired or gone out of business. All aim to be the next Yahoo! or Netscape, but you never know what can happen when sausage gets hurled into zero g.

COMPANY	DOES WHAT?
1-800-BATTERIES	Retailer of batteries and accessories for mobile professionals over the Internet
2ND CENTURY COMMUNICATIONS	Provider of telephone services, Internet access, and data and video services using an ATM-based platform
24/7 MEDIA	Provider of online advertising networks
280	Provider of Internet communications service
401K FORUM	Provider of integrated retirement planning and mutual-fund allocation advice via the Internet
800.COM	Retailer of consumer electronics over the Internet
ADAUCTION.COM	Provider of an online auction for Internet ad space
ADFORCE	Provider of Internet-targeted marketing services
ADKNOWLEDGE	Provider of products and services to help advertisers, agencies, and publishers manage and evaluate online advertising
ADONE CLASSIFIED NETWORK	Operator of a centralized marketplace for newspaper classified advertising on the World Wide Web
ADVANCED ACCESS	Provider of direct-marketing services
ADVERTISING COMMUNICATIONS INTERNATIONAL	Provider of automated Internet delivery service for high-value files

COMPANY	DOES WHAT?
AGE WAVE COMMUNICATIONS	Provider of online marketing and advertising services targeting senior citizens
AKAMAI TECHNOLOGIES	Provider of services to improve speed of Internet access
ALIBRIS	Retailer of out-of-print, used, and rare books
ALLAPARTMENTS	Provider of national apartment listings and relocation services for consumers via the Internet
ALLEGIANCESTORES. COM	Developer of affinity-group Web sites
ALTRA ENERGY TECHNOLOGIES	Developer of software and services for marketing within the energy industry
AMAZON.COM	Retailer of books via the Internet, offering a searchable database containing over a million titles
AMPLIFIED.COM	Provider of an Internet store enabling customers to purchase and download songs as well as create custom-compilation CDs delivered by mail
AMULET	Developer of a Web-based automated information retrieval research agent
ANCESTRY.COM	Provider of genealogy resources on the Web
ANDOVER ADVANCED TECHNOLOGIES	Developer of a network of Web sites that provide news, information, products, and services to technology-oriented users
APPLICA	Provider of application services that concentrate on a holistic set of application hosting and management services for electronic businesses
ART.COM	Provider of framed and unframed art
@BACKUP	Provider of online PC backup targeted for small businesses and mobile professionals
@PLAN	Provider of Internet marketing services
ATWEB	Provider of online Web site maintenance and promotional services
AUDIBLE	Provider of a system that delivers recorded spoken audio programming via the Internet
AUTOBYTEL.COM	Developer of Internet-based purchasing program for new and used vehicles and related consumer services, including automotive financing, leasing, and insurance

COMPANY	DOES WHAT?
AUTOLINES	Retailer of used automobiles via the Internet
AUTOWEB.COM	Provider of an Internet shopping service for new and used cars
AVULET	Provider of information technology training over the Internet
BE FREE	Provider of affiliated network sales solutions for the Internet
BEYOND.COM	Reseller of software to individuals and businesses through the Internet
BIGBOOK	Developer of online services for consumer-oriented business information
BINARY COMPASS ENTERPRISES	Provider of online point-of-sale consumer research
BIZTRAVEL.COM	Provider of Internet travel content for frequent business travelers
BLUEDOT.COM	Provider of event publicity over the Internet
BRAINPLAY.COM	Provider of children's software over the Internet
BRANDDIRECT MARKETING	Provider of direct response marketing
BROADBAND ASSOCIATES	Provider of interactive Webcasting services to corporate customers via the Internet and private IP networks
BUILDING BLOCKS INTERACTIVE	Provider of online home-design product information
BUILDNET	Developer of Web site that maintains a database of over 900,000 pages of building industry and home improvement resources, companies, and industry related business opportunities
BUY.COM	Retailer of computers and associated products over the Internet
BUYDIRECT.COM	Operator of an online software store
CAMPUS LINK	Provider of low-cost computer networking capacities to dorm rooms, administrative offices, classrooms, and laboratories
CAREERBUILDER	Provider of online products to help job seekers find jobs and employers find potential candidates
CDNOW	Retailer of compact discs and other music-related products online

COMPANY	DOES WHAT?
CENTRAAL	Developer of an intuitive Internet navigation system
CHEMCONNECT	Publisher and provider of information and services pertaining to the chemical industry, such as connecting commercial and chemical buyers and sellers and building online global trading
CHEMDEX	Provider of Web-based sales channel for various science research fields
CHIP SHOT GOLF	Retailer of custom-built, tour-quality clubs over the Internet
CITYAUCTION	Provider of person-to-person online auctions featuring geographic targeting
CLASSIFIEDS2000	Provider of classified advertising content and search technology
CLASSROOM HOLDINGS	Provider of curriculum integration training and curriculum content production for educational Internet use
COLLEGIS	Manager of an information-technology program for universities and colleges
COLORADO PEN COMPANY	Retailer and direct marketer of specialty pens and fine writing instruments and accessories
COMMERCEINC	Provider of business-to-business content serving as a resource for the estimated 11 million small businesses in the United States
COMPARENET	Provider of up-to-date product comparison information via the Internet
COMPUTER LITERACY BOOKSHOPS ONLINE	Reseller of computer and technical books over the Internet
COMPUTERJOBS STORE	Provider of online career resources
CONCENTRIX	Provider of outsourcing for marketing and fulfillment
CONDUCENT	Developer of "push" technology service capable of delivering advertisements to PC software applications
CONTEXT INTEGRATION	Provider of consulting services for the client/server industry
CONVENE INTERNATIONAL	Provider of online education services and software services available for geographically dispersed communications

COMPANY	DOES WHAT?
COOK EXPRESS	Developer of an online grocery store focusing on convenient meal solutions, solutions that can be delivered the same day
COOKING.COM	Developer of an online cooking site for shopping, advice, and recipes
CREATIVE CATALOG CONCEPTS	Developer of an online gift catalog
CRITICAL PATH	Provider of e-mail hosting solutions for Internet service providers (ISPs), Web-hosting companies, and corporations
CUSTOMER INSITES	Provider of Web site effectiveness measurement
CYBER DIALOGUE	Provider of online market research
CYBERGOLD	Provider of real time cash microtransactions over the Internet
CYBERIAN OUTPOST	Retailer of 17,000 computer products, namely hardware and software, over the Internet
CYBERMEALS	Provider of online information on restaurants
CYBERSMITH	Operator of a chain of interactive and online store cafes
CYBERSTATE UNIVERSITY	Provider of online network-certification training to individuals and corporations
CYBERSYSTEM TECHNOLOGIES	Developer and operator of virtual malls on private Internet protocol networks
CYBORGANIC	Provider of Internet services, namely Web consulting, development, online community chat rooms, and Web-based publishing and collaboration services
CYVEILLANCE	Provider of technologies that protect companies owning well-known brands against devaluation and loss of market share due to misuse on the Internet
DAOU SYSTEMS	Designer and developer of health care information networks
DATAMATIX	Provider of electronic commerce services
DEJANEWS	Supplier of a World Wide Web interface to Usenet, an electronic public-message service that hosts 90,000 discussion and news groups
DELLA & JAMES, THE GIFT REGISTRY	Provider of online gift-registry services to the bridal marketplace

COMPANY	DOES WHAT?
DIGITAL CHEF	Retailer of gourmet food and kitchenware over the Internet
DIGITAL EVOLUTION	Provider of customized multimedia databases for a variety of applications
DIGITAL INSIGHT	Developer of Internet sites designed for financial institutions
DIGITAL ISLAND	Provider of a high-performance applications network designed to provide worldwide deployment of Internet applications
DIGITAL MARKET	Provider of intermediary services for the communication channels between electronic-component buyers and distributors
DIGITAL THINK	Developer and provider of interactive, collaborative courses via the World Wide Web
DIRECT MEDICAL KNOWLEDGE	Provider of in-depth, independent, customized medical and health information to consumers through their managed care plans
DOUBLECLICK	Provider of an Internet advertising network
DOZIER ELECTRONIC COMMERCE SOLUTIONS	Provider of Electronic Data Interchange (EDI) services
DRUGSTORE.COM	Retailer of online local drugstore products
DVD EXPRESS	Retailer of DVD (digital versatile disk) videos and software on the Internet
E TICKET	Acquirer of online rights to branded content and publisher of Web sites based on this content
EAGLE RIVER INTERACTIVE	Developer of online interactive marketing Web sites and software
EARTHWEB	Provider of an Internet service that locates Java sites, resources, and applications
eBAY	Provider of person-to-person auction services on the World Wide Web
EC	Provider of easy-to-use, low-cost solutions for back-office business-to-business electronic commerce
ECLIPSE TRADING	Provider of after-hours online equities trading
ECONOMETRICS	Provider of online consumer demographic information

COMPANY	DOES WHAT?
EDUCATIONAL STRUCTURES BY ACC	Provider of custom Internet curriculum that includes an extensive online library of lesson plans and educational resources in mathematics, social studies, science, and language arts
EGROUPS	Provider of branded Web-based services and tools to enable consumers and businesses to operate online communities
E-LOAN	Multilender Internet mortgage company offering a variety of loan products to users over the Web
EMAGINET	Provider of Internet service that allows companies to identify consumers' specific interests and preferences in order to motivate and reward them with targeted and personalized electronic incentives (e-centives) such as discounts, promotions, and reward points
EMAIL CHANNEL	Provider of demographics-based e-mail hosting, database distribution, and response-management services
EMAIL PUBLISHING	Provider of e-mail subscription management services to magazine, newspaper, and newsletter publishers
EMPLOYEASE	Provider of Internet-based human resource and employee benefits administration services for small- and mid-sized companies
ENCODING.COM	Provider of encoding and optimization of audio and video for the Internet
ENGAGE GAMES	Provider of multiplayer games via the Internet and most major online services
e-NICHE	Developer of solutions to rectify the transactional and informational inefficiencies faced by buyers and sellers in specialized secondary markets
E-STAMP	Developer of secure electronic-commerce platform designed to postage-enable every Internet-connected personal computer
eTOYS	Retailer of toys on the Internet
ETRADE	Provider of online discount brokerage services
EVERGREEN INTERNET	Developer of commerce-enabled, interactive sites on the Web

COMPANY	DOES WHAT?
EXODUS COMMUNICATIONS	Provider of services enabling customers to outsource the management and day-to-day operations of their Internet and intranet servers
EXTRAPRISE GROUP	Provider of a comprehensive suite of consulting services for organizations building business-critical Internet, intranet, and extranet applications
FAIRBANKS SYSTEMS GROUP	Provider of online backup storage
FAITH MOUNTAIN	Provider of mail-order shopping services for clothing and home collectibles
FASTPARTS	Provider of component buy-and-sell transaction services to the semiconductor and circuit-board assembly industry
FAXNET	Provider of telecommunications facsimile services
FAXSAV	Provider of a variety of business-to-business fax-transmission services
FINANCIAL ENGINES	Developer and marketer of impartial, Internet-based investment advisory services for individuals and the finance industry
FIREFLY GREETINGS	Provider of an online card-sending service
FLYCAST	Provider of online advertising
FOGDOG SPORTS	Retailer of sporting goods over the Internet
FOUR11	Provider of Internet White Pages directory service for locating e-mail addresses
FREEMARK COMMUNICATIONS	Provider of free e-mail service to consumers
FURNITURE.COM	Distributor of fine wholesale and retail furniture via the Internet
GARDEN ESCAPE	Provider of gardening resources, including retail products and information, to home gardeners via the Internet
GEOCITIES	Provider of free personal home pages and free e-mail accounts on the Web
GIGA INFORMATION GROUP	Provider of information-technology consulting services, including market research, analysis, and advice
GREENBERG NEWS NETWORKS	Developer of a desktop communication tool for the medical industry

COMPANY	DOES WHAT?
GREENTREE NUTRITION	Provider of comprehensive, online, personalized and health-related information and supplies
GREET STREET	Provider of personalized greeting card delivery service via the Internet
GRIC COMMUNICATIONS	Developer of Internet-based communications and settlement solutions for industry-leading ISPs
GROUP CORTEX	Provider of high-end Internet strategy, application development, and consulting services
GROUPSERVE	Provider of interactive communications and collaboration services on the Internet
HEALTHDESK	Developer of a health care management and information system
HEALTHEON	Provider of Internet-based health care information services for HMOs and medical and dental offices
HIGHWAY TO HEALTH	Provider of health care locator services for travelers, both domestically and internationally
HIRESYSTEMS	Provider of Web-based hiring-management, applicant-tracking, and résumé-processing services
HOMEGROCER.COM	Retailer of grocery items over the Internet
HOMESHARK	Provider of a home mortgage loan Web site
HOMESTEAD TECHNOLOGY	Provider of a service that enables end-users to collaboratively build Web sites online
HORIZON LIVE DISTANCE LEARNING	Provider of online training over the Internet
HOTMAIL	Developer of e-mail technology and provider of e-mail services
HOT OFFICE	Provider of Web-based intranet service for small businesses, especially those with collaboration needs, multiple offices, mobile workers, telecommuters, and virtual offices
HUMAN CODE	Developer of interactive, multimedia Internet, and intranet solutions for the consumer, business, and education markets
iATLAS	Provider of business information available on the Internet through its search engine
IKONIC	Provider of interactive media and Internet development services

COMPANY	DOES WHAT?
IMAGEX	Developer of private, password-protected Web sites enabling customers to order from a collection of company-branded templates of marketing and promotional printed materials
IMPROVENET	Provider of an Internet-based service for home and building services
IMPULSE! BUYNETWORK	Provider of an electronic-commerce site for name-brand products and services through an affiliated distributed network
IMX MORTGAGE EXCHANGE	Provider of mortgage information over the Internet to retail and wholesale professionals
iNAME	Provider of third-party e-mail services
INFINITE MUSIC	Developer of Internet radio stations
INFOBEAT	Developer of a proprietary e-mail distribution engine that allows for very high throughput of free e-mail messages
INFONAUTICS	Developer and marketer of online reference services
INFORMATION AMERICA	Developer and producer of a database of public record information accessible through online network
INPART DESIGN	Provider of component data and CAD content on the Internet
INQUIRY.COM	Provider of an online research service with information on companies in the software and hardware industries
INQUISIT	Provider of an online news service that delivers information to its subscribers
INSTILL	Provider of electronic-transaction and information services for the food-service industry
INSURANCE HOLDINGS OF AMERICA	Developer of an Internet-based processing system that provides multiple company distribution technology in the insurance industry
INSWEB	Facilitator of online insurance transactions
INTELLIGENT SYSTEMS FOR RETAILING	Retailer of groceries over the Internet
INTELLIMATCH	Provider of an online job-search service
INTELLIPOST	Provider of an Internet-based direct-mail delivery system

COMPANY	DOES WHAT?
INTERNAP NETWORK SERVICES	Provider of high-quality, fault-tolerant Internet network infrastructure and connectivity services
INTERNATIONAL COMPUTER SECURITY ASSOCIATION	Provider of private online training, seminars, and public forums that address information and communications security issues
INTERNATIONAL MEDICAL COMMUNICATIONS	Provider of a celebrity-driven, health care-based, electronic-commerce business
INTERNET BUSINESS ADVANTAGES	Provider of Internet consultation services for businesses
INTERNET GIFT REGISTRIES	Provider of online gift-registry services for consumers and the retail industry
INTERNET TELEPHONY EXCHANGE CARRIER	Provider of services to the Internet-telephony service provider market
INTERNET TRAVEL NETWORK	Provider of an Internet service that facilitates interaction between travelers and their local travel agent
IN TOUCH GROUP	Provider of music retail stores using the global infrastructure of the Internet to provide music retailers a state-of-the-art online store
INTRAWARE	Provider of intranet software solutions and services to IT departments in corporations worldwide
INUNITY	Developer and provider of a range of digital solutions that meet regulatory requirements for electronic prospectus delivery and other compliance issues for the financial services industry
INVENTA	Provider of Internet consulting and systems integration
iPASS	Provider of third-party settlement for Internet services, global Internet roaming, corporate remote access, Internet telephony, and other emerging Internet-based applications
iPRINT	Developer of an electronic-commerce environment specifically designed to customize mass market custom printing over the Internet
I/PRO	Provider of World Wide Web traffic verification, analysis, and research
iSHIP.COM	Developer of a Web site that allows businesses and individuals to choose the best method to ship, track, and manage information about packages

COMPANY	DOES WHAT?
iSYNDICATE	Provider of services that allow content creators to syndicate their news, columns, photos, tools, games, comics, and software to Web sites
I-SYSTEMS	Provider of Internet services
iXL ENTERPRISES	Provider of multimedia and Web services for corporations
KNOT	Provider of wedding services and information Web site
LIMITRADER SECURITIES	Developer of an electronic, corporate bond-trading system
LINKEXCHANGE	Provider of advertising services on the Internet
LIQUID MARKET	Developer of electronic-commerce services
LOOKSMART	Provider of Internet search capabilities
LOOPNET	Developer of an Internet-based commercial real estate exchange
LOT21	Advertising agency specializing in Internet campaigns
LYNK SYSTEMS	Provider of electronic payment and cash-advance services for small- to mid-sized merchants
M3 TECHNOLOGIES	Supplier of advanced composite materials and components to the semiconductor capital-equipment, flat-panel, robotics, precision motion-control, and optical-systems industries
MAINSPRING COMMUNICATIONS	Provider of Internet advisory services including collaborative, on-site work sessions, in-depth research reports, and reality-based case studies to help companies assess the business impact of Internet strategies
MATCHLOGIC	Provider of services and tracking for World Wide Web advertising
MEDIA METRIX	Provider of market research focused on Internet audience measurement
MEDSCAPE	Provider of online information for the medical community
MERIDIAN EMERGING MARKETS	Provider of online information pertaining to financial data, news, and analytics on global emerging market companies
MINDERSOFT	Developer of a database marketing system that uses an Internet "push" technology to deliver personalized reminders to consumers based on a user's profile and a company's proprietary content

COMPANY	DOES WHAT?
MODERN AGE BOOKS	Provider of electronic editions of best-selling business and computer books
MOTHERNATURE.COM	Provider of online vendor services for natural products
MOVIESTREET	Developer of specialty electronic-retailing businesses targeting large demographic audiences
MULTEX.COM	Provider of online brokerage services
MUSIC CONNECTION	Provider of custom-compiled music CDs over the Internet
N2K	Provider of new media entertainment and online information services
NARROWLINE	Provider of advertising transaction and information services for the Internet market
NARUS	Developer of network analysis tools for network service providers (NSPs)
NEOFORMA	Provider of medical product and service information on the World Wide Web
NET EARNINGS	Provider of financial services to small businesses via the Internet
NET2000 COMMUNICATIONS	Provider of telecommunications services and organizational consulting
NETBUY	Distributor of standard electronic components over the Internet
NETCENTIVES	Developer of Internet marketing tools
NETDOX	Provider of secure, electronic message delivery over the Internet
NETFLIX	Retailer and renter of digital video disk (DVD) over the Internet
NETS INC.	One of the largest business-to-business marketplaces on the Internet
NEXTCARD	Marketer of credit cards to consumers over the Internet
nFRONT	Provider of full-service Internet banking solutions for community banks
NOOSH	Developer of Web-based marketplace for commercial printing
OMEGA PERFORMANCE	Provider of performance improvement and interactive learning for the retail and commercial banking, insurance, transportation, and telecommunications industries

COMPANY	DOES WHAT?
ONELIST.COM	Provider of an online e-mail list system and services
ONLINE INTERACTIVE	Provider of an online commerce service
ONLINE RESOURCES & COMMUNICATIONS	Developer and marketer of online banking and financial-transaction systems used primarily by nonmoney center banks and financial institutions
ONLINELEARNING. NET	Provider of distance-learning programs in continuing education
ONSALE	Facilitator of online, interactive, retail auctions
OUTPOST NETWORK	Provider of Internet greeting card and post office services
PAYMENTNET	Provider of Internet-based, automated, real time payment-processing services for the electronic commerce industry
PEAPOD	Provider of interactive, online grocery shopping and delivery service
PEGASUS SYSTEMS	Provider of transaction processing services to the hotel industry
PEOPLELINK	Supplier of OEM communications services to Web sites and ISPs
PERSONAL COMMUNICATIONS INTERACTIVE	Provider of mass-market, interactive, voice-communications services
PHYSICIANS' ONLINE	Provider of online information service for physicians and managed care organizations
PINK DOT	Provider of a grocery delivery service
PIVOT TECHNOLOGIES	Provider of remote network, system, and asset management services
PLANETALL	Provider of an Internet-based day-planner and personal-reminder service
PLANETRX	Provider of online pharmacy services
PLANETU	Developer of consumer-oriented Internet promotion services
POINTCAST	Developer of an online service using "push" technology providing news, stock quotes, weather, and other information
POPPY TYSON INTERACTIVE	Developer of sales and marketing solutions via diskette, CD-ROM, or online services

COMPANY	DOES WHAT?
PORTERA SYSTEMS	Developer and host of business portals
POST COMMUNICATIONS	Provider of Web-based marketing solutions designed to build online customer loyalty and improve profitability
POWER AGENT	Provider of a narrow-cast advertising system for the Internet
POWERADZ.COM	Provider of online advertising channels for regional media companies
PREVIEW TRAVEL	Marketer of travel and vacation packages via the Internet
PRIVASEEK	An informediary providing Internet consumers with complete control over personal information
PRIZEPOINT ENTERTAINMENT	Provider of an online game center where users compete for prizes
PROCARD	Provider of specialized credit-card–based transaction services
PRODUCT PARTNERS	Provider of international merchandising and fulfillment for online commerce sites
QPASS	Provider of an outsource solution for content commerce
QUESTLINK SYSTEMS	Provider of employment database and employment information service
QUESTLINK TECHNOLOGY	Provider of online technical reference information for the worldwide community of design engineers
QUIKPAGE	Provider of Internet advertising for small companies
QUOTE.COM	Provider of financial market data to Internet users
RAPIDAUTONET	Developer of e-commerce in automotive aftermarket
REALSELECT	Provider of multimedia advertising services
REDGATE COMMUNICATIONS	Provider of new-media marketing services
REEL.COM	Retailer of cult, classic, blockbuster, foreign language, and art-house movies via an online video store
RELEASE SOFTWARE	Distributor of Internet software
RELEVANT KNOWLEDGE	Provider of Internet demographics and tracking services
REMARQ	Provider of Usenet services for corporate, ISP, and individual clients

COMPANY	DOES WHAT?
REQUISITE TECHNOLOGY	Developer of a computerized system that streamlines the corporate purchasing process for nonproduction goods and services
REVERE GROUP	Provider of systems integration and technology consulting
ROCKETTALK	Developer of Internet voice messaging software
ROWECOM	Provider of an electronic-commerce solution that enables enterprises to manage purchases of knowledge resources including magazines, newspapers, journals, and books, through an intranet or the Internet
SANDPIPER NETWORKS	Provider of Internet and system-software architecture, implementation, and maintenance services
SAPIENT HEALTH NETWORK	Provider of direct online access to information concerning disease-specific patient groups
SAVESMART	Provider of an interactive consumer-promotion program with an Internet delivery system that provides targeted marketing based on consumer profiles
SCIENT	Provider of professional services that help companies integrate electronic-commerce strategies into their business plans
SERVICE INTELLIGENCE	Provider of customer-service training and measurement
SERVICE METRICS	Provider of Internet performance-measurement services
SERVICE RESOURCES	Provider of single-source facility management services to the retail industry
SITEMATIC	Provider of automated Web site publishing services
SMARTAGE	Provider of a suite of Internet advertising services for small- to mid-sized businesses
SMARTERKIDS.COM	Provider of an online retail store designed to assist parents in purchasing educational products for their children's specific needs
SNAP TECHNOLOGIES	Provider of Internet-based services, and developer of software that enables students to apply electronically for college admissions, financial aid, and scholarships

COMPANY	DOES WHAT?
SOCIALNET	Provider of Internet-based social-networking services offering core products in the romance, personal, local community, and professional areas
SOFTWARE BUYLINE	Provider of electronic marketing, sales, and distribution solutions for personal computer products
SONNET FINANCIAL	Developer of foreign-exchange software
SPARKS.COM	Retailer of personalized greeting cards online
SPEECH MACHINES	Provider and developer of an automatic, Internet-based dictation-transcription service
SPINNER.COM	Provider of audio content on the Internet
STAMPS.COM	Developer of electronic software solutions for postage metering
STARMEDIA NETWORK	Provider of communications, information, entertainment programming, and retail services to an online audience in Spanish and Portuguese
STOCKPOWER	Provider of online financial transaction, affinity-marketing, and communication services
STUDENT ADVANTAGE	Provider of discounts, information, and services available to students
SUPERSITE.NET	Developer and provider of super Web sites that serve users in specific industries
SUPPLYBASE	Developer of Internet-based manufacturing directories
SURPLUS SOFTWARE INTERNATIONAL	Marketer and retailer for publishers', distributors', and retailers' overstocked, overproduced, factory refurbished, or distressed inventories
TALKCITY	Creator and operator of high-quality original Internet programming for the consumer market with a focus on community and audience participation
TECHBOOKS	Provider of electronic publishing services to publishers of academic publications, online databases, and Internet content providers
TELTECH	Provider of an online information service for research and knowledge-management consulting services
THIRD AGE MEDIA	Provider of products and services for active older adults via Web sites, a syndicated news service, outbound e-mail programs, content partnerships, research programs, events, and commerce services

COMPANY	DOES WHAT?
TICKETSLIVE	Provider of online ticketing service
TIMESHIFT	Provider of software and network technology for accessing and managing enhanced communication services
TOPICA	Provider of Internet messaging services
TOYSMART	Retailer of children's educational toys
TRADING EDGE	Developer of software for Internet securities trading
TRANSACTOR NETWORKS	Provider of enabling e-commerce technology in the form of free Web-based service that analyzes merchant order forms and constructs a simplified, standardized point-and-click front end to purchasing online
TRAVELMATION	Provider of an online information service for use by corporate travelers with personal computers
TUNE-UP.COM	Operator of an online PC anti-virus service center
U.S. INTERACTIVE	Provider of consulting and development services for Internet advertising
UNIVERSAL LEARNING TECHNOLOGY	Distributor of educational software and information
USA.NET	Provider of consumer and commercial electronic-messaging services on the Internet
USINTERNETWORKING	Provider of Internet-based outsourcing services and software integration
USWEB	Provider of Web-related professional services
USWEB LEARNING	Provider of training and certification programs for the Internet and Internet technologies
VERISIGN	Issuer of digital IDs or confidential digital identification numbers for secure commercial online transactions
VERTICALNET	Creator of online business-to-business industrial communities
VIAGRAFIX	Developer and producer of technology-based IT training and graphics software products
VIANT	Provider of a variety of services for Internet product development
VICINITY CORPORATION	Supplier of private label Yellow Pages and geo-enabled (mapping) services on the World Wide Web
VIDEOGATE TECHNOLOGIES	Provider of live, online electronic commerce services between goods and service providers and consumers

COMPANY	DOES WHAT?
VINNET	Provider of online registration and titling of cars between car dealers, motor-vehicles departments, and banks
VIP CALLING	Provider of telecommunications services to carriers and telephony resellers globally
VIRTUAL VINEYARDS	Provider of gourmet food and wine service via the Internet
VISTO CORPORATION	Developer of Java-infrastructure software that allows individuals to gain access to programs without storing additional software
VITA SYSTEMS	Provider of a Web-based business administration solution designed for high-growth, middle-market companies that need a simple, secure, flexible, and low-cost approach to managing common business functions
VSTREAM	Provider of media-on-demand services, using Internet streaming technologies on behalf of Fortune 500 companies worldwide
WALL STREET ON DEMAND	Provider of investment research for individual investors, including information on stocks and mutual funds
WEBLEY SYSTEMS	Provider of voice-activated, unified messaging and electronic personal-assistant services
WEBMD	Provider of Internet-based health care services
WHEN.COM	Developer of a scalable, consumer-oriented Internet calendar and event network that provides fast, secure, free personal calendars and event information via a Web browser
WHITTMAN-HART	Provides strategic IT consulting services
WIT CAPITAL	Provider of online investment banking and brokerages
WNP COMMUNICATIONS	Provider of broadband communications
WORLDPRINTS.COM	Retailer of posters, notecards, and other image-based products over the Internet
WORLDRES	Provider of a free, online hotel reservation service
WORLDVIEW SYSTEMS	Provider of customized electronic destination information and software to travel agents

COMPANY	DOES WHAT?
WYND COMMUNICATIONS	Provider of wireless e-mail services for the hand-held and portable computer market
YOYODYNE ENTERTAINMENT	Developer of online promotional programs such as games, contests, and sweepstakes for customer acquisition and retention
ZING NETWORKS	Provider of multimedia content for the World Wide Web during download time delays

Angels Among Us
Alternatives
to Venture Capital

Chapter Eight

THIS CHAPTER IS brief because *Zero Gravity* focuses more on venture capital than on alternative financing. Before I get into the snapshot of non-VC funding, keep in mind that not getting venture funding doesn't mean that any other funding is going to be second-rate. Don't feel bad if the VCs don't believe in your plan. The obvious benefit of not having venture money at the start is that you retain more equity. Sometimes not getting a VC's short attention span means that your firm may be at the ultra seed stage and not in need of the VC machine to get you up and running. This is known as the "funding gap": you're too small for VCs to put money into. How's that?

For the venture capitalists it's just as easy to put $5 million to work as $500,000. Average VC investments run about $2 million to $3 million at start-up. If you need $250,000 they may pass on that alone, creating the funding gap between what VCs want to invest and what entrepreneurs may be able to pool from their own resources.

Another thing: venture capital isn't for everyone. It's not always a fast track to instant IPO and adoration. The success of your business doesn't rely on a VC but on you and your team. VCs can help, but don't overestimate them. Of ten start-ups that get funding, only about two will generate a 10× return to the VCs. Two more will probably fail, and the rest will try to be sold to larger companies for their technology or expertise. So, don't view funding as the summit, but rather, one summit of many to aim for.

Another point is that VCs are people, too, trying to scramble and make things happen for their existing investments, and the VC answers to the institutional investors who demand fairly high ROI. So they don't always "get it" when you give your pitch. Keep in mind that their agenda is to see huge returns on their investments, and with the sheer volume of pitches they see, they may not notice the gem in your idea. If you think about the two of every ten investments being home runs, then you can see why VCs are so picky. Even after all the due diligence, some of their investments will not pan out.

If VCs don't invest right away, it's not the end of your company dreams. I can hear you say, "I went to five VCs and none were interested." HotMail went to twenty-one VCs before Draper Fisher Jurvetson finally said yes. Twenty-one! Other start-ups never took VC money at all.

Cisco couldn't get any VCs interested in its early days. There can be half a dozen reasons why you may not. One is the funding gap— maybe you need too little for a VC to look at. If so, you may want to consider the alternatives before approaching a VC. It all depends on your goals and capital needs at that moment. Other reasons include a market not ready for your product or service; the venture capitalists may be following the herd of other venture capitalists and investing in other areas; or maybe the opportunity you're presenting isn't fleshed out enough.

The alternatives to venture capital are bootstrapping, friends and family, angels, private placements, and corporate investors. I won't discuss bank loans or small business grants, but those may be options also. Another thing to consider is *venture leasing* to save costs on your office space, and so on. Venture leasing gives your landlord warrants or options in your firm instead of full rent. Admittedly, my focus is more on capital raising than capital borrowing or capital savings. By all means, though, look at the spectrum and use what makes sense for you with a mix that keeps the lights on.

Bootstrapping describes funding your start-up yourself through savings, loans, credit cards, and piggy banks. It comes from the expression "Pull yourself up by the bootstraps," which is a roundabout way of saying "Do it yourself." Quite simply, bootstrapping is when you scrape together the capital you may have at your own disposal and put it into creating a company, or into putting up an initial Web site with which you can demo and attract investors. Bootstrapping is quite common, with or without any venture capital coming into play. Bootstrappers often go on to raise venture capital or other financing. So this is not always an either/or scenario.

The great thing about bootstrapping is that you control your destiny. No outside investors are e-mailing or calling you with the latest fad-of-the-week advice. The downside to bootstrapping is that these small amounts of capital (credit cards, small bank loans) often run out quickly. Sometimes an entrepreneur will mortgage a house (although I don't recommend that, unless you can afford to live without a house, can take having your spouse walking out on you, and perhaps your kids and dog doing the same).

Let's look at an example of a mixture of funding from bootstrapping and friends and family, since these two methods of raising capital often come together.

Se habla español? Latin American portal network Starmedia was founded by Fernando Espuelas and Jack Chen in 1996 with $600,000 seed funding the two had saved from their well-paying jobs. Simple idea: provide portal sites for Latin America, an underserved segment of the growing Web—at least they thought so. They made the calls at dozens of VCs and not one VC invested. None. Nada.

Meanwhile, the growing company became a beast and each of these founders maxed out credit cards and savings to keep the fledgling going. The amazing thing is that in the course of the next year, Starmedia became a VC darling. Chase Capital Partners, Flatiron Partners, BancBoston Robertson Stephens, Intel, GE Equity Capital Group, Platinum Venture Partners, and others gladly came on board so that more than $100 million was raised, the record setter for private money raised by an Internet start-up to date. As Naveen Jain said, this is a typical story in the crazy world of raising capital—when

Infospace.com: Friends, Family, and Some Good Advice

Q&A

WEB CONTENT, COMMERCE wholesaler-distributor Infospace.com founder Naveen Jain financed the firm in 1996 entirely with his own and his friends' and family's money, barely over $1 million. He never took professional venture money. By the time Infospace.com went public, Naveen owned about 50 percent of the company. Early in 1999 when INSP stock continued its ascent, Naveen's personal stake in his dream had become worth more than $1 billion.

In the early days how did you finance Infospace?
Jain: With friends' and family's funds. The reason is that most VCs are very short-term horizon. They like to look at the exit strategy before they even enter. And we were interested in building the company for the long term rather than the short term. Sometimes when you work with a VC you end up making short-term decisions that could turn out to be bad long-term decisions. Also, you see situations where VCs force you into the latest hype. It could be "push" (Internet broadcasting of news) or Java. Then everything has to be Java. If the VC exit is two or three years and yours is four or five years, that may make a difference also.

How much did you initially raise?
Jain: We put in about $1 million in 1996. And since we didn't have that much money, it forced us into a very creative way of doing business. We always focused on revenue, always focused on coming up with a new business model that makes you money as opposed to continues to lose your money. So by doing that, we became profitable in our first full year of operation.

How many financing rounds did you do?
Jain: We did friends and family and only one angel investor. He came in just before we went public, three months before we filed for our initial public offering. Absolutely no venture round, just one angel. We became profitable this way quickly since we knew it was our money and not someone else's. Our business model had to generate results quickly. We had our content partners pay us money, our distributors pay us money, had the advertiser pay us money. It's real interesting when you don't have money how quickly you learn how to make money.

All this was driven from a very simple philosophy that I learned from my mother: when I was leaving home she said, "It doesn't matter how much money you make in life, just remember one thing—always spend less than what you earn." Always make sure you spend less than you're earning. If you're building a company the same business model should apply.

How many employees did you start with?
Jain: We started with seven or eight employees.

You were with Microsoft before. Did these employees also come from Microsoft—that helped, having experienced people?
Jain: That's right.

What have you learned along the way in financing an Internet business? What tips do you have for those entrepreneurs starting out?
Jain: Try to finance through friends and family if they are able to help. If they cannot, then seek alternatives. But every penny you take at the beginning is more expensive today

(continued)

than tomorrow. The more you delay taking the money, the more money you can keep in your pocket (in equity). The more you can build the company on your own funds, I think it's the best thing you can ever do. That helped me keep 50 percent of the company. That proves to the world that you can take the risk and build the company. It allows you to create an atmosphere that you don't need the money. It's funny that everyone wants to give you money when you don't need it and not give you money when you do.

You did a secondary offer shortly after going public to keep the zero to 6,000 miles-per-hour growth?
Jain: We needed to be able to fund this hyper growth and always have cash on hand to be able to do the things we wanted to do. Secondly, we wanted some liquidity for our shareholders. At the same time, large institutional investors wanted to build a very large position in the company. And they have a very hard time acquiring the stock, especially if the stock doesn't have a large float.

What was your initial valuation?
Jain: We started at $20 million valuation so when we raised $1 million it was just 5 percent of the company.

they needed money, it couldn't be found; when they didn't need it, the capital came flowing in. That reminds me of legendary investor Warren Buffett, who borrows money when the money supply is available even if he doesn't yet need it—because when the money supply is tight borrowing (debt) isn't that attractive.

Another important observation I've made these past five years in the Internet investing realm: Many investors are followers but few are leaders. Said another way, there are fewer risk-takers than not. Because leading requires risk—risk of the unknown. The part great venture capitalists and any investor, for that matter, realize is that reward comes in equal measure to risk. If investors want 100× return they cannot be thinking inside the box.

Angels Among Us

BEYOND BOOTSTRAPPING, FRIENDS, and family is the loose but powerful world of angels. What's an *angel*? A high-net-worth individual who invests alone or in groups. It may truly feel like someone with wings when all you've got is a prayer. So be it.

Angels make up one of the least-known but most active Internet investor groups. In any given year angels invest more than twice in dollar terms what the venture capitalists do. Estimates are that the Internet sector sees more than $10 billion invested by angels alone. If you recall the funding gap, that implies a high number of deals if you think about $10 billion divided by $500,000 per deal or so.

Angels may be more attractive than friends and family because in the Internet or tech space an angel is often a successful CEO or founder of a company. They are normally successful enough to have enough liquidity for investing in the thing they know best: technology start-ups. That's advantageous for you, making available not only the cash you need, but also a few clues about how to start a company. Many angels have done so and know how to develop one. They're operational people, entrepreneurs themselves. Venture capitalists are professional investors—a key difference to remember. Both have their pros and cons.

Many times successful CEOs find that re-investing allows them to share advice, establish contacts, form alliances. In some ways you may find angels more flexible than VCs because their ROI is to themselves and not pension funds. Their hands-on experience may help you avoid mistakes, and their connections could open up strategic allies you couldn't reach solo.

How do you find an angel? Your friends and family may provide a route to angels through their contacts and coworkers. Angels come in all shapes and sizes, and many have entertained them unawares. For example, if you have a Web site up and running you may never know who has seen it, tried it, and thinks it's compelling to them as an investment. Or you do a demo at a trade show and catch the eye of a high-tech exec that sees promise. Marc Andreessen invested in Replay TV after happening on the company because it was so close to Netscape's corporate headquarters. More than geography, something else attracted Marc to it—Replay's technology for capturing TV for playback whenever a viewer wanted it.

One of the immediate advantages of angels lies in their ability to move extremely quickly, to kick the tires on your dream, and to decide fairly rapidly to invest or not—a week or two sometimes. Since angels aren't professional investors per se, they are able to offer more favorable terms than a VC can in many cases. Angels do want a return on the investment to be great, as would any investor, but they have less pressure for stellar performance.

Not all angels are angels. Some can be devils, so beware. A drawback for you to consider is the level of involvement an angel can bring. VCs will set goals and work hard, usually with you, to ensure some chance of success, since they are accountable for the capital they invest. Angels may be prudent investors but may not be able to give you the time or resources to develop the firm quickly. Or they may get too involved and believe the company is their new hobby and sidetrack your entire plan.

An example of a bootstrap/angel-funded company that didn't take venture capital was Web direct marketer, community provider Xoom.com. Founder Chris Kitze had experienced success after starting and selling a few high-tech pre-Internet and Internet firms before embarking on Xoom.com. That helped give him some experience to draw on. One firm he sold was an early (1994–95) popular Internet site that rated the best Web sites, Point Communications, which Lycos acquired in the early days of the Internet.

That sale allowed Chris to have a small amount of capital to start Xoom. He then financed it from angel investors, a challenging task, to be sure. Chris considered venture money at later stages, but the VCs (with their high ROI demands) didn't invest at the valuation Chris was asking. Soon after Xoom's IPO the company's market value jumped past $1 billion. VCs could have made perhaps 5× return in about six months.

Without their capital Chris and his talented team made it happen. By bootstrapping and scrambling to get angels to keep the lights on, Chris managed to hold onto about a third of Xoom personally, much more than he would have had if the VCs had invested. Another key point was Chris and cofounder Laurent Massa's seasoned management experience. They didn't necessarily need the advice of VCs in the way a rawer start-up with first-timers would. The angels believed in Xoom from the early days. They stood by Xoom and happily saw the value increase and their investment returned.

Rather than go one-on-one and try to arrange a half dozen angels, a better approach is to find a group that works together in a club-like manner. There are several nationwide groups in the United States and more appearing internationally.

The solo angel is out there, but bands of angels are quite common. By far the best-known group is the Silicon Valley dream team with the apropos name, Band of Angels™. I use them as a prototypical or best example of what a band can do. On the following pages, you'll get a glimpse into these heaven-sent miracle-makers in the box that follows.

Private Placements

A PRIVATE PLACEMENT is a finance animal that should be tackled only with the assistance of a securities lawyer. A private placement can be done at any stage of a firm's life, whether the company is private or public. CyberCash, the Web-based transaction processing firm, has long been public but has done private placements several times now.

In this case the entrepreneur or company often prepares a document telling prospective investors what the firm does, the risks, goals, and market. It also lists the shares it's planning to sell, price per share, shares outstanding, and use of the proceeds. Benefits of a private placement include perhaps getting a better valuation for the firm. You could be dealing with just a few investors and can raise a large amount efficiently if done correctly.

One of the key drawbacks of doing a private placement is the cost of financing, as the broker who raises this is paid what can be a high fee.

Corporate Investor

YOU PROBABLY WOULDN'T guess, but in 1998 Intel invested more than $300 million in start-ups. Oracle started a VC fund in 1999.

The Band Of Angels™

120 Former or Current High-Tech Executives
➤ Successful track record in new company formation
➤ Common interest in early stage investing
➤ Desire to be actively involved with young companies
➤ Substantial personal wealth
➤ Gather monthly at a dinner for the Band to consider investment in three companies
➤ Active participation (board, management, business development)

The Basics of the Band
➤ Founded January 1995
➤ Number of founding members: 12
➤ Membership today: 120
➤ Average amount invested monthly: $1.1M
➤ Total amount invested: $45M
➤ Companies invested into: about 100
➤ What firms have they founded? Maybe you've heard of a few of these firms:

— Cirrus Logic	— Sierra Semiconductors
— Symantec	— Logitech
— National Semiconductor	— McKenna Group
— DSP Group	— C-Cube
— Rasna	— Genentech
— Silicon Valley Bank	— Prism Solutions
— California Microwave	— Xilinx
— DataQuest	— Meridian Data Systems
— VLSI Technologies	— Vector Graphic
— Power Computing	— Resound
— Cadence Design	— KLA-Tencor
— Advanced Cardiovascular	— Nellcor Systems

How The Band of Angels™ Works:

ALL COMPANIES MUST be invited to present, and the process is fairly straightforward: a Band member must see your pitch or hear your business plan and then invite you to present to the larger group. That's outlined in the chart on page 192.

The Band invests in a wide spectrum of fields, including many opportunities in the Internet field. Knowing the break-out can help you decide if this Band is your band. The good news is that the majority of the investments the group has done so far, more than sixteen deals, are in the networking field. On the other hand, the so-called Consumer Internet was about half that, an example of how the Band bets on smaller, more techno-centric deals rather than trying to fund the larger, consumer Internet plays.

The nice thing about angels is that if they can fund that small seed round and get things started for you, it can attract the VCs later. Having angel groups like The Band of Angels™ invest doesn't keep VCs out of the deal. In fact, VCs often invest in later rounds after the angels have done a lot of the upfront risk work and developed the firms. Companies in which the Band invested no more than $40 million total have gone on to raise more than $180 million in additional financing, according to the group.

I provide this one club as an example, but many of the angel groups act in a similar fashion. The formulas may differ slightly, but usually it goes like this: informal introductions, a dinner or presentation to the wider group, and then a yes or no fairly quickly.

What do I do if I live light years from Silicon Valley and can't find an angel group? While many areas of the U.S. and globe don't have as high a profile bunch of dreamweavers, you'd be surprised at the popularity of angel groups. See *steve-harmon.com* for a list of links.

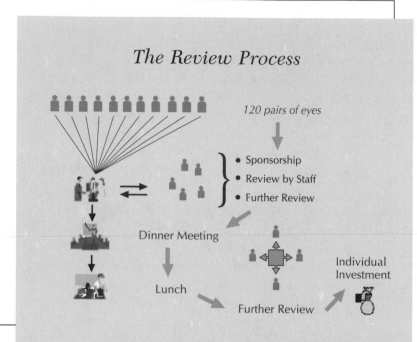

Source: The Band of Angels ™

Microsoft invests in venture funds. AOL has its own Greenhouse venture effort for incubating start-ups that complement AOL. Corporations are active investors more than ever in the Internet space. They do so to keep a finger on the pulse, to get an early look at new things, to acquire start-ups and add them to their own offerings, or simply to make investments.

Before you blast off an e-mail to them with an executive summary, consider that corporate investors have different requirements than professional investors in the VC world. Corporate investors want to know first how your company benefits their company. Is there a synergy between them? An example: Network Solutions, the public domain name registrar, invested a small amount in Web firm Centraal. Centraal makes software that lets people type in "book" or other natural-language words in the URL line of the browser and it finds those Web sites associated with the terms. In that scenario, you can have a long string of *http://www.thinkofalongcompanyname-here.com* users simply type in "car" and perhaps autoweb.com pops up. You can see how that system makes the domain speculator game less valuable than the game of buying the top slot from Centraal in the natural-language world most people may prefer.

As an entrepreneur, however, keep in mind that the corporate investor's goal is to further its own corporate efforts. That may or may not further your goals or could create a situation where the corporation fuses your ideas into its own and leaves you without the value you sought in the first place.

For great finance resources relating to venture capital and Internet investing please see *http://www.steve-harmon.com*. See you in zero gravity.

Steve Harmon's Zero Gravity Web Resource*

* See www.steve-harmon.com for these handy
links of Internet venture capital

The Venture Capital Rolodex

3i

3i claims to be Europe's leading venture capital company. Its main activity is investing in start-up companies, growing businesses, management buy-outs, management buy-ins, and share purchases. 3i has a network of 29 offices in Europe serving business locally. Its continental Europe network extends throughout the U.K., France, Italy, Germany, and Spain. There is a field office in Singapore and affiliated operations in Japan.

London
Patrick Sheehan *Technology@3i.com*
3i plc
91 Waterloo Road
London SE1 8XP
Telephone: 44 (0)171-928-3131
Fax: 44 (0)171-928-0058

Singapore
Jane Crawford *singapore@3i.com*
08/04 The Exchange
20 Cecil Street
Singapore
Telephone: + 65 438 3131
Fax: + 65 536 2429
Web site: *http://www.3i.com.sg*

Tokyo
Paul Vickery
3iBJ, Bancho Kaikan 5F 12-2 Gobancho
Chiyoda-ku, Tokyo 102
Telephone: + 81 3-3239-5670
Fax: + 81 3-3239-6828
Web site: *www.3i.com*

21st Century Internet Venture Partners

Featured in Chapter 2 of *Zero Gravity*.

Two South Park, Second Floor
San Francisco, CA 94107 US
Telephone: 415-512-1221
Fax: 415-512-2650
E-mail contacts:
J. Neil Weintraut, General Partner *n.weintraut@21vc.com*
Peter Ziebelman, General Partner *peterz@21vc.com*
Jennifer Croft, Office Manager *jcroft@21vc.com*
Melissa Batchelder *mbatchelder@21vc.com*
Web site: *www.21st-century.com*

Accel Partners

Good U.S. East Coast-headquartered venture firm. Did Real Networks and UUNET, among others.

Administrative Office:
One Palmer Square
Princeton, NJ 08542
Telephone: 609-683-4500
Fax: 609-683-0384
E-mail contacts:
Jim Breyer   *jbreyer@accel.com*
Bud Colligan   *bcolligan@accel.com*
Jim Flach   *jflach@accel.com*
Bruce Golden   *bgolden@accel.com*
Garry Hallee   *ghallee@accel.com*
Gene Hill   *ghill@accel.com*
Mitch Kapor   *mkapor@accel.com*
John Partridge   *jpartridge@accel.com*
Arthur Patterson   *apatterson@accel.com*
Joe Schoendorf   *jschoendorf@accel.com*
Carter Sednaoui   *csednaoui@accel.com*
Jim Swartz   *jswartz@accel.com*
Peter Wagner   *pwagner@accel.com*
Webmaster   *webmaster@accel.com*

Palo Alto:
428 University Avenue
Palo Alto, CA 94301
Telephone: 650-614-4800
Fax: 650-614-4880
General Information:
info@accel.com
Web site: *www.accel.com*

Access Technology Investors LP (North Coast)

Invests in companies in Michigan, Ohio, Indiana, and other Midwestern states.
206 S. Fifth Avenue, Suite 550
Ann Arbor, MI 48104
Telephone: 734-662-7667
Fax: 734-662-6261
Web site: *http://www.accven.com*
Web site: *http://www.northcoastvc.com*

Advanced Technology Ventures

Petstore.com and a growing list of Internet investments.
281 Winter Street, Suite 350
Waltham, MA 02154
Telephone: 781-290-0707
Fax: 781-684-0045
485 Ramona Street, Suite 200
Palo Alto, CA 94301
Telephone: 650-321-8601
Fax: 650-321-0934
E-mail: *info@atv-ventures.com*
Web site: *http://www.atv-ventures.com*

Advantage Capital Missouri Partners

A diverse investment range across media/technology.
One Penn Plaza, 42nd Floor
New York, NY 10119
Telephone: 212-273-7250
Fax: 212-273-7249

E-mail: *ajoe@advantagecap.com*
Web site: *http://www.advantagecap.com*

Advent International Corp.

One of the largest venture firms in the world with $3 billion under management globally. One of their top guys was a speaker at my conference in London and quite knowledgeable.

USA
Andrew I. Fillat
Advent International
75 State Street
Boston, MA 02109
Telephone: 617-951-9400
Fax: 617-951-0566

John J. Rockwell
Advent International
2180 Sand Hill Road, Suite 420
Menlo Park, CA 94025
Telephone: 650-233-7500
Fax: 650-233-7515
London
John D. Bernstein
Advent International plc
123 Buckingham Palace Road
London SW1W 9SL
England
Tel: 44 171-333-0800
Fax: 44 171-333-0801
Singapore
Derrick M.C. Lee
Advent International/SEAVI
331 North Bridge Road
#05-04/06 Odeon Towers
Singapore 188720
Telephone: 65 339-9090
Fax: 65 339-8247
Hong Kong

Raymond Lo
Advent International
Suite 1415, Two Pacific Place
88 Queensway
Hong Kong
Telephone: 852 2978-9300
Fax: 852 2826-9247
Jakarta
Samuel K.H. Chia
P.T. Seavi Indonesia Venture
Bapindo Plaza Tower II, 22nd Floor
Jl. Jendral Sudirman Kav. 54
Jakarta 12190
Indonesia
Telephone: 62 21-526-6845
Fax: 62 21-526-6843
Buenos Aires
Ernest G. Bachrach
Advent International
25 de Mayo 555 24th Floor
1002 Buenos Aires
Argentina
Tel: 54 1-310-8900
Fax: 54 1-310-8910
Web site: *www.adventinternational.com*

Alpine Technology Ventures
Invests in only Silicon Valley firms.
   20300 Stevens Creek Blvd., Suite 495
   Cupertino, CA 95014
   Telephone: 408-725-1810
   Fax: 408-725-1207
   E-mail: *kathryn@alpineventures.com*
   Web site: *http://www.alpineventures.com*

APV Technology Partners II
Focuses on seed and early stage investments with large technology
corporations in information technology.

E-mail contacts:

William Stewart, President, Asia Pacific Ventures *will@apvtp.com*

Spencer Tall, Executive VP, Asia Pacific Ventures *spencer@apvtp.com*

Helen Ingerson, APV Technology Managing Member *helen@apvtp.com*

535 Middlefield Road, Suite 150

Menlo Park, CA 94025

Telephone: 650-327-7871

Fax: 650-327-7631

E-mail: Christine Lien Choi, Research Analyst *christine@apvtp.com*

Web site: *http://www.apvco.com*

Arbor Partners

Focuses on electronic commerce and knowledge management software.

130 South First Street

Ann Arbor, MI 48104

Telephone: 734-668-9000

Fax: 734-669-4195

E-mail: *info@arborpartners.com*

Web site: *www.arborpartners.com*

Arch Venture Partners

Invests nationally in U.S. specialty materials and chemicals, biotechnology, medical products, communication, and information technology.

Chicago

8735 West Higgins Road, Suite 235

Chicago, IL 60631

Telephone: 773-380-6600

Fax: 773-380-6606

E-mail: *info@archventure.com*

Seattle

1000 Second Avenue, Suite 3700

Seattle, WA 98104

Albuquerque

1155 University Blvd., SE

Albuquerque, NM 87109

Telephone: 505-843-4293

Fax: 505-843-4294

E-mail: *cwb@archventure.com*
New York
45 Rockefeller Plaza, Suite 2520
New York, NY 10020
Telephone: 212-262-7260
Fax: 212-397-1782
E-mail: *mjm@archventure.com*
Web site: *http://www.archventure.com*

Aspen Ventures
Seed and early stage investing in information technology companies.
E-mail contacts:
Alexander Cilento *alex@aspenventures.com*
E. David Crockett *dcrockett@aspenventures.com*
Stephen Fowler *stephen@aspenventures.com*
Thad Whalen *twhalen@aspenventures.com*
1000 Fremont Avenue, Suite 200
Los Altos, CA 94024
Telephone: 650-917-5670
Fax: 650-917-5677
Web site: *http://www.aspenventures.com*

Asset Management Company
Not many Internet investments so far, but a few notables.
2275 E. Bayshore Road, Suite 150
Palo Alto, CA 94303
Telephone: 650-494-7400
Fax: 650-856-1826
E-mail: postmaster@assetman.com
Web site: *www.assetman.com*

Atlas Venture
Seeks enterprise software, data/telecommunications, e-commerce, and life sciences companies (particularly biopharmaceutical and medical device companies). Geographic focus is East and West Coast companies close to Boston and Menlo Park. Some European investments, especially in Benelux, France, Germany, Switzerland, and the United Kingdom.

Menlo Park
Eric Archambeau *earchambeau@atlasventure.com*
2420 Sand Hill Road, Suite 102
Menlo Park, CA 94025
USA
Telephone: 650-233-3072
Fax: 650-234-8202
Boston
Barry Fidelman (617-859-9290 Ext 224) *bfidelman@atlasven-ture.com*
Ron Nordin (617-859-9290 Ext 240) *rnordin@atlasventure.com*
Jeff Warren (617-859-9290 Ext 241) *jwarren@atlasventure.com*
222 Berkeley Street
Boston, MA 02116
USA
Telephone: 617-859-9290
Fax: 617-859-9292
E-mail: *boston@atlasventure.com*
London
Christopher Spray (44 171-292-0316) *cspray@atlasventure.co.uk*
Graham O'Keeffe (44 171-292-0300) *gokeeffe@atlasventure.co.uk*
Gerard Montanus (44 171-292-0300) *gmontanus@atlasventure.nl*
4 Cork Street
London W1X 1PB
United Kingdom
Telephone: 44 171-292-0300
Fax: 44 171-292-0301
E-mail: *london@atlasventure.co.uk*
Paris
Jean-Yves Quentel (33 1 45-23-41-20) *jquentel@atlasventure.fr*
Philippe Claude (33 1 45-23-41-20) *pclaude@atlasventure.fr*
32 bis, boulevard Haussmann
75009 Paris
France
Telephone: 33 1 45-23-41-20
Fax: 33 1 45-23-41-21
E-mail: *paris@atlasventure.fr*
Naarden (Amsterdam)
Gerard Montanus (31 35-695-4800) *gmontanus@atlasventure.nl*

P.O. Box 5225
1410 AE Naarden
The Netherlands
Telephone: 31 35-695-4800
Fax: 31 35-695-4888
E-mail: *amsterdam@atlasventure.nl*
Munich
Bernhard Schmid (49 89-458745-17) *bschmid@atlasventure.de*
Werner Dreesbach (49 89-458745-20) *wdreesbach@atlasven-ture.de*
Alexander Bruehl (49 89-458745-13) *abruehl@atlasventure.de*
Axel Bichara (49 89-458745-19) *abichara@atlasventure.de*
Widenmayerstrasse 16
D-80538 Munich, Germany
Telephone: 49 89-458-45-0
Fax: 49 89-4587-45-45
E-mail: *munich@atlasventure.de*
Web site: *http://www.atlasventure.com*

Austin Ventures

Texas has been a hotbed of Internet start-ups around Austin,
Texas. This venture firm has been involved with a lot of deals
in that region; Vignette and Deja.com are two examples.
114 West 7th Street, Suite 1300
Austin, TX 78701
Telephone: 512-479-0055
Fax: 512-476-3952
E-mail: *moreinfo@ausven.com*
Web site: *http://www.austinventures.com*

Bachow & Associates, Inc.

Invests in technology, communications, service businesses, manufac-
turing, and vertical software.
Bala Plaza East, Suite 502
Bala Cynwyd , Pennsylvania 19004 US3
Telephone: 610-660-4900
Fax: 610-660-4930
E-mail: *info@bachow.com*
Web site: *www.bachow.com*

BankAmerica Ventures

One of the largest banks—big and not agressive in investing in the Internet vet.

James C. Deichen
Senior Vice President
555 California Street, Suite 5507
San Francisco, CA 94104
Telephone: 415-953-5532
Fax: 415-622-2514
Web site: *http://corp.bankamerica.com/capital_raising/home.html*

BancBoston Robertson Stephens

Does equity, equity-related and debt securities for both public and private companies.

555 California Street
San Francisco, CA 94104
Tel: 888-275-7726
E-mail: *stuart_clark@rsco.com*
Web site: *http://www.rsco.com*

Beer & Partners

U.K.-based investors doing venture capital of between £100,000 and £500,000.

Beer & Partners
The Bell House
57 West Street
Dorking
Surrey
RH4 1BS
UNITED KINGDOM
Fax: +44 0 1306 884999
E-mail: *beerprt@netcomuk.co.uk*
Web site: *www.beer.com*

Ben Franklin Technology Center of SE Pennsylvania

Funding programs specifically designed to assist start-up, early and medium stage technology-based companies, and community-centered businesses.

3624 Market Street
Philadelphia, PA 19104
Telephone: 215-382-0380
Fax: 215-387-6050
E-mail: bftc@benfranklin.org
Web site: *http://www.benfranklin.org*

Benchmark Capital

One of the more agressive; landed eBay, with a great return.
2480 Sand Hill Road, Suite 200
Menlo Park, California 94025 US
Telephone: 650-854-8180
Fax: 650-854-8183
If you have an idea you'd like to bounce off them or a question about
funding, please feel free to contact one of their partners:
Dave Beirne: *dbeirne@benchmark.com*
Bruce Dunlevie: *bdunlevie@benchmark.com*
Kevin Harvey: *kharvey@benchmark.com*
Bob Kagle: *rkagle@benchmark.com*
Andy Rachleff: *arachleff@benchmark.com*
For general questions, send e-mail to *info@benchmark.com.*
Web site: *www.benchmark.com*

Business Angel Site

U.K.
http://www.venturesite.co.uk/

Cambridge Technology Capital Fund

Based in Southern California.
11512 El Camino Real, Suite 215
San Diego, CA 92130
Telephone: 619-259-7869
Fax: 619-259-7909
E-mail: barryr@ctp.com
Web site: *http://www.ctc.ctp.com*

Capital Access Partners

Provides advisory services and obtains expansion capital for early stage firms.

E-mail contact:
John Hammer *capital@inch.com*
320 E. 46th St. 16th Floor
New York , New York 10017 USA
Web site: *www.inch.com/~capital/cap.html*

Carlyle Venture Partners

A global player with $1.4 billion invested.
Washington D.C.
Carlyle Venture Partners
1001 Pennsylvania Ave., N.W.
Suite 220 South
Washington , D.C. 20004 US
Telephone: 202-347-2626
Fax: 202-347-1818
Hong Kong
Carlyle Asia
Telehone: 852 2878-7000
Fax: 852 2878-7007
London
Carlyle Europe
20 Berkeley Square
London W1X 6NB
United Kingdom
Telephone: 44 171-894-1200
Fax: 44 171-894-1600
Milan
Carlyle Europe
CEP Advisors Srl
Via dell'Arcivescovado 1
20122 Milano, Italy
Main: 39 02 89012107
Fax: 39 02 86991301
Munich
Carlyle Europe

Residenzstrafle 18
D-80333 M¸nchen Germany
Main: 49 89 29 19 580
Fax: 49 89 29 19 5858
Paris
Carlyle Europe
112, avenue Kleber
75116 Paris France
Main: 33 1 53 70 35 20
Fax: 33 1 53 70 35 30
Web site: *www.thecarlylegroup.com*

CeBourn, Ltd.

Offers advisory services to IT, telecommunication, and basic industry enterprises.

Please e-mail business plans to:
assistant@cebourn.com
E-mail links for the Management Team:
derrin@cebourn.com
ron@cebourn.com
beth@cebourn.com
One Norwest Center
1700 Lincoln St. Suite 3700
Denver, CO 80203-4537 USA
Telephone: 303-832-8220
Fax: 303-832-8232
Web site: *www.cebourn.com*

Charter Venture Capital

Manages over $300 million of capital and invests in emerging growth, technology-based companies in data networking, telecommunications, enterprise software, systems and peripherals, Internet software, and electronic commerce.

525 University Avenue, Suite 1500
Palo Alto, CA 94301
Telephone: 650-325-6953
Fax: 650-325-8811
E-mail: info@charterventures.com

Web site: *http://www.charterventures.com*

CMGI @Ventures

Behind Lycos, Geocities, NaviSite, Furniture.com, and others.
  East Coast
  Guy Bradley *gbradley@cmgi.com*
  Three Burlington Woods Drive
  Fourth Floor
  Burlington, MA 01803
  Tel: 781-238-5220
  Fax: 781-229-2526
  Marc Poirier *mpoirier@cmgi.com*
  Three Burlington Woods Drive
  Fourth Floor
  Burlington, MA 01803
  Tel: 781-238-5234
  Fax: 781-229-2526
  David S. Wetherell
  100 Brickstone Sq.
  Andover, MA 01810
  West Coast
  Jonathan D. Callaghan *jcallaghan@cmgi.com*
  3000 Alpine Road
  Menlo Park, CA 94028
  Tel: 650-233-0333
  Fax: 650-233-0506
  Brad Garlinghouse *bgarlinghouse@cmgi.com*
  3000 Alpine Road
  Menlo Park, CA 94028
  Tel: 650-233-0333
  Fax: 650-233-9657
  Peter Mills
  3000 Alpine Road
  Menlo Park, CA 94028
  Tel: 650-233-0333
  Fax: 650-233-0506
  Web site: *www.cmgi.com*

Connecticut Innovations Inc.

Invests in high technolgy companies in Connecticut.

999 West Street
Rocky Hill, CT 06067
Telephone: 860-563-5851
Fax: 860-563-4877
E-mail: *info@ctinnovations.com*
Web site: *http://www.ctinnovations.com*

Convergence Partners

Invests only in companies with a management team based in the United States at the time of the investment.

3000 Sand Hill Road, Building 2, Suite 235
Menlo Park, CA 94025
Telephone: 650-854-3010
Fax: 650-854-3015
E-mail: *info@convergencepartners.com*
Web site: *http://www.convergencepartners.com*

Crescendo Ventures (formerly IAI)

Focuses on information technology, communication services, and health care.

E-mail contacts:
R. David Spreng *dspreng@iaiventures.com*
Anthony S. Daffer *tdaffer@iaiventures.com*
Lorraine Fox *lfox@iaiventures.com*
Jeffrey R. Hinck *jhinck@iaiventures.com*
Lane Brostrom *lbrostrom@iaiventures.com*
800 LaSalle Ave, Suite 2250
Minneapolis, MN 55402
Telephone: 612-607-2800
Fax: 612-607-2801
505 Hamilton Ave, Suite 315
Palo Alto, CA 94301
Telephone: 650-470-1200
Fax: 650-470-1201
Web site: *www.iaiventures.com*

Crosspoint Venture Partners

Crosspoint has been pretty active in the 'Net space. They seem to "get it."

E-mail contacts:

General *partners@crosspointvc.com*

John Mumford *jmumford@crosspointvc.com*

Seth Neiman *sneiman@crosspointvc.com*

Rich Shapero *rshapero@crosspointvc.com*

The Pioneer Building

2925 Woodside Road

Woodside, CA 94062

Telephone: 650-851-7600

Fax: 650-851-7661

Southern California:

Bob Hoff *bhoff@crosspointvc.com*

Barbara Lubash *blubash@crosspointvc.com*

Don Milder *dmilder@crosspointvc.com*

Crosspoint Venture Partners

18552 MacArthur Blvd, Suite 400

Irvine, CA 92612

Telephone: 949-852-1611

Fax: 949-852-9804

Web site: *http://www.crosspointvc.com*

Cubic Egg

Invests between £20,000 and £300,000 in U.K.-based start-ups.

88 Kingsway,

London, WC2B 6AA

UK

Telephone: +44 0 171-242-5068

Fax: +44 0 171-209-1236

E-mail: *enquiries@cubicegg.com*

Web site: *www.cubicegg.com*

Draper Fisher Associates Fund III LP

Invests only in U.S.-based information technology companies. Probably one of the most aggressive investors in the Internet space.

400 Seaport Court, Suite 250

Redwood City, CA 94063
Telephone: 650-599-9000
Fax: 650-599-9726
Web site: *http://www.drapervc.com*

El Dorado Ventures
Interested in emerging Internet commerce technology companies.
2400 Sand Hill Road, Suite 100
Menlo Park, CA 94025
Telephone: 650-854-1200
Fax: 650-854-1202
E-mail: *edv@eldoradoventures.com*
Web site: *www.eldoradoventures.com*

Embryon Capital
Geographical preference: 3-hour travel time of Washington, D.C.
Contacts:
Tim Webb, Founding Partner
Will Tobey, Partner
Philip B. Smith, Partner
7903 Sleaford Place
Bethesda, MD
20814 US
Telephone: 301-656-6837
Fax: 301-656-8056
E-mail: *info@embryon.com*
Web site: *www.embryon.com*

Encompass Group Inc.
Manages $70 million. Specializes in providing technology companies
with a bridge to Asia.
777 108th Avenue NE, Suite 2300
Bellevue, WA 98004
Telephone: 425-468-3900
Fax: 425-468-3901
E-mail: *info@evpartners.com*
Web site: *http://www.encompassventures.com*

Enterprise Partners

Strong regional orientation toward investing in California companies. Broad range of investments.

La Jolla
7979 Ivanhoe Avenue, Suite 550
La Jolla, California 92037-4519
Telephone: 619-454-8833
Fax: 619-454-2489

Newport Beach
5000 Birch Street, Suite 6200
Newport Beach, California 92660-2143
Telephone: 949-833-3650
Fax: 949-833-3652
E-mail: *afrenz@ent.com*
Web site: *http://www.ent.com*

FBR Technology Venture Partners LP

Focuses mainly on Internet, electronic commerce investments around Washington, D.C.

1001 19th Street North
Arlington, VA 22209
Telephone: 703-312-9755
Fax: 703-312-9655
E-mail: *greichers@fbr.com*
Web site: *www.fbrcorp.com/vc/*

First Analysis Corporation

Over $450 million in venture capital funds with a leaning toward Information Technology.

E-mail contacts:
Alex Kim, Associate *akim@facvc.com*
Dennis Yang, Associate *dyang@facvc.com*
The Sears Tower, Suite 9500
233 South Wacker Drive
Chicago , IL 60606 US
Telephone: 312-258-1400
Fax: 312-258-0334
E-mail: *info@facvc.com*

Web site: *www.facvc.com*

Fluke Capital Management
Likes the the Pacific Northwest.
　E-mail contacts:
　Dennis Weston *weston@flukecapital.com*
　Kevin Gabelein *gabelein@flukecapital.com*
　11400 Southeast 6th St., Suite 230
　Bellevue, WA 98004-6469
　Telephone: 425-453-4590
　Fax: 425-453-4675
　Web site: *http://www.flukecapital.com*

Foundation Capital
A wide swath of interest in technology and the Internet.
　70 Willow Road, Suite 200
　Menlo Park, CA 94025
　Telephone: 650-614-0500
　Fax: 650-614-0505
　Web site: *http://www.foundationcapital.com*

Geocapital Partners
Industry focus in information technology.
　2 Executive Drive, Suite 820
　Fort Lee, New Jersey 07024
　Telephone: 201-461-9292
　Fax: 201-461-7793
　E-mail: *investments@geocapital.com*
　Web site: *www.geocapital.com*

Greenfield Technology Ventures
Seed and first-round funding and "roll up your sleeves" style expertise.
　668 High Street
　Palo Alto, CA 94301
　Telephone: 650-322-8584
　Fax: 650-853-1748
　E-mail: *jallen@gftv.com*

Web site: *http://www.gftv.com*

Grotech Capital Group

The majority of these partnerships are located in the mid-Atlantic and Southeastern regions of the United States and include investments in companies in the early, emerging firms in the e-commerce area.

9690 Deereco Road, Suite 800
Timonium, MD 21093
Telephone: 410-560-2000
Fax: 410-560-1910
E-mail: *sgogol@grotech.com*
Web site: *http://www.grotech.com*

Hambrecht & Quist Venture Capital

The investment bank also does some venture investments.

E-mail contact:
Julie Harshberger *jharshberger@hamquist.com*
One Bush Street, 18th Floor
San Francisco, CA 94104
Telephone: 415-576-3300
Fax: 415-677-7747
Web site: *http://www.hamquist.com*

Herald Investment Management Limited

Specializes in achieving capital growth through investing in quoted companies in the areas of technology and media: information technology, communications, broadcasting, e-commerce, business intelligence, Internet, networking, and telephony.

England
12 Charterhouse Square
London EC1M 6AX
Telephone: 0171 553 6300
Fax: 0171 490 8026
Ireland
George' Dock House
International Financial Services Centre
Dublin 1
Ireland

E-mail: *info@heralduk.com*
Web site: *www.heralduk.com*

Hummer Winblad Venture Partners

Featured in Chapter 2 of *Zero Gravity*.
E-mail contacts:
John Hummer, partner *jhummer@humwin.com*
Ann Winblad, partner *awinblad@humwin.com*
Mark Gorenberg, partner *mgorenberg@humwin.com*
Dan Beldy, associate *dbeldy@humwin.com*
2 South Park, 2nd Floor
San Francisco, CA 94107
Telephone: 415-979-9600
Fax: 415-979-9601
Web site: *http://www.humwin.com*

Idanta Partners

Invests in information technology: advanced cellular/digital communications devices, data compression software, electronic system virtual prototyping software, knowledge discovery software, minicomputers, remote access connectivity devices, removable storage drives, semiconductor capital equipment, tape drives, value-added reseller of mechanical software.
4660 La Jolla Village Drive #850
San Diego, CA 92122 USA
Telephone: 619-452-9690
Fax: 619-452-2013
Web site: *www.idanta.com*

idealab!

Venture incubator for starting and growing Internet businesses. Founded in March 1996 by entrepreneur Bill Gross. Start-ups include CitySearch, GoTo.com, eToys, WeddingChannel, Tickets. com, IntraNetics and Cooking.com.
130 West Union Street
Pasadena, CA 91103
Telephone: 626-585-6900
Fax: 626-535-2701

Web site: *www.idealab.com*

Information Technology Ventures LP

ITV specializes in early-stage information technology companies within the western United States, but also invests outside of the region with co-investors.

3000 Sand Hill Road
Building One, Suite 280
Menlo Park, CA 94025
Telephone: 650-854-5500
Fax: 650-234-0130
E-mail: *main@itventures.com*
Web site: *http://www.itventures.com*

Innocal

Early stage investors in electronics, software, communications, and health care, with some high-growth businesses in other viable industries also considered.

Contact:
Eric S. Harrison, Associate *eharrison@innocal.com*
Telephone: 714-850-6784
Principal office:
Plaza Tower, Suite 1270
600 Anton Blvd
Costa Mesa, CA 92626
Telephone: 714-850-6784
Fax: 714-850-6798
Satellite office:
Park 80 West/Plaza One
Saddle Brook, NJ 07663
Telephone: 201-845-4900
Fax: 201-845-3388
Web site: *www.innocal.com*

Institutional Venture Partners

Manages over $1 billion in venture capital, making it one of the bigger firms. IVP's goal is to invest in leading early stage companies with advanced technology in information and life sciences. IVP also selectively invests in later stage opportunities. Areas: Internet and communications infrastructure companies, e-commerce, entertainment, and publishing.

3000 Sand Hill Rd Bldg 2, Suite 290
Menlo Park, CA 94025
Telephone: 650-854-0132
Fax: 650-854-5762
E-mail: *infotech@ivp.com*
Web site: *http://www.ivp.com*

International Capital Partners

Provides expansion and acquisition capital in the form of equity and securities linked to equity in smaller growth companies. Preferably, these companies are public companies valued under $150 million.

300 First Stamford Place
Stamford, CT 06902
Telephone: 203-961-8900
Fax: 203-969-2212
E-mail: *ICP@intcapital.com*
Web site: *http://www.intcapital.com*

Intersouth partners

Invests primarily in the Raleigh/Durham Research Triangle area of North Carolina and Austin, Texas, and surrounding cities. Portfolio interests include biotechnology and computer technologies and software.

Southeast
1000 Park Forty Plaza, Suite 290
Research Triangle Park, NC
Southwest
6907 N. Capital of Texas Highway, Suite 220
Austin, TX
E-mail: *info@intersouth.com*
Web site: *www.intersouth.com*

Kleiner Perkins Caufield & Byers

Chapter 2 of *Zero Gravity* describes KP. It's considered the leading venture firm for Internet investments with Amazon.com, Netscape, and Chemdex to its credit, among many more.

Menlo Park
2750 Sand Hill Road
Menlo Park, CA 94025
Telephone: 650-233-2750
Fax: 650-233-0300

San Francisco
Four Embarcadero Center, Suite 1880
San Francisco, CA 94111
Telephone: 415-421-3110
Fax: 415-421-3128
E-mail: *webmaster@kpcb.com*
Web site: *http://www.kpcb.com*

Kline Hawkes California LP

Likes later-stage venture deals, change of control situations, and industry consolidations. California focus, but also some other U.S. interests. Range: $2 million to $6 million in the health care, information technology, telecommunications, and service industries.

11726 San Vicente Boulevard, Suite 300
Los Angeles, CA 90049
Telephone: 310-442-4700
Fax: 310-442-4707
E-mail: *general@klinehawkes.com*
Web site: *www.klinehawkes.com*

Labrador Ventures

Invests in early stage, private companies pursuing opportunities in digital technologies—information, communications, software, media/entertainment, and semiconductors. During the last three years fifteen of twenty-two investments have been related to the Internet.

400 Seaport Court, Suite 250
Redwood City, CA 94063
Telephone: 650-366-6000

Fax: 650-366-6430
E-mail: *lkubal@labrador.com*
Web site: *www.labrador.com*

Levy Trajman Management Investment Inc.

Focus on fast-growth, high-tech companies located in the Boston and
Silicon Valley areas, Israel, and India.
67 South Bedford St., 400W
Burlington, MA 01803 USA
Telephone: 781-229-5818
Fax: 781-229-1808
E-mail: *info@ltmi.com*
Web site: *www.ltmi.com*

Mandeville Partners

Telecommunications, including cable television and MMDS/hardwire
system development in Latin America.
12121 Wilshire Boulevard, Suite 1041
Los Angeles, CA 90049
Telephone: 310-442-7880
Fax: 310-442-7890
Contacts:
David A. Eisner
Jonathan D. Lloyd
Rory S. Phillips
Peter A. Roussak
Sean M. Thorpe
E-mail: *newbusiness@mandevillepartners.com*
Web site: *http://mandevillepartners.com*

Mayfield Fund

Looks at businesses that solve mission-critical problems by providing
software-based middleware, tools, applications, online services, and
Internet-based online services that provide education and entertainment to mass market consumers.
2800 Sand Hill Road
Menlo Park, CA 94025
Telephone: 650-854-5560

Fax: 650-854-5712
E-mail: *info@mayfield.com*
Web site: *http://www.mayfield.com*

Menlo Ventures

Interested in high technology, Internet, semiconductor, software, and communications.
  3000 Sand Hill Rd Bldg 4, Suite 100
  Menlo Park, CA 94025
  Telephone: 650-854-8540
  Fax: 650-854-7059
  E-mail contacts:
  Sonja L. Hoel, General Partner *sonja@menloventures.com*
  Mark A. Siegel, General Partner *mark@menloventures.com*
  Web site: *www.menloventures.com*

Mid-Atlantic Venture Funds

Invests in companies in the Mid-Atlantic, but will consider others.
  Headquarters
  Frederick J. Beste III, Partner *Fred@MAVF.com*
  Glen R. Bressner, Partner *Glen@MAVF.com*
  Thomas A. Smith, Partner *Tom@MAVF.com*
  Ben Franklin Technology Center
  Lehigh University
  125 Goodman Drive
  Bethlehem, PA 18015
  Telephone: 610-865-6550
  Fax: 610-865-6427
  Virginia
  Marc F. Benson, Partner *Marc@MAVF.com*
  William E. Quigley, Associate *William@MAVF.com*
  1801 Reston Parkway
  Suite 203
  Reston, VA 20190
  Telephone: 703-904-4120
  Fax: 703-904-4124
  Web site: *http://www.mavf.com*

Mission Ventures

Southern California; semiconductor, software, hardware, wireless, and Internet technologies.

11512 El Camino Real, Suite 215
San Diego, CA 92130-2046 USA
Telephone: 619-259-0100
Fax: 619-259-0112
E-mail: *ted@missionventures.com*
Web site: *http://www.missionventures.com*

Mohr Davidow Ventures

Specializes in making early-stage investments in companies with a strong information technology component. An example would be CriticalPath, a provider of outsourced e-mail solutions to corporations.

2775 Sand Hill Road, Ste. 240
Menlo Park, CA 94025
Telephone: 650-854-7236
Fax: 650-854-7365
Contacts:
Rob Chaplinksy *rchaplinsky@mdv.com*
Nancy Schoendorf *nancys@mdv.com*
Bill Davidow *whd@mdv.com*
George Zachary *gzachary@mdv.com*
Teresa Engelhard *tengelhard@mdv.com*
Geoffrey Moore *gmoore@mdv.com*
Jon Feiber *jdf@mdv.com*
Donna Novitsky *dnovitsky@mdv.com*
Michael Solomon *msolomon@mdv.com*
Derek Proudian *derek@mdv.com*
Web site: *www.mdv.com*

Morgan Stanley Venture Partners

Invests primarily in later-stage high-growth IT and health care, with a lot of interest in enterprise software, communications and network infrastructure, and information services.

New York
Guy L. de Chazal, General Partner

M. Fazle Husain, General Partner
Debra Abramovitz, Chief Operating Officer
Ghassan Bejjani, Principal
Noah Walley, Vice President
David Hammer, Financial Associate
Aaron Broad, Venture Associate
Gary Stein, Sr. Venture Associate
Philip R. Dur, Venture Associate
1221 Avenue of the Americas
33rd Floor
New York, NY 10020
Telephone: 212 762-7900
Fax: 212 762-8424
E-mail: *msventures@ms.com*
Menlo Park
Robert J. Loarie, General Partner
William J. Harding, General Partner
Scott S. Halsted, General Partner
Jeffrey J Booth, Vice President
Peter Chung, Venture Associate
Patrick Gallagher, Venture Associate
John F. Ryan, Venture Associate
Grace Voorhis, Venture Associate
John Eberhardt, Venture Analyst
3000 Sand Hill Road
Building 4, Suite 250
Menlo Park, CA 94025
Telephone: 650-233-2600
Fax: 650-233-2626
E-mail: *msventures@ms.com*
Web site: *http://www.msvp.com*

Morgenthaler Ventures

Manages $600 million. One of the older venture firms, begun in 1968, funding more than 150 companies, two-thirds of which are now public or part of public entities: information technology and health care as well as later stage management-led buyouts.

Northeast

629 Euclid Ave., Suite 700
Cleveland, OH 44114
Telephone: 216-621-3070
Fax: 216-621-2817
West Coast
2730 Sand Hill Road, Suite 280
Menlo Park, CA 94025
Telephone: 650-233-7600
Fax: 650-233-7606
Southeast
Satellite Office
3200 Habersham Road
Atlanta, GA 30305
Telephone: 404-816-0051
Fax: 404-816-0685
E-mail: *tlaufik@morgenthaler.com*
Web site: *www.morgenthaler.com*

Murphree and Company Inc.

Southwest focus, with offices in Houston, Austin, and Albuquerque. Its newest fund, Murphree Venture Partners,IV, has special emphasis on information technologies—both software and hardware—materials technologies, and medical devices.

Houston
1100 Louisiana, Ste. 5225
Houston, TX 77002
Telephone: 713-655-8500
Fax: 713-655-8503
Albuquerque
1155 University Blvd. SE
Albuquerque, NM 87106
Telephone: 505-843-4277
Fax: 505-843-4278
Austin
221 West Sixth, Suite 1750
Austin, Texas 78701
Telephone: 512-236-1535
Fax: 512-472-3053

E-mail: Geoffrey T. Tudor in Austin *tudor@murphco.com*
Web site: *http://www.murphco.com*

Needham Capital Partners
Needham & Company specializes in technology, health care, and specialty retailing.
New York
Needham Capital Partners
445 Park Avenue
New York, NY 10022
Telephone: 212-371-8300
Fax: 212-371-8702
Boston
Needham Capital Partners
One Post Office Square, Suite 3710
Boston, MA 02109
Telephone: 617-457-0910
Menlo Park
Needham Capital Partners
3000 Sand Hill Road, Building 2
Suite 190
Menlo Park, CA 94025
Telephone: 650-854-9111
Tel Aviv, Israel
Needham Capital Partners
Balance Holdings, Ltd.
Dr. Joseph Abramoff
3A Jabotinsky St.
Diamond Tower
Ramat Gan, Israel
Telephone: 972-3-575-5674
E-mail: *kkenny@needhamco.com*
Web site: *www.needhamco.com*

New York State Science & Tech. Foundation
99 Washington Avenue, Suite 1731
Albany, NY 12210
Telephone: 518-473-9741

Fax: 518-473-6876
E-mail: *bmalone@empirestate.ny.us*

Newbury Ventures

Primarily seeks investments in communications and health care companies in these areas: communications technologies, remote access, broadband switching and transmission, semiconductor chip design, network and service management, Internet content, multimedia conferencing, security and encryption, bandwidth management, photonics, application provisioning tools, and wireless access technologies.

E-mail contacts:
Bruce J. Bauer *bruce@newburyven.com*
Michael W. Loughry *mike@newburyven.com*
Jay B. Morrison *jay@newburyven.com*
Jacqueline M. Larkin *jacqueline@newburyven.com*
Andree N. Merchant *andree@newburyven.com*
535 Pacific Avenue
San Francisco, CA 94133
Telephone: 415-296-7408
Fax: 415-296-7416
Newbury Ventures Contacts:
Ossama R. Hassanein *ossama@newburyven.com*
Colleen E. Young *colleen@newburyven.com*
Tuan Tran-Palmer *tuan@newburyven.com*
One First Street, Suite 12
Los Altos, CA 94022
Telephone: 650-947 8200
Fax: 650-947 0733
E-mail: *jacqueline@newburyven.com*
Web site: *http://www.newburyven.com*

Newcap Partners Inc.

Focuses on serving the corporate finance needs of emerging companies. They are especially interested in software and information services.

Suite 1135, 5777 West Century Boulevard
Los Angeles, CA 90045-569
Telephone: 310-645-7900

Fax: 310-215-1025
E-mail: *turney@newcap.com*
Web site: *http://www.newcap.com*

Newtek Ventures

Likes companies that design and manufacture products that promise significant price/performance advantages over existing technologies. Investments are also made in technology-oriented service and software businesses. Areas of interest include: medical devices, electronics—semiconductor equipment/lasers/optics, computers/communications, software application products, telecommunications, Internet goals and content, medical software and services.

San Franciso
500 Washington Street, Suite 720
San Francisco, CA 94111
Telephone: 415-986-5711
Fax: 415-986-4618
Menlo Park
3000 Sand Hill Road
Building 3, Suite 140
Menlo Park, CA 94025
Telephone: 415-854-9744
Fax: 415-854-9749
E-mail: *hall@newtekventure.com*
Web site: *http://www.newtekventure.com*

Newvista Capital LLC

Early-stage, information technology companies managed by minority and women entrepreneurs; NVC also works with the management of its investments to build successful growth companies of real value, especially in Internet communities, Internet technology, software, and networking.

540 Cowper Street, Suite 200
Palo Alto, CA 94301
Telephone: 650-329-9333
Fax: 650-328-9434
E-mail: *fgreen@nvcap.com*
Web site: *http://www.nvcap.com*

Norwest Venture Partners

Norwest Venture Capital has invested in more than 300 companies since its founding in 1961. The firm has a national presence, maintaining offices in Palo Alto, Boston, and Minneapolis. Norwest invests primarily in technology and health care, with some selective investments in consumer services. Actively manages more than $500 million. Forty percent of Norwest's capital distribution is made to software and Internet technologies.

Palo Alto

Kevin G. Hall *khall@norwestvc.com*

Promod Haque *phaque@norwestvc.com*

George J. Still, Jr. *gstill@norwestvc.com*

Colin R. Savage *csavage@norwestvc.com*

Paul Vabakos *pvabakos@norwestvc.com*

245 Lytton Avenue, Suite 250

Palo Alto, CA 94301

Telephone: 650-321-8000

Fax: 650-321-8010

Minneapolis

Daniel J. Haggerty *dhaggerty@norwestvc.com*

John P. Whaley *jwhaley@norwestvc.com*

2800 Piper Jaffray Tower

222 South Ninth Street

Minneapolis, MN 55402

Telephone: 612-667-1650

Fax 612-667-1660

Boston

Ernest C. Parizeau *eparizeau@norwestvc.com*

Blair Whitaker *bwhitaker@norwestvc.com*

Wellesley Office Park

40 William Street, Suite 305

Wellesley, MA 02181

Telephone: 781-237-5870

Fax: 781-237-6270

Web site: *http://www.norwestvc.com*

Novak-Biddle Venture Partners

Provides equity financing and assistance to the management of young information technology companies.

1897 Preston White Drive
Reston, VA 20191
Telephone: 703-264-7904
Fax: 703-264-1438
E-mail: *info@novakbiddle.com*
Web site: *http://www.NovakBiddle.com*

Oak Investment Partners

Including follow-on investments, likes to invest $4 to $60 million or more in six to eight special situation investments each year. Oak has the ability to sponsor investment amounts well in excess of $60 million through its network of outside resources.

Palo Alto
Partners: Bandel Carano, Fred Harman
Key Focus: Information Technology
525 University Avenue
Suite 1300
Palo Alto, CA 94301
Telephone: 650-614-3700
Fax: 650-328-6345

Westport
Partners: Ed Glassmeyer, Seth Harrison, Ann Lamont, Ginger More
Key Focus: Information technology, healthcare
1 Gorham Island
Westport, CT 06880
Telephone: 203-226-8346
Fax: 203-227-0372

Minneapolis
Partners: Jerry Gallagher, Cathy Agee
Key Focus: Retail industry
4550 Norwest Center
90 South Seventh Street
Minneapolis, MN 55402
Telephone: 612-339-9322
Fax: 612-337-8017
E-mail: *bizplans@oakinv.com*

Web site: *http://www.oakinv.com*

Olympic Venture Partners

Makes equity investments in early stage technology-based companies primarily in the western third of North America, while maintaining a leading market share position in the Pacific Northwest. Specific emphasis is on firms in the software, life sciences, Internet, communications, and health care sectors. OVP usually originates and leads its investments, taking an active role in assisting the management and growth of the portfolio company.

Seattle
George Clute *clute@ovp.com*
Bill Miller *miller@ovp.com*
Chad Waite *waite@ovp.com*
Bill Funcannon *funcannon@ovp.com*
2420 Carillon Point
Kirkland, WA 98033
Telephone: 425-889-9192
Fax: 425-889-0152
Portland
Gerry Langeler *langeler@ovp.com*
340 Oswego Pointe Drive, Suite 200
Lake Oswego, Oregon 97034 US
Telephone: 503-697-8766
Fax: 503-697-8863
E-mail: *info@ovp.com*
Web site: *www.product.com/olympic*

Onset Ventures

Focuses on seed and early-stage investing in business-to-business markets. In addition, they specialize in on-site "incubations"—working one-on-one with entrepreneurs to develop business concepts and launch new companies. Based in the Silicon Valley and Austin, Texas, they primarily fund companies located in those regions.

Menlo Park
2490 Sand Hill Rd.
Menlo Park, CA 94025
Telephone: 650-529-0700

Fax: 650-529-0777
E-mail: *menlopark@onset.com*
Austin
ONSET Ventures
8911 Capital of Texas Highway
Building II, Suite 2310
Austin, Texas 78759
Telephone: 512.349.2255
Fax: 512.349.2258
E-mail: *austin@onset.com*
Web site: *http://www.onset.com*

Partech International
Provides financing in the United States, Europe, and Japan. Invests in Internet and technology-enabled business-to-business services, electronic commerce, outsourced business applications, and life sciences with particular focus on health care information technology and services, and medical devices.

    San Francisco
Partech International
50 California St., Suite 3200
San Francisco, CA 94111
Telephone: 415-788-2929
Fax: 415-788-6763
Paris
Partech International SA
42, Avenue Raymond Poincare
75116 Paris - France
Tel.: +33 0 1 53 65 65 53
Fax: +33 0 1 53 65 65 55
Tokyo
Partech International Co., Ltd.
SVAX TT Building
3-11-15, Toranomon, Minato-Ku
Tokyo 105-0001 - Japan
Tel.: +81 3 5470 6495
Fax: +81 3 5470 6498
Web site: *http://www.partechintl.com*

Patricof & Co. Ventures Inc.

Computer hardware and software: consumer-goods and services; business services; financial services; health care industry-devices, services, and therapeutics; industrial goods and services; Internet services; semiconductors and electronics; retailing; telecommunications infrastructure and services.

New York
Patricof & Company Ventures Inc.
445 Park Avenue
New York, NY 10022
Tel: 212-753-6300
Fax: 212-319-6155

California
Patricof & Company Ventures Inc.
2100 Geng Road, Suite 150
Palo Alto, CA 94303
Telephone: 650-494-9944
Fax: 650-494-6751

Pennsylvania
Patricof & Company Ventures Inc.
Executive Terrace Building
455 South Gulph Road, Suite 410
King of Prussia, PA 19406
Telephone: 610-265-0286
Fax: 610-265-4959
Web site: *http://www.patricof.com*

England
Apax-Leumi Partners Ltd
15 Portland Place
London W1N 3AA
U.K.
Telephone: 44-171-872-6300
Fax: 44-171-636-6475
4 Park Square East
Leeds LS1 2NE
U.K.
Telephone: 44-113-242-3040
Fax: 44-113-242-3047

Web site: *http://www.apax.co.uk*
Scotland
Apax Partners & Co. Asset Management Ltd.
28 Melville Street
Edinburgh EH3 &HA
Scotland
Telephone: 31 225-7300
Fax: 31 225-7311
Germany
Apax-Leumi Partners Ltd
Möhlstrasse 22
D-81675 Munich
Germany
Telephone: 49 89-998-9090
Fax: 49 89-998-90932
Web site: *http://www.apax.de*
Israel
Apax-Leumi Partners Ltd
2 Weizmann Street
IBM Building, 10th floor
P.O. Box 33031
Tel Aviv 61330
Israel
Telephone: 972 3-696-5990
Fax: 972 3-696-5977
Web site: *http://www.apax.co.il/*
Spain
Apax Partners & Co. SA Corporate Finance
Principe de Vergara
33-3_ Dcha
E-28001 Madrid
Spain
Telephone: 34 1-578-0660
Fax: 34 1-578-0115
Ireland
Apax Partners & Co. Capital Ltd.
10 Fitzwilliam Square
Dublin, 2

Republic of Ireland
Telephone: 353 1-661-2671
Fax: 353 1-661-3057
France
Apax Partners and Cie Ventures
45, Avenue Kléber
75784 Paris Cedex 16
France
Telephone: 33 1 53-65-0100
Fax: 33 1 53-65-0101
Web site: *http://www.apax.partners.com.fr*
Switzerland
Apax Partners and Company AG
Bahnhofstrasse 17
CH-8702 Zollikon/Zürich
Switzerland
Telephone: 41 1-391-5268
Fax: 41 1-391-5935
Web site: *http://www.apax.de*

Piper Jaffray Ventures Inc.

Medical devices, health care services and technology. Piper Jaffray Ventures currently manages three major funds: Piper Jaffray Healthcare Funds I and II, and Piper Jaffray Technology Fund. The Piper Jaffray Technology Fund (PJTF) is investing in high-growth, technology-based service companies. Members of the PJTF portfolio produce new or substantially enhanced services to businesses and/or consumers by employing emerging software and communications capabilities.

Minneapolis
Piper Jaffray Tower
222 South Ninth Street
Minneapolis, MN 55402
Telephone: 612-342-6000
Fax: 612-342-8514
Menlo Park
2500 Sand Hill Road
Suite 200

Menlo Park, CA 94025-7016
Telephone: 650-233-2260
Telephone: 800-981-1203
76 Cannon St 011-44
London, UK EC4N 6AE
Telephone: 171-489-9902
Web site: *www.piperjaffray.com*

Platinum Venture Partners

Two-thirds of PVP's investments are Internet and information technology related, with the other third in branded consumer products
and services.

1815 South Meyers Road, 5th Floor
Oakbrook Terrace, IL 60181
Telephone: 630-620-5000
Fax: 630-691-9134
E-mail: *pvpinfo@platinum.com*
Web site: *http://www.platinumventures.com*

Primedia Ventures

PRIMEDIA Ventures is a subsidiary of PRIMEDIA Inc., and was orga-
nized in March 1998 to invest in early-stage Internet companies and other
technology opportunities in such areas as commerce services, enterprise
software applications, distance learning, and advertising-related technologies.

PRIMEDIA Ventures
745 Fifth Ave., 21st Floor
New York, NY, 10151
Telephone: 212-745-1203
Fax: 212-610-9422
E-mail: *busplans@primediaventures.com*
Web site: *http://www.primediaventures.com*

Primus Capital Fund

Primus has a strong portfolio interest in information technology and
consumer services, without regional limitations.

5900 Landerbrook Dr. Suite 200
Cleveland, OH 44124

Telephone: 440-684-7300
Fax: 440-684-7342
E-mail: *srothman@primusventure.com*
Web site: *http://www.primusventure.com*

Rand Capital

Rand Capital is venturing forth into the IT venture capital area.
Business plans can be mailed to:
Allen Grum, President
2200 Rand Building
Buffalo NY 14203
USA
No Web site or e-mail information at this time.

Red Rock Ventures

Western U.S. location preferred. Portfolio interest in business-to-
business, e-commerce, and knowledge management and data mining.
525 University Avenue Suite 600
Palo Alto, CA 94301
Telephone: 650-325-3111
Fax: 650-321-2902
E-mail: *mailto:info@redrockventures.com*
Web site: *www.redrockventures.com*

Redleaf Venture Management

Primary strategy is to develop high-growth, Internet technology-oriented businesses by actively assisting people who have the ideas and personal qualities to build new enterprises with significant growth and market leadership potential. Robert von Goeben specializes in Internet
marketing and content and was responsible for taking one of the most
popular music companies, Geffen Records, online in 1993. John Kohler
brings over twenty years of technology industry and business experience
to Redleaf. He has invested heavily in technology product formation
and has been concentrating on Internet start-ups since 1995.
Contacts:
Robert von Goeben, *Director rvg@redleaf.com*
John Kohler, Managing Director *john@redleaf.com*
Saratoga (CA)

Redleaf Venture Management, L.L.C.
14395 Saratoga Avenue, Suite 130
Saratoga, CA 95070
Telephone: 408-868-0800
Fax: 408-868-0810
Seattle
Redleaf Venture Management, L.L.C.
Northwest Office
800 5th Avenue
Suite 4100
Seattle, WA 98104
Voice: 206-447-1350
Fax: 206-447-1351
E-mail: *nancy@redleaf.com*
Web site: *http://www.redleaf.com*

RWI Group
Software, telecommunications, health care and the Internet.
720 University Avenue, Suite 103
Palo Alto, CA 94301
Telephone: 650-833-4980
Fax: 650-833-4983
E-mail: *dlucas@rwigroup.com*
Web site: *www.rwigroup.com*

Scripps Ventures
Internet, e-commerce, business-to-business, content and media technologies and companies.
Contact:
Benjamin Burditt, Senior Vice President
bburditt@scrippsventures.com
200 Madison Avenue
New York, NY 10016
Telephone: 212-293-8709
Fax: 212-293-8716
Web site: *www.scrippsventures.com*

Seapoint Ventures

Serves as a point for Oak Investment Partners, Sevin Rosen Funds, and Venrock Associates in Pacific Northwest information technology companies.

Contacts:
Thomas S. Huseby
direct: 425-637-5602
mobile: 206-369-3632
E-mail: *tom@seapointventures.com*
Susan P. Sigl
direct: 425-637-5604
mobile: 425-417-6083
E-mail: *susan@seapointventures.com*
777 108th Avenue N.E.
Suite 1895
Bellevue, Washington 98004
Telephone: 425-455-0879
Fax: 425-990-8810
Web site: *Seapoint Ventures*

Sequoia Capital

Profiled in Chapter 2 of *Zero Gravity*. Strong investments in information technology, computers, software, and Internet technologies. Its biggest hits include Yahoo! and Cisco.

E-mail contacts:
Michael Moritz, Information technology *moritz@sequoiacap.com*
Don Valentine, Computers, semiconductors *dtv@sequoiacap.com*
3000 Sand Hill Rd Bldg 4, Suite 280
Menlo Park, CA 94025
Telephone: 650-854-3927
Fax: 650-854-2977
E-mail: *sequoia@sequoiacap.com*
Web site: *www.sequoiacap.com*

Sevin Rosen Funds

Focuses on the "information sciences" area, where their investments include software, semiconductors, data communications, telecommunications, and information services.

Dallas
13455 Noel Rd Suite 1670
Dallas, TX 75240
Telephone: 972-702-1100
Fax: 972-702-1103
Palo Alto
169 University Avenue, Suite 200
Palo Alto, California 94301
Telephone: 650-326-0550
Fax: 650-326-0707
E-mail: *info@srfunds.com*
Web site: *http://www.srfunds.com*

Sierra Ventures

Focuses on early stage health care, information technology-related companies, and service businesses.
3000 Sand Hill Rd Bldg 4, Suite 210
Menlo Park, CA 94025
Telephone: 650-854-1000
Fax: 650-854-5593
E-mail: *info@sierraven.com*
For funding requests, please send a business proposal to:
funding@sierraven.com
Web site: *www.sierraven.com*

Sigma Partners

Invests primarily in technology-based companies: computers, electronics, software, and communications.
Menlo Park
2884 Sand Hill Road, Suite 121
Menlo Park, CA 94025
Telephone: 415-854-1300
Fax: 415-854-1323
Boston
20 Custom House Street, Suite 830
Boston, MA 02110
Telephone: 617-330-7872
Fax: 617-330-7975

Web site: *www.sigmapartners.com*

Sofinnova Inc.

Invests in U.S. West Coast, Europe, and Israel in early-stage and start-up teams in both information technology and life sciences.

E-mail and direct contacts:

Alain Azan 415-597-5754 *azan@sofinnova.com*

Robert Carr 415-597-5753 *carr@sofinnova.com*

Dr. Michael Powell 415-597-5755 *powell@sofinnova.com*

Nathalie Auber 415-597-5758 *auber@sofinnova.com*

General *info@sofinnova.com*

San Francisco

Sofinnova, Inc.

140 Geary Street, 10th floor

San Francisco, CA 94108

Telephone: 415-597-5757

Fax: 415-597-5750

Paris

Sofinnova S.A. *sofinnova-partners@sofinnova.fr*

51, rue St. Georges

75009 Paris, France

Telephone: 33.1.44-53-53-00

Fax: 45-26-78-92

Web site: *www.sofinnova.com*

Softbank Technology Ventures

Makes privately negotiated equity and equity-related investments in companies attempting to capitalize on opportunities in digital information technology, including Internet communications, commerce, and content. SOFTBANK Technology Ventures is affiliated with *SOFTBANK Corporation, which* bought one-third of Yahoo! at its IPO and has many Internet investments globally.

E-mail contacts:

Gary Rieschel *Gary@sbvc.com*

Scott Russell *srussell@zd.com*

333 West San Carlos, Ste 1225

San Jose, CA 95110

Telephone: 408-271-2265

Fax: 408-271-2270
Charley Lax *clax@sbvc.com*
10 Langley Road
Suite 202
Newton Center, MA 02159
Telephone: 617-928-9300
Fax: 617-928-9305
Bradley Feld *brad@sbvc.com*
P.O. Box E
Eldorado Springs, CO 80025
Telephone: 303-494-3242
Fax: 303-494-7642
Web site: *http://www.sbvc.com*

Techfarm, Inc.

Assists in starting, financing, growing, organizing, and taking public start-ups with semiconductor and software technology.
111 W. Evelyn Avenue
Suite 101
Sunnyvale, CA 94086
Telephone: 408-720-7080
Fax: 408-720-7090
E-mail: *kak@techfarm.com*
Web site: *www.techfarm.com*

Technology Crossover Ventures (TCV)

Founded in June 1995 by seasoned venture capital and investment professionals Jay Hoag and Rick Kimball, the firm focuses exclusively on information technology, investing in expansion-stage private enterprises, as well as select public situations.
West
575 High Street
Suite 400
Palo Alto, CA 94301
Telephone: 650-614-8200
Fax: 650-614-8222
Northeast
160 West 86th Street, Suite 12B

New York, NY 10024
Telephone: 212-277-3900
Fax: 212-277-3901
East
56 Main Street, Suite 210
Millburn, NJ 07041
Telephone: 973-467-5320
Fax: 973-467-5323
E-mail: *tnewby@tcv.com*
Web site: *www.tcv.com*

Technology Funding Venture Partners
Interest in information technologies, e-commerce, and semiconductor technologies.
2000 Alameda de las Pulgas Suite 250
San Mateo, CA 94403
Telephone: 650-345-2200
Fax: 650-345-1797
Web site: *http://www.techfunding.com*

Technology Gateway Partnership LP
Managed by Ventana Global. International basis, with a strong Latin American presence. Focuses on detection systems, electronic niche markets; hardware and software peripherals; Internet-related technologies; LAN devices and associated software; semiconductor equipment and related industries; telecommunications and wireless technologies, etc.
USA
Karen Kitridge *kkitridge@ventanaglobal.com*
18881 Von Karman Avenue
Tower 17, Suite 1150
Irvine, CA 92612
Telephone: 714-476-2204
Fax: 714-752-0223
F. Duwaine Townsen *ventana@ventanaglobal.com*
8880 Rio San Diego Drive
Suite 500
San Diego, CA 92108

Telephone: 619-291-2757
Fax: 619-295-0189
Mexico
Carlos de Rivas *derivas@ventanaglobal.com*
Paseo de Los Tamarindos
400-B Piso 10
Bosques de Las Lomas, C.P. 05120
Mexico
Telephone: 525-258-0176
Fax: 525-258-0186
Chile
Alvaro Alliende Edwards
Gerente General *alliende@ventanaglobal.com*
Marchant Pereira 201
Piso 9
Santiago
Chile
Telephone: 011-56-2-269-3245
Fax: 011-56-2-274-7955
E-mail: *ventana@ventanaglobal.com*
Web site: *http://www.ventanaglobal.com*

Technology Management & Funding, L.P.

Looks for companies with breakthrough technology that can alter or change the competitive dynamics of an industry. The technology must also be proprietary, proven, have multiple applications, and address major markets. TMF's expanding portfolio consists of companies worldwide in industries ranging from software, electronics, and industrial components to environmental, telecommunications, and biotechnology.

Dr. Anthony C. Warren President, COO
Mary E. Pappas Associate VP, Contact for Admissions
Technology Management & Funding, L.P.
707 State Rd.
Princeton, NJ 08540
E-mail: *tmfinfo@tmflp.com*
Web site: *www.tmflp.com*

Telesoft Partners

A Sterling Payot company. Sterling Payot has a strong international presence, particularly in Europe and the United States, with portfolio interests in telecommunications, Internet technologies, and e-commerce.

222 Sutter Street
San Francisco, CA 94108
Telephone: 415-274-4500
Fax: 415-274-4545
E-mail: *arjun@telesoftvc.com*
Web site: *www.telesoftvc.com*

Telos Venture Partners

Invests in information technology, semiconductor, and communications companies. In information technology, Telos is primarily interested in client/server enterprise computing applications that enhance corporate productivity by exploiting the Internet and private intranet computing model, especially in the electronic commerce and knowledge management fields. In the communications market, Telos invests in companies whose products improve the capacity, performance, and functionality of communication networks. Such companies typically offer components, software, or systems in the following areas: Access xDSL, wireless local loop and wireless comm, transmission backbone carrier equipment, switching routers, switches, and network management quality of service and performance management.

USA
Bruce R. Bourbon, 408-982-5820
Athanasios "AK" Kalekos, 408-982-5822
Paul Ansl, 408-982-5821
Shari M. Rooney, Ofc Admin, 408-982-5800
2350 Mission College Blvd., Suite 1070
Santa Clara, CA 95054
Telephone: 408-982-5800
Fax: 408-982-5880
Israel
Ron Kenneth, General Manager
Ackerstein Bldg.

103 Medinat Ha'yehudim St.
P.O.B. 12756
Herzelia 46733, Israel
Telephone: +972-9-957-1002
Fax: +972-9-957-1675
Portable: +972-50-485-293
U.S. voice mail: 408-982-2800
Web site: *www.telosvp.com*

Tribune Ventures

Operations in television and radio broadcasting, publishing, education, and interactive ventures. Looks for new media and technology businesses related to Tribune's core publishing, broadcasting, and education businesses. Interest in Internet-based media and electronic commerce, business-to-business information services, education, digital television and interactive direct marketing.

435 N. Michigan Avenue
Chicago, Illinois 60611 US
Telehone: 312-222-3893
Fax: 312-222-5993
E-mail contacts:
David Kniffin, Director *David Kniffin*
Shawn Leutchens, Manager *Shawn Luetchens*
Web site: *www.tribune.com/ventures/ventures2.html*

Trident Capital

Invests in content providers, transaction processors, application software, and Internet products and services.

2480 Sand Hill Rd, Suite 100
Menlo Park, CA 94025
Telephone: 650-233-4300
Fax: 650-233-4333
E-mail: *shall@tridentcap.com*
administrator@tridentcap.com
Web site: *http://www.tridentcap.com*

TVM Techno Venture Management

Leads investments in Germany and co-invests as part of a venture capital syndicate in selected other European countries. In the United States TVM will act as a lead investor or co-investor.

USA

Web site: *http://www.tvmvc.com*

TVM Techno Venture Management Limited Partnership

An international venture capital firm managing more than $400 million in committed capital. TVM has made investments in over 140 communication technology, information technology, and biotechnology companies.

Boston

TVM Techno Venture Management

101 Arch Street

Suite 1950

Boston, MA 02110

USA

Tel.: +1-617-345 9320

Fax: +1-617-345 9377

E-mail: *info@tvmvc.com*

Germany

TVM Techno Venture Management GmbH & Co. KG

Denninger Str. 15

81679 Munich

Deutschland

Tel.: +49-89-998 992-0

Fax: +49-89-998 992-55

E-mail: *info@tvmvc.de*

Web site: *www.tvmvc.com*

US Venture Partners

Focuses primarily on western U.S.-based interests in data communications, Internet and intranet hardware and software, networking products, semiconductors, enterprise and client productivity software, and electronic design automation software.

E-mail contacts:

Semiconductor technology: Irwin Federman *federman@usvp.com*

Network technology: Steve Krausz *skrausz@usvp.com*

Computers and software: Marc Friend *mfriend@usvp.com*

Computers, semiconductor technology: Lucio Lanza
llanza@usvp.com
Internet and networking: Stuart Phillips *stu@usvp.com*
2180 Sand Hill Rd. Suite 300
Menlo Park, CA 94025
Telephone: 650-854-9080
Fax: 650-854-3018
E-mail: *sbanke@usvp.com*
Web site: *http://www.usvp.com*

Vanguard Venture Partners
Specializes in seed and early-stage high-technology investments, with
a particular interest in information technology and the Internet.
Palo Alto
525 University Ave., Suite 600
Palo Alto, CA 94301
Telephone: 415-321-2900
Fax: 415-321-2902
Houston
1330 Post Oak Blvd., Suite 1550
Houston, TX 77056
Telephone: 713-877-1662
Fax: 713-877-8669
E-mail: *info@vanguardventures.com*
Web site: *http://www.vanguardventure.com*

Venglobal Capital
Targets investments in early stage companies in Silicon Valley, focus-
ing on software, communications, and semiconductor technology.
E-mail contacts:
Gary Cheng *gcheng@venglobal.com*
Phil Mak *philmak@venglobal.com*
5201 Great America Parkway, Suite 320
Santa Clara, CA 95054
Telephone: 408-982-2551
Fax: 408-982-2558
Web site: *www.venrock.com*

Venrock Associates

Founded as the venture capital arm of the Rockefeller family. Focuses on early stage companies in information technology with investments in Intel, Apple, Stratacom, Spyglass, CheckPoint Software, Visual Networks, and DoubleClick, as well as in health care.

East Coast
Joseph E. Casey 212-649-5790 *jec@venrock.com*
David R. Hathaway 212-649-5787 *drh@venrock.com*
West Coast
Brian D. Ascher 650-651-9394 *bda@venrock.com*
Terence Garnett 650-561-9173 *tg@venrock.com*
Ray A. Rothrock 650-561-9397 *rar@venrock.com*
Anthony Sun 650-561-9178 *as@venrock.com*
New York
30 Rockefeller Plaza, Suite 5508
New York, New York 10112 US
Telephone: 212-649-5600
Fax: 212-659-5788
Menlo Park
2492 Sand Hill Road, Suite 200
Menlo Park, CA 94026
Telephone: 650-561-9580
Fax: 650-561-9180
Web site: *www.venrock.com*

Venture Resources

An industrial design and technology development consultancy.
James Goldberg
Venture Resources
242 Bonnie Way
Glen Ellen, CA 95442
Telephone: 707-975-0237
Fax: 707-939-1659
E-mail: *jimm@linex.com*
Web site: *http://www.linex.com/venres/*

Vertex Management III Ltd.

Invests in seed and early stage Israeli and Israel-related private companies engaged in the technology sector. The Vertex III Venture Fund, managed by Vertex Management (III) Ltd., is part of the Vertex Venture Group, which manages approximately $500 million of venture capital.

1 Hashikma Street
Savyon, 56530
Israel
Telephone: 972-2-535-7621
Fax: 972-3-535-7622
E-mail: Alan Feld, Vice President *afeld@vertexmgt.co.il*
Web site: *www.vertexisrael.co.il*

Vision Capital

Targets European-based technology companies who are seeking to enter the U.S. capital and product markets and U.S. companies with premier venture backing seeking to enter the European market. Partners and investors in Europe and the U.S. execute this trans-Atlantic investment strategy.

USA
3000 Sand Hill Road
Building Four, Suite 230
Menlo Park, CA 94025
Telephone: 650-854-8070
Fax: 650-854-4961
Europe
10, Rue du Vieux-Collège
1204 Geneva
Switzerland
Telephone: 41-22-312-3333
Fax: 41-22-312-3366
E-mail:*dag@visioncap.com*
Web site:*http://www.visioncap.com*

Voyager Capital

Invests in information technology companies located primarily in the Pacific Northwest and other high-technology areas on the West Coast.

800 Fifth Ave., Suite 4100
Seattle, WA 98104
Telephone: 206-470-1180
Fax: 206-470-1185
E-mail: *info@voyagecap.com*
Web site: *www.voyagercap.com*

Walden Group of Venture Capital Funds

Affiliated with the Walden International Investment Group (WIIG). The combined organizations manage funds in excess of U.S. $1.2 billion. The funds include regional, global, and industry specific funds. Since its founding in 1974 Walden has invested in over 300 companies worldwide in the areas of semiconductors, communications, software, new media and information technology, health care, biotechnology, and specialty retailing.

750 Battery Street, 7th Floor
San Francisco, CA 94111
Telephone: 415-391-7225
Fax: 415-391-7262
E-mail: *swilder@wiig.com*
Web site: *http://www.waldenVC.com*

Weiss, Peck & Greer Venture Partners

Since 1971 has managed $600 million of committed capital with investments in more than 180 companies. Lead investors in early and expansion stage information technology and life sciences companies. U.S. focus.

E-mail contacts:
Peter Nieh (software, comm, info svcs) *pnieh@wpgvp.com*
Gill Cogan (software, comm, semi-cond) *gcogan@wpgvp.com*
Philip D. Black (info tech) *pblack@wpgvp.com*
Barry Eggers (networking) *eggers@wpgvp.com*
555 California Street, Suite 3130
San Francisco , CA 94104 US
Telephone: 415-622-6864
Fax: 415-989-5108
Web site: *www.wpgvp.com*

Worldview Technology Partners

Investments in telecommunications, semiconductors, and software, with Asian focus, with personnel in Tokyo, Singapore, Taiwan, and Hong Kong.

Palo Alto
Worldview Technology Partners
Michael Orsak, General Partner and Co-Founder
435 Tasso Street, Suite 120
Palo Alto, CA 94301
Telephone: 650-322-3800
Fax: 650-322-3880
E-mail: *morsak@worldview.com*
jameswei@worldview.com

Tokyo
Worldview Technology
Venture Capital Co. Ltd.
Shishido Bldg. 6F 1-15-14
Sakai, Musashino-shi
Tokyo, Japan 180
Telephone: 81-422-55-2007
Fax: 81-422-55-2014
E-mail: *tanaka@worldview.co.jp*

Singapore
Worldview Technology Asia Pte. Ltd.
16 Raffles Quay
#37-02 Hong Leong Building
Singapore 048581
Telephone: 65-221-7388
Fax: 65-221-7366
E-mail: *terence@worldview.com*

Index

About Bloomberg

Bloomberg L.P., founded in 1981, is a global information services, news, and media company. Headquartered in New York, the company has nine sales offices, two data centers, and 80 news bureaus worldwide.

Bloomberg Financial Markets, serving customers in 100 countries around the world, holds a unique position within the financial services industry by providing an unparalleled combination of news, information, and analytic tools in a single package known as the BLOOMBERG® service. Corporations, banks, money management firms, financial exchanges, insurance companies, and many other entities and organizations rely on Bloomberg as their primary source of information.

BLOOMBERG NEWS℠, founded in 1990, offers worldwide coverage of economies, companies, industries, governments, financial markets, politics, and sports. The news service is the main content provider for Bloomberg's broadcast media, which include BLOOMBERG TELEVISION®— the 24-hour cable television network available in ten languages worldwide—and BLOOMBERG NEWS RADIO™—an international radio network anchored by flagship station BLOOMBERG NEWS RADIO AM 1130℠ in New York.

In addition to the BLOOMBERG PRESS® line of books, Bloomberg publishes BLOOMBERG® MAGAZINE, BLOOMBERG PERSONAL FINANCE™, and BLOOMBERG WEALTH MANAGER™.

To learn more about Bloomberg, call a sales representative at:

Frankfurt:	49-69-920-410
Hong Kong:	852-977-6000
London:	44-171-330-7500
New York:	1-212-318-2000
Princeton:	1-609-279-3000
San Francisco:	1-415-912-2960
São Paulo:	5511-3048-4500
Singapore:	65-438-8585
Sydney:	61-29-777-8686
Tokyo:	81-3-3201-8900

About the Author

Steve Harmon is a prominent stock analyst, a pioneer in the field of Internet investment, and CEO of e-harmon.com, an Internet investing firm. CBS.MarketWatch.com named him one of the "Best of Wall Street." His comments appear on a number of finance Web sites: Yahoo! Finance, Upside.com, and Silicon Investor (techstocks.com). Bill Gates, John Doerr, Esther Dyson, and many Internet executives and thousands of investors follow Harmon's analysis.